Communications in Computer and Information Science 2089

Series Editors

Gang Li ⓘ, *School of Information Technology, Deakin University, Burwood, VIC, Australia*

Joaquim Filipe ⓘ, *Polytechnic Institute of Setúbal, Setúbal, Portugal*

Zhiwei Xu, *Chinese Academy of Sciences, Beijing, China*

Rationale

The CCIS series is devoted to the publication of proceedings of computer science conferences. Its aim is to efficiently disseminate original research results in informatics in printed and electronic form. While the focus is on publication of peer-reviewed full papers presenting mature work, inclusion of reviewed short papers reporting on work in progress is welcome, too. Besides globally relevant meetings with internationally representative program committees guaranteeing a strict peer-reviewing and paper selection process, conferences run by societies or of high regional or national relevance are also considered for publication.

Topics

The topical scope of CCIS spans the entire spectrum of informatics ranging from foundational topics in the theory of computing to information and communications science and technology and a broad variety of interdisciplinary application fields.

Information for Volume Editors and Authors

Publication in CCIS is free of charge. No royalties are paid, however, we offer registered conference participants temporary free access to the online version of the conference proceedings on SpringerLink (http://link.springer.com) by means of an http referrer from the conference website and/or a number of complimentary printed copies, as specified in the official acceptance email of the event.

CCIS proceedings can be published in time for distribution at conferences or as postproceedings, and delivered in the form of printed books and/or electronically as USBs and/or e-content licenses for accessing proceedings at SpringerLink. Furthermore, CCIS proceedings are included in the CCIS electronic book series hosted in the SpringerLink digital library at http://link.springer.com/bookseries/7899. Conferences publishing in CCIS are allowed to use Online Conference Service (OCS) for managing the whole proceedings lifecycle (from submission and reviewing to preparing for publication) free of charge.

Publication process

The language of publication is exclusively English. Authors publishing in CCIS have to sign the Springer CCIS copyright transfer form, however, they are free to use their material published in CCIS for substantially changed, more elaborate subsequent publications elsewhere. For the preparation of the camera-ready papers/files, authors have to strictly adhere to the Springer CCIS Authors' Instructions and are strongly encouraged to use the CCIS LaTeX style files or templates.

Abstracting/Indexing

CCIS is abstracted/indexed in DBLP, Google Scholar, EI-Compendex, Mathematical Reviews, SCImago, Scopus. CCIS volumes are also submitted for the inclusion in ISI Proceedings.

How to start

To start the evaluation of your proposal for inclusion in the CCIS series, please send an e-mail to ccis@springer.com.

Raffaele Di Fuccio · Giusi Antonia Toto
Editors

Psychology, Learning, Technology

Second International Conference, PLT 2022
Foggia, Italy, November 17–18, 2022
Revised Selected Papers

Editors
Raffaele Di Fuccio
Università Telematica Pegaso
Rome, Italy

Giusi Antonia Toto
University of Foggia
Foggia, Italy

ISSN 1865-0929　　　　　　　　ISSN 1865-0937　(electronic)
Communications in Computer and Information Science
ISBN 978-3-031-81705-2　　　ISBN 978-3-031-81706-9　(eBook)
https://doi.org/10.1007/978-3-031-81706-9

© The Editor(s) (if applicable) and The Author(s), under exclusive license
to Springer Nature Switzerland AG 2025

This work is subject to copyright. All rights are solely and exclusively licensed by the Publisher, whether the whole or part of the material is concerned, specifically the rights of translation, reprinting, reuse of illustrations, recitation, broadcasting, reproduction on microfilms or in any other physical way, and transmission or information storage and retrieval, electronic adaptation, computer software, or by similar or dissimilar methodology now known or hereafter developed.
The use of general descriptive names, registered names, trademarks, service marks, etc. in this publication does not imply, even in the absence of a specific statement, that such names are exempt from the relevant protective laws and regulations and therefore free for general use.
The publisher, the authors and the editors are safe to assume that the advice and information in this book are believed to be true and accurate at the date of publication. Neither the publisher nor the authors or the editors give a warranty, expressed or implied, with respect to the material contained herein or for any errors or omissions that may have been made. The publisher remains neutral with regard to jurisdictional claims in published maps and institutional affiliations.

This Springer imprint is published by the registered company Springer Nature Switzerland AG
The registered company address is: Gewerbestrasse 11, 6330 Cham, Switzerland

If disposing of this product, please recycle the paper.

Preface

The rapid evolution of technology and learning is offering new ways to new knowledge and educational practice. This is evident also in the educational and clinical psychology field, which benefits from technology elements and at the same time provides new inputs for designing technological prototypes and tools. Technology can play a crucial supportive role in improving the quality and outcomes of learning. Likewise, technology can help people in meeting their psychological needs in everyday life, promoting human well-being.

The Psychology, Learning, and Technology Conference (PLT) aimed to explore learning paths that incorporate digital technologies in innovative and transformative ways and the improvement of the psychological and relational life, in this triple helix between psychological studies, educational and pedagogical practices, and technology opportunities. The conference included topics about the methodology of application of ICT tools in psychology and education: from the intersection between emotion and learning to the application of artificial intelligence in education; from teaching, learning, and assessment strategies and practices to new frontiers in Technology Enhanced Learning.

PLT aimed to become a meeting point for researchers in education, psychology, and computing, and for all those who have an interest in the future of learning with technology. The Conference advanced a set of scientific knowledge and methodologies of intervention that can be purposefully applied to the design and development of technologies that support the learning process.

PLT engaged researchers, practitioners, educational developers, and entrepreneurs to address current challenges and advances in the field.

July 2025   Raffaele Di Fuccio

Organization

General Chairs

Giusi Antonia Toto — University of Foggia, Italy
Raffaele Di Fuccio — University of Foggia, Italy

Program Committee

Paola Angelelli	Università del Salento, Italy
Elena Barberà	Universitat Oberta de Catalunya, Spain
Linda Cassibba	Università di Bari, Italy
Giovanna Celia	Università di Foggia, Italy
Raffaele Di Fuccio	Università di Foggia, Italy
Stefano Di Tore	Università di Salerno, Italy
Chiara Valeria Marinelli	Università di Foggia, Italy
Antonio Javier Criado Martín	International University of La Rioja, Spain
Lucia Monacis	Università di Foggia, Italy
Paola Palladino	Università di Foggia, Italy
Annamaria Petito	Università di Foggia, Italy
Tiziana Quarto	Università di Foggia, Italy
Angelo Rega	IRFID, Italy
Thomas Ryan	Nipissing University, Canada
Dolores Rollo	Università di Parma, Italy
Francesco Sulla	Università di Foggia, Italy
Giusi Antonia Toto	Università di Foggia, Italy
George Ubachs	EADTU, Italy
Leonardo Carlucci	Università di Foggia, Italy
Eliana Brunetti	University of Naples Federico II, Italy
Caterina Artuso	Università di Genova, Italy
Piergiorgio Guarini	Università di Foggia, Italy
Francesca Vizzi	Università del Salento, Italy
Stefania Fantinelli	Università di Foggia, Italy
Pierluigi Zoccolotti	Sapienza University of Rome, Italy
Milvia Cottini	Free University of Bozen-Bolzano, Italy
Mauro Cozzolino	Università di Salerno, Italy
Guendalina Peconio	Università di Foggia, Italy
Martina Rossi	Università di Foggia, Italy

Ciro Esposito   Università di Foggia, Italy
Marco di Furia   Università di Foggia, Italy
Francesca Finestrone   Università di Foggia, Italy
Martina Cangelosi   Università degli Studi di Bologna, Italy
Marika Iaia   Università di Salerno, Italy

Contents

Digital Psychology and Digital Settings

Evaluation of Essays and Comments for Developing Critical Thinking
Ability During a University Course 3
    Minoru Nakayama, Satoru Kikuchi, Masaki Uto, and Hiroh Yamamoto

Proposal of an Online Strength-Based CBT Intervention Model
in Hospitalized Patients with COVID-19: Promotion of Psychological
Well-Being and Prevention of Post-COVID Emotional Symptoms
in Italian Medical Setting 18
    Melania Severo, Antonella Calvio, Melania Rita Difino,
    Annalisa Zaffino, Salvatore Iuso, Donato Lacedonia,
    and Annamaria Petito

The Relationship Between Fluid Intelligence and Memory and How
to Measure it with Technological Tools 30
    Fulvia Francesca Campo, Francesco Carlomagno, and Elvira Brattico

New Digital Technologies for Psychotherapy 47
    Giusi Antonia Toto and Pierpaolo Limone

Advances in Technology Enhanced Learning and Teaching

Intersectionality Between Open Educational Resources and Sustainable
Development Goals: Future Perspectives 63
    Piergiorgio Guarini, Martina Rossi, Francesco Pio Savino,
    and Francesca Finestrone

Italian Teachers and TPACK-G: An Exploratory Study of Its Relationship
with Attitudes Towards DGBL and Digital Self-efficacy 78
    Roberta Renati, Natale Salvatore Bonfiglio, Maria Lidia Mascia,
    Dolores Rollo, and Maria Pietronilla Penna

Traditional, Flipped Learning, or Blended Learning Classroom: Which
Method Improves Students' Engagement in Gamified Digital Storytelling
Environment? 91
    Vahid Norouzi Larsari

Training Teachers to "Play Seriously": Testing a Game Design Activity
for Assessment During a Teacher Training Course 101
   Marco di Furia, Guendalina Peconio, and Benedetta Ragni

Bilingualism and Second Language Learning

Bilingualism and Second Language Learning through the Use of Social
Robots: A Scoping Review 117
   Carla Cirasa and Daniela Conti

Reading Profile in Deaf Adults 142
   Francesca Vizzi, Pierluigi Zoccolotti, Marika Iaia, Paola Angelelli,
   and Chiara Valeria Marinelli

Game-Based Learning and Innovative Teaching Environments

Comparison of Traditional and Virtual Reality Learning in Children
with ADHD 159
   Alessandro Frolli, Sonia Ciotola, Clara Esposito, Francesco Cerciello,
   Angelo Rega, and M. C. Ricci

Exploratory Study of the Effects of Digital Storytelling Using Tangible
User Interfaces on Acquired Knowledge About a Story in a Group
of Primary School Children 168
   Francesco Sulla, Stefania Fantinelli, Clarissa Lella, Ciro Esposito,
   and Raffaele Di Fuccio

Virtual Reality and Learning in Children with SEN 183
   Alessandro Frolli, Clara Esposito, Francesco Cerciello, Sonia Ciotola,
   Angelo Rega, and M. C. Ricci

Game-Based Assessment: Between Goals and Psychometric Rigor 192
   Gianluigi Serio, Michela Balsamo, and Leonardo Carlucci

Author Index 205

Digital Psychology and Digital Settings

Evaluation of Essays and Comments for Developing Critical Thinking Ability During a University Course

Minoru Nakayama[1(✉)], Satoru Kikuchi[2], Masaki Uto[3], and Hiroh Yamamoto[2]

[1] Tokyo Institute of Technology, Meguro, Tokyo, Japan
`nakayama@ict.e.titech.ac.jp`
[2] Shinshu University, Matsumoto, Nagano, Japan
[3] The University of Electro-Communications, Chofu, Tokyo, Japan
`uto@ai.is.uec.ac.jp`

Abstract. Sentences in student's essay and comments were analysed to examine the feasibility of evaluating ability of critical thinking disposition (CTD) by measuring this ability based on texts in a university class. Two approaches, such as term dependency in texts and automated essay scoring using a machine learning technique (BERT), were employed to predict writing performance and CTD factor scores. The results, which are based on the term dependency reflect the levels of essay scores and factor scores, and illustrate the relationships between dependency and ability level using corresponding analysis of these frequencies. A machine learning based approach can predict accurately essay and comment scores from these texts, however, the prediction for CTD factor scores needs further improvements.

Keywords: Critically Thinking Attitude · Essay report · Lexical analysis · Automate essay scoring

1 Introduction

In addition to the catastrophic geophysical events such as volcanic eruption, earthquake and Tsunami that are experienced around the world, the current abnormal weather pattern triggers serious natural disasters, floods, heat waves and forest fires. In these situations, appropriate information processing capabilities and proper decision making responsibility are required if early and adequate evacuation and emergency responses are to be facilitated [7, 9].

One of the abilities requiring development in order to better adapt to these situations is critical thinking disposition (CTD), which is a generic skill for understanding the immediate state of a situation, processing knowledge, and making better and faster decisions as a result. One of the authors has been conducting a large scale class which

---

This research was partially supported by the Japan Society for the Promotion of Science (JSPS), Grant-in-Aid for Scientific Research (KAKEN, 21K18494: 2021–2023).

teaches these skills in a face-to-face or online learning course. Human cognition and information processing techniques are used in the course [17, 18]. In particular, online discussions and essay report assignments are systematically given to the participants throughout the course. In regards to the understanding of the topics taught during the course, the effectiveness of online discussion was confirmed experimentally [10, 11]. The contents of discussion were also analysed using lexical analysis [16, 22]. As essay reports have been widely used in various types of learning assessments, some lexical analysis techniques are introduced to the evaluation [16, 18]. A modern natural language processing system is also introduced in order to provide efficient and accurate evaluation of learning performance or to support improvement in writing ability [8, 29, 31]. Therefore, appropriate essay performance assessment procedures should be developed and their effectiveness evaluated. In regards to the educational aim of the course, the appropriate presentation of information should be examined by the students themselves, using an essay assessment system. The self-improvement process enhances the presentation of information when students understand what their own level of CTD ability is by using the system with summaries of their own essays. Currently, with many people voicing their own opinions and making observations on social media platforms, a proper support system may be able to provide participants with their level of CTD ability using these written communications.

This paper introduces two types of approaches to the estimation of CTD factor scores using individual essay texts and natural language processing techniques such as term dependency in the texts and automated essay scoring techniques. The following topics will be addressed.

1. Features of frequency of terms dependency are extracted in order to examine the relationship between ability of CTD factors and features of essay reports regarding issues investigated by individual students.
2. The feasibility of estimating essay performance and CTD factor scores using an automated essay scoring system is examined.

2 Related Works

2.1 Critical Thinking Disposition Development

Generally, the discussion of various topics with peers has been thought to encourage and cultivate critical thinking ability [6]. Critical thinking disposition is a set of generic skills or a key competence [27], which is essential for communication, and for the development of writing skills [24]. This thinking ability may also contribute to an aptitude for analysis or scientific reasoning. Therefore, many programs at institutes of higher education introduce various activities that develop these skills. In particular, these skills and aptitudes are key to producing the best of human behaviour during natural disasters and the crises that result from these events [25, 35].

The online learning environment of MOOCs at institutes of higher education can provide the ideal opportunity for this development of online discussions [30]. During these activities, critical thinking aptitude contributes to the number and quality of postings in online discussions [4, 10]. One of the authors has analysed discussion activity promoting critical comments and encouraging suggestions in two types of discussions during a fully online course at a graduate level course [20]. Another analysis of online discussions using a bulletin boards during a blended learning course was organised [14]. In both cases, the practice was useful and the activity enhanced participant's knowledge, though the effectiveness was unclear since the number of participants was limited.

Also, the personal characteristics of participating students affected their learning activity regarding critical thinking disposition, and so causal analyses was conducted to evaluate key factors and learning activities [14–16].

2.2 Essay Text Analysis Using Conventional NLP Technique

As essay reports have been used and evaluated in various types of learning, a detailed assessment of ability should be made using a lexical analysis techniques such as morphological term frequency and document similarity as a basic text mining techniques [16, 18, 21]. Term dependency in sentences is also analysed to represent the features of the content [23]. Essay assessment using document similarity was applied using learning support systems and learning analytics [32].

The lexical characteristics of essay reports were analysed to evaluate critical thinking disposition ability [18]. As the characteristics of CTDs may be related to the style of writing and document structuring ability, content analysis of essays should be introduced in order to help developing these abilities. These features may also aid in the development of literacy.

2.3 Automated Essay Scoring

As mentioned above, the essay task is widely used in large classes, so that rating these documents is often discussed. To handle this issue, natural language processing techniques have been applied to automated essay scoring such as the JESS system [8] which evaluates three aspects of essay documents or the Erater system [3]. For the test assessment system, accurate short-answer scoring techniques have been studied [12].

Recently, machine learning techniques have been applied to document assessments and scoring systems [1, 29]. In particular, BERT (Bidirectional Encoder Representations from Transformers) is widely applied to document content analysis including essay scoring [2, 13, 26, 28, 34, 36]. In addition to this approach, accuracy enhancing approaches such as using item response theory (IRT) have been studied [31, 33]. The feasibility of estimating the latent ability such as critical thinking disposition using the above scoring system has not been investigated or confirmed, however.

3 Course and Survey Method

3.1 Course Styles

The responses of participants were surveyed during a bachelor course at a Japanese university. Ordinarily, the class was organised as a blended learning course, consisting of online discussion in addition to 15 weekly face-to-face class sessions [14, 16, 17]. All participants were asked to research and summarise a human cognitive problem based on an individual experience of each of the students as a part of a field study project. Since 2020, the format had to change to a fully online learning style course due to the COVID-19 pandemic. The detailed formats are as follows:

Blended Style. The survey was conducted during a university freshman course titled "Psychology of Natural Disaster Mitigation and Prevention", and involved over 300 students in various disciplines. This instruction style was based on a conventional large scale lecture. Additionally, various types of learning activities are required, such as essay reports, weekly tests, and online discussion activities, since one of the aims of the course is the development of critical thinking skills.

Fully Online Style. The lecturer recorded videos of his lectures in advance, and the video clips for each session were delivered using the university LMS (Moodle learning management system). All participants joined the course flexibly as off-campus students, and there were no face-to-face lecture room classes. All communications such as assignment submissions, online tests, essay report reviews and follow-up surveys were conducted using the LMS. Learning performance was evaluated using online tests such as short writing tests which asked about course session topics and practices as well as the weekly tests conducted in a blended learning style.

3.2 Survey Metrics

The surveys consisted of the following metrics of individual participants: four factor scores for critical thinking disposition (CTD), and additional characteristics of each student participant. The surveys and analysis were approved by an ethics committee at the university where the surveys took place.

Critical Thinking Disposition (CTD). In order to measure the participant's critical thinking attitude, a Japanese inventory set developed in a previous study [5] was used. The metric consists of four factor structures which use a 5 point Likert scale (1–5), consisting of Awareness of logical thinking (CTD-1), Inquiry-mindedness (Inquisitiveness) (CTD-2), Objectiveness (Objectivity) (CTD-3), and Evidence-based judgement (CTD-4).

These metrics were surveyed twice during the course during its first and the second halves. The scores of the 2nd survey are used in the following analysis.

Table 1. Mean of grades of all essays and factor scores of CTD (N = 275)

Score category / Factors	Mean	STD
Essay grade	79.9	7.0
CTD-1: Awareness of Logical thinking	2.78	0.59
CTD-2: Inquiry mindedness	3.88	0.65
CTD-3: Objectiveness	3.68	0.56
CTD-4: Evidence-based judgement	3.47	0.63

Table 2. Number of participants in the three levels (N = 275)

Levels	Rep	CTD-1	CTD-2	CTD-3	CTD-4
Low	74	2(48)	3(37)	3(62)	3(79)
Middle	123	3(104)	4(99)	4(91)	4(90)
High	78	4(26)	5(42)	5(25)	5(9)
Missing	0	87	87	87	87

Student's Characteristics. Most learning behaviours are often explained by student's characteristics, so that the following characteristics are also surveyed for every participant in each course were also surveyed: Personality (Big5), information-processing style (IPS), literacy of science and technology (LST), personal preparation for any natural disasters.

3.3 Essay Report Assessments

Some essay reporting tasks were assigned to all participants in order to conduct an overall assessment for the final grade. The main essay task was to pick up a problem concerning human perception in daily life by observing something such as a posted sign or a particular situation in one's neighbourhood, and to suggest procedures which would provide an improvement. Using a picture taken of a situation and pointing out the reasons why misunderstandings occur, ideas for improvements and revisions to existing procedures are introduced and summarised in essay reports.

Additional short comment essays were required, in order to summarise participant's own opinions during two short talks which were given by two external lecturers invited to the class.

These individual essays were required to be submitted via the LMS platform used to manage the online course. The lecturer's marks were provided to participants using the system.

4 Term Frequency Analysis of Essay Reports

A phrase based text analysis was applied to the set of essays which were summarised during the fully online course.

4.1 Text Analysis of Essay Reports

Every essay report on a 2021 fully online course, consisting of Japanese text characters, was processed using text analysis. During pre-processing, the texts were extracted from the student's essay reports. In order to extract terms from the texts, Japanese morphological analysis was applied. After that, a dependency analysis was conducted on all texts [23], and the frequency of term dependency relationships was extracted [19]. Though

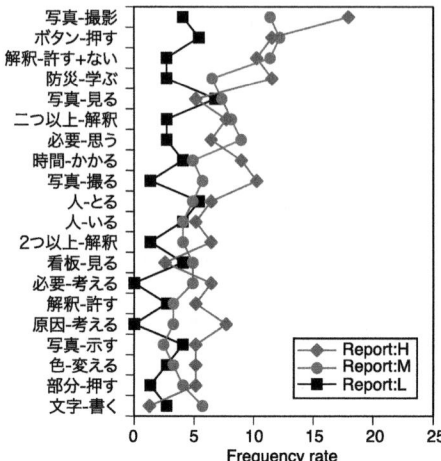

Fig. 1. Frequent phrases in essay reports by assessment grade

the length of the essays and their presentation styles differed between individuals, these features were compared and the differences between extracted texts compared as a group.

The categories for comparing the features of presentations in essay reports were created using overall rating scores of essay reports or levels of factor scores of CTD. The simple statistical means and STDs are summarised in Table 1. Regarding distribution, all valid participants are classified into three levels (Low, Middle and High), as shown in Table 2.

4.2 Dependencies in Essay Reports

The dependency relationships of the three levels of essay reports are extracted and summarised using frequency order evaluation in Fig. 1. The vertical axis shows pairs of dependencies in Japanese, and the horizontal axis represents the frequencies of the dependency of the three levels of the evaluation. The top four to ten pairs show relatively higher frequencies. The frequency relationships contain the themes in the essay reports, such as "photo taking", "learning mitigation", and also the descriptions about problems discovered are also listed.

These frequencies for the three levels of essay assessment (H,M,L) are summarised in Table 2. The number of participants in the groups differs, and so the frequencies are standardised by equalising the number of participants. As shown in Fig. 1, the frequencies in the top four relationships increase with the level of essay assessment, and the frequencies for the High and Middle groups are higher than ones for the Low group. Some differences in these figures are observed. They provide evidence that essay report text dependencies are affected by the ratings of the essay reports.

These changes are also examined for CTD factor score levels, and the results are summarised in Fig. 2. Though overall trends of frequency changes are almost the same, some specific differences between factor scores are present. In some cases, the frequencies for low levels of the factor scores are higher than the ones for other levels. These may

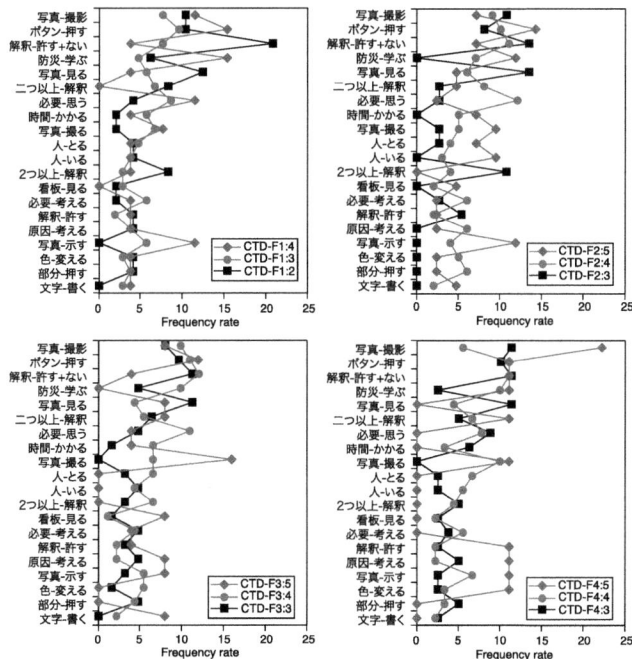

Fig. 2. CTD factor score levels of frequent phrases in essay reports

also be evidence that factor scores represent the frequency of dependency of sentence texts in essay reports.

4.3 Corresponding Analysis

In the previous section, the relationship between ability and presentation of essay reports is unclear because the frequencies of the dependencies are simply compared. In order to introduce a quantitative measurement, corresponding analysis is applied to the frequency of each level of student's ability.

Figure 3 shows a two-dimensional mapping result of analysis of the relationship in Fig. 1. Both dimensional scales represent features of frequencies. The diameter of the circle represents the frequency. The dark coloured circles represent the level of assessment scores of essay reports for "Report L", "Report M" and "Report H". The smaller circles represent each dependency relationship. Again, the central circle represents "Report M", and the overlapping relationships may be the frequently of use of a word or sets of words in these essay reports, such as phrases used as explanations of situations. Some relationships are located near "Report H", and these note phrases used to describe the purposes of the essays.

The illustration format was applied to the relationship between the dependency frequencies of levels of CTD factor scores. The results in response to Fig. 2 are summarised in Fig. 4. In the results for CTD-1 and CTD-2, the three levels are well distributed in a two-dimensional space. Therefore, some specific phrases of dependencies in response

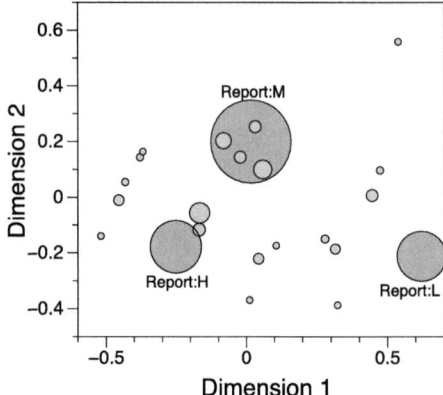

Fig. 3. Two dimensional illustration of corresponding analysis of report ratings

to the levels of factor scores are displayed. For CTD-3 and CTD-4, another space may be required to represent the dependencies. As is a common tendency, the dependency of the phrase "a photo shows" is located near the factor scores for the High level. The phrase introduces an author's interpretation and opinion of the contents of the photo.

5 Assessment Score Estimation Using Essay Texts

Student's essays can be evaluated using an automated rating system such as natural language processing using BERT. The techniques are extend to evaluate factor scores of CTD which is shown in Table 3, the possibility to estimate critical thinking ability is examined using several essays which were produced over two years of a blended learning course.

5.1 Prediction Procedure Using the BERT System

As mentioned in the Sect. 2, BERT is a pre-trained language model which has achieved a high level of performance in various natural language tasks including automated essay scoring and automated short-answer grading. This technique has been applied to the 6 essays submitted by each student and graded according to ratings given by the instructor (0~100).

An outline of the architecture of the model is illustrated in Fig. 5. It consists of transformers for BERT and a linear layer for estimating scores using sequences of words ($w_{j1} \sim w_{jnj}$) in a document j. The transformer block of BERT is constructed with multi-head attention and a feed-forward network of multi-layered connections which is called as transformer encoders. In this analysis, a *base*-sized BERT model was pre-trained using a Japanese corpus[1] and fine-tuned using the AdamW optimizer. The detailed prediction procedure is based on the previous works [31, 33], where a subtokenizer is applied to the essay texts, these word sequences and the BERT is applied to the model instructor's

---

[1] https://huggingface.co/cl-tohoku/bert-base-japanese-v2.

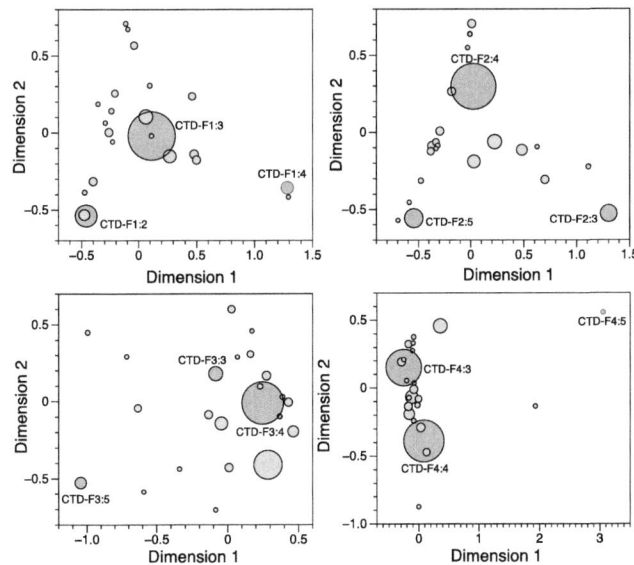

Fig. 4. Two dimensional illustration of corresponding analysis of CTD factor score levels

Table 3. CTD Factor scores during a blended learning course

Factors	2018FY(N = 238)		2019FY(N = 257)	
	Mean	STD	Mean	STD
CTD-1: Awareness of Logical thinking	2.72	0.68	2.76	0.60
CTD-2: Inquiry mindedness	3.86	0.68	3.88	0.63
CTD-3: Objectiveness	3.53	0.67	3.66	0.56
CTD-4: Evidence-based judgement	3.39	0.67	3.47	0.66

essay scores, as shown in Fig. 5. Here, a special token [CLS] represents the beginning of each input sequence. Performance is evaluated using a 5-fold cross validation procedure, and is evaluated using correlation coefficients of the instructor's ratings and quadratic weighted Kappa (QWK: 0~1), which is considered as an ordinal scale [29]. (Table 4)

5.2 Essay Score Prediction Performance

Estimation performance was evaluated using a 5-fold setting which is based on a trained model that used 4-subsets and tested with a remainder set. The results of QWK are summarised in Table 5 and correlation coefficients (r) are summarised in Table 6. Both results show the highest performance shows using Comment3 and Comment4, and the lowest performance shows using Comment1. These coefficients are practically constant across the 5 fold settings. The most prediction performances show the possibility of making predictions using an automated scoring.

Table 4. Statistics of student's essays

Essays	Characteristics			Grades	
	N	Text size	Morpheme	Mean	SD
Report1	227	2200.9(77.2)	466.0(16.5)	78.4	11.7
Comment1	214	1023.4(31.0)	226.1(7.2)	65.9	8.9
Comment2	234	459.6(21.9)	107.4(5.0)	81.0	13.2
Report2	341	1914.5(57.9)	426.0(12.6)	79.7	7.7
Comment3	313	649.2(26.7)	149.9(6.6)	74.0	6.6
Comment4	340	652.7(29.8)	152.0(6.8)	74.7	8.2

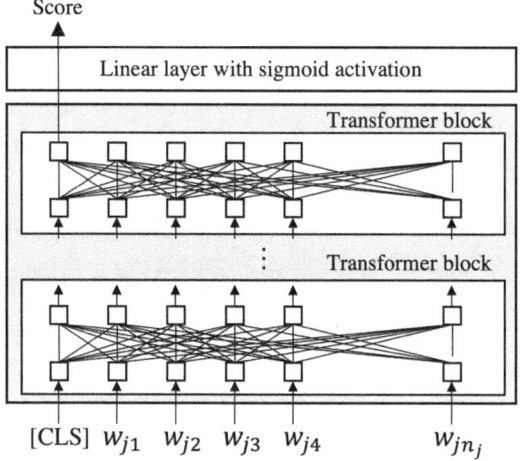

Fig. 5. A BERT-based model for estimating scores [33]

The major report essays (Report1 and Report2) present significant coefficients, but the coefficients seem a little bit weak, however. In order to confirm the prediction ability, scatter-grams between the instructor's scores and the estimations are summarised in Fig. 6 in Report1 and Fig. 7 for Comment3. As shown in the figures, some estimations have some deviations in their scores which may influence the metrics. Also, the instructor may give consideration to the ratings to major report essays in the final grade, or lower ratings may be given to some essays due to delayed submission etc. These ratings also influence the estimation performance.

Table 5. QWK

QWK	Fold1	Fold2	Fold3	Fold4	Fold5	Mean
Report1	0.44	0.34	0.42	0.45	0.56	0.44
Comment1	0.27	0.30	0.31	0.23	0.35	0.29
Comment2	0.48	0.67	0.65	0.60	0.62	0.61
Report2	0.37	0.31	0.24	0.39	0.29	0.32
Comment3	0.73	0.83	0.79	0.79	0.64	0.76
Comment4	0.76	0.75	0.74	0.72	0.82	0.76

Table 6. Correlation coefficients between lecturer's grades and estimation scores

r	Fold1	Fold2	Fold3	Fold4	Fold5	Mean
Report1	0.46	0.27	0.68	0.52	0.58	0.50
Comment1	0.38	0.33	0.38	0.28	0.34	0.34
Comment2	0.46	0.66	0.68	0.62	0.56	0.60
Report2	0.45	0.43	0.24	0.47	0.32	0.38
Comment3	0.75	0.82	0.81	0.84	0.67	0.78
Comment4	0.77	0.80	0.75	0.73	0.83	0.78

5.3 Possibility of Predicting Factor Scores of CTD

The prediction of essay scoring is usually possible for the set of essays from the course using the BERT technique. For the next step, the technique is used to estimate CTD factor scores as well as essay scores. The correlation coefficients of estimation performance are summarised in Table 7. In this table, coefficients which are not significant represented in brackets. Most coefficients are not significant and remain around 0 (r:-0.14~0.19).

Table 7. Correlation coefficients between factor scores and estimated scores of essay texts

r	N	CTD-1	CTD-2	CTD-3	CTD-4
Report1	210	(0.06)	0.19	(0.05)	(−.01)
Comment1	214	−.14	(−.04)	(0.02)	(−.12)
Comment2	182	(0.12)	(−.07)	−.13	(−.04)
Report2	256	(−.05)	(−.06)	(0.08)	0.15
Comment3	234	0.13	(0.01)	(0.06)	(0.09)
Comment4	257	(−.05)	(−.01)	(−.02)	(0.01)

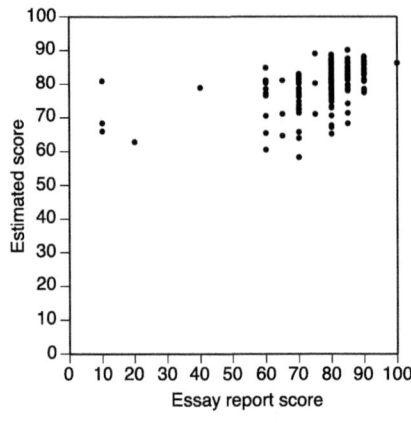 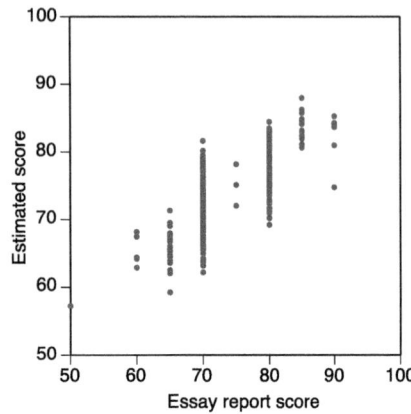

Fig. 6. Prediction result in Report1 ($r = 0.46$) **Fig. 7.** Prediction result in Comment3 ($r = 0.78$)

A detailed analysis of CTD-F2 using scatter-gram is shown in Fig. 8. In comparison with the means and deviations, the estimated factor scores do not vary greatly from the original scores. Most scores can be estimated within a possible range of values, but these do not correlate with the original values.

6 Discussion

Feature extraction based on a corresponding analysis for essay texts shows a relationship between essay scores and some factor scores. However, it is not possible to accurately estimate individual scores. This technique can be applied to any texts of essays or documents.

The BERT-based approach can estimate essay scores, but some deviation in performance is observed. In comparing the estimation performance between sets of assigned essays, essay volume may affect the performance. In order to confirm the factor of text volume, a scatter-gram between quantity of text and estimation coefficients is summarised in Fig. 9. As mentioned in Tables 5 and 6, short comments such as Comment2∼4 show high co-efficiency. When the text volume is larger than 1000 (bytes), coefficients (r) remain under 0.5. Though the relationship seems unclear, the text volume may influence the estimation accuracy.

The CTD factor scores are latent values, while essay scoring is based on the texts presented. The difference may influence these estimation performance. Critical thinking aptitude may be observed using certain measures, therefore the possibility of estimating essay scores should be confirmed in a further study.

The factor score estimating approaches can be used for learning support of participants if individual essay scores could be estimated using their own text. While learners summarise essays or comments which help develop their CTD ability, every participant consults with the system to confirm the validity of their presentation. Of course, appropriate instruction and support procedures for participants should be considered in advance.

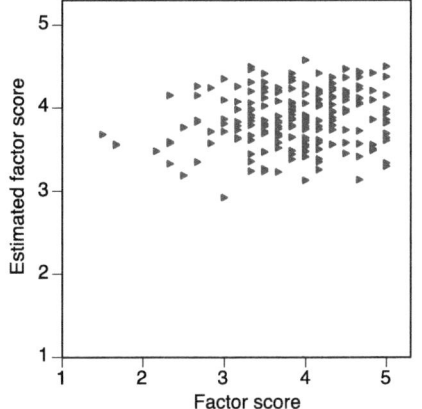

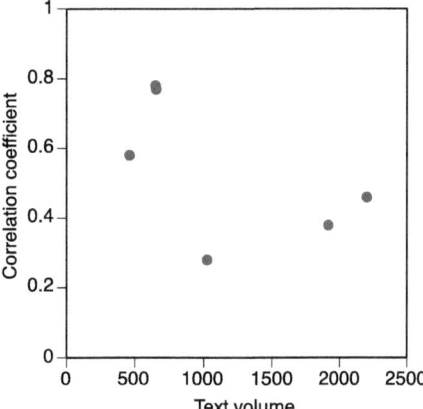

Fig. 8. Prediction of CTD-2 (F2: Inquiry mindedness) ($r = 0.19$)

Fig. 9. Correlation coefficients using text size

These topics will be subjects of our further study.

7 Summary

The possibility of estimating essay scores and scores of factors of critical thinking disposition (CTD) are examined using term dependency and a pre-trained BERT model on student's essay reports and comments during fully online and blended style courses for developing CTD abilities. The following results were obtained.

1. The frequency of dependencies in text presentations of student's essays is affected by essay assessment levels and CTD factor scores. These dependencies in essays can be used as an index of ability.
2. The frequency of dependencies can be extended to multi-dimensional measurements using a corresponding analysis. When features are mapped, the relationships between dependency and ability level are comparable quantitatively in a two-dimensional plane.
3. BERT-based automated essay scoring as a pre-trained machine-learning approach was introduced to estimate essay and comment scores and CTD factor scores. Though the essay scores can be estimated with certain accuracy, estimation performance for CTD factor scores remained at a low level.

An appropriate approach to estimating CTD ability in referring the results of the above analysis should be developed. The establishment of a detailed procedure will be the subject our further study.

Acknowledgement. Parts of Sect. 4 were presented at the Learning Analytics Symposium on International Conference Information Visualisation 2022 [19]. The authors appreciate the discussions and comments by reviewers which were provided at the presentation.

References

1. Cozma, M., Butnaru, A.M., Ionescu, R.T.: Automated essay scoring with string kernels and word embeddings. In: Proceedings of the 56th Annual Meeting of the Association for Computational Linguistics, pp. 503–509 (2018)
2. Devlin, J., Chang, M.W., Lee, K., Toutanova, K.: BERT:pre-training of deep bidirectional transformers for language understanding. In: Proceedings of NAACLHLT2019, pp. 4171–4186 (2019)
3. Powers, D.E., Burstein, J.C., Chodorow, M., Fowles, M.E., Kukich, K.: Stumping E-Rater: challenging the validity of automated essay scoring (2001). https://www.ets.org/Media/Research/pdf/RR-01-03-Powers.pdf
4. Ekahitanond, V.: Promoting university students' critical thinking skills through peer feedback activity in an online discussion forum. Alberta J. Educ. Res. **59**(2), 247–265 (2013)
5. Hirayama, R., Kusumi, T.: Effect of critical thinking disposition on interpretation of controversial issues: evaluating evidences and drawing conclusions. Jpn. J. Educ. Psychol. **52**, 186–198 (2004)
6. Höppner, C., Whittle, R., Bründl, M., Buchecker, M.: Linking social capacities and risk communication in Europe: a gap between theory and practice. Nat. Haz. **64**(2), 1753–1778 (2012)
7. Hppner, C., Whittle, R., Brndle, M., Buchecker, M.: Linking social capacities and risk communication in Europe: a gap between theory and practice? Nat. Haz. **64**, 1753–1778 (2012)
8. Ishioka, T., Kameda, M.: JESS: An automated Japanese essay scoring system. Bull. Comput. Stat. Japan **16**(1), 3–19 (2003)
9. Kawamoto, S., Nakayama, M., Saijo, M.: Using a scientific literacy cluster to determine participant attitudes in scientific events in japan, and potential applications to improving science communication. JCOM **12**(1), 1–12 (2013)
10. Kusumi, T., Tanaka, Y.: A development of critical thinking ability during a class of English for specific purpose. In: Proceedings of JAEP Annual Meeting, pp. PF2–35 (2008)
11. Leh, A., Kremling, J., Nakayama, M.: Effects of the blog and discussion board on online teaching and learning. In: Proceedings of Society for Information Technology and Teacher Education International Conference, pp. 574–579 (2012)
12. Liu, T., Ding, W., Wang, Z., Tang, J., Huang, G.Y., Liu, Z.: Automatic short answer grading via multiway attention networks. In: Isotani, S., Mill'an, E., Ogan, A., Hatings, P., McLaren, B., Luckin, R. (eds.) Artificial Intelligence in Education (AIED 2019). LNAI (LNAI), vol. 11626, pp. 169–173 (2019)
13. Lun, J., Zhu, J., Tang, Y., Yang, M.: Multiple data augmentation strategies for improving performance on automatic short answer scoring. In: Proceedings of the Tenth AAAI Symposium on Educational Advances in Artificial Intelligence (EAAI-20), pp. 13446–13453 (2020)
14. Nakayama, M., Kikuchi, S., Yamamoto, H.: The relationship between student's characteristics and online discussion activity. In: Proceedings of 17th European Conference on E-Learning, pp. 417–423. Athens, Greece (2018)
15. Nakayama, M., Kikuchi, S., Yamamoto, H.: Analysis of lexical features of online postings during a blended learning course. In: Proceedings of ITHET, pp. 1–5 (2019)
16. Nakayama, M., Kikuchi, S., Yamamoto, H.: Lexical analysis of online discussion in a blended learning course. In: Proceedings of 6th European Conference on Social Media, pp. 223–230. Brighton, UK (2019)
17. Nakayama, M., Kikuchi, S., Yamamoto, H.: Development of critical thinking disposition during a blended learning course. In: Proceedings of 19th European Conference on E-Learning, pp. 358–364. Berlin, Germany (2020)

18. Nakayama, M., Kikuchi, S., Yamamoto, H.: The feasibility of evaluating critical thinking disposition using features of essay reports. In: Proceedings of ITHET2021, pp. 1–6 (2021)
19. Nakayama, M., Kikuchi, S., Yamamoto, H.: Phrase features in essay report sentences for developing critical thinking ability in a fully online course. In: Proceedings of 2022 26th International Conference Information Visualisation (IV), pp. 240–244 (2022)
20. Nakayama, M., Leh, A., Santiago, R.: Relationships of student experience and student characteristics in a graduate-level flipped classroom. In: Proceedings of 2nd European Conference on Social Media, pp. 348–353. Porto (2015)
21. Nakayama, M., Mutsuura, K., Yamamoto, H.: Note-taking evaluation using network illustrations based on term co-occurence in a blended learning environment. Int. J. Distance Educ. Technol. **14**, 77–91 (2016)
22. Nakayama, M., Yamamoto, H., Santiago, R.: The role of essay tests assessment in e-learning: a Japanese case study. Electron. J. e-Learn. **8**, 173–178 (2010)
23. NTT-Data Suuri: Text Data Mining Studio (2013)
24. OECD: Testing student and university performance globally: OECD's AHELO (2014). http://www.oecd.org/edu/ahelo
25. Reuter, C., Stieglitz, S., Imran, M.: Social media in conflicts and crises. Behav. Inf. Technol. **39**, 40–46 (2013)
26. Rodriguez, P.U., Jafari, A., Ormerod, C.M.: Language models and automated essay scoring. arXiv, pp. 1–17 (2019)
27. Rychen, D., Salganik, L.: Key Competencies for a Successful Life and a Well-Functioning Society. Hogrefe & Huber Publishers, Boston (2003)
28. Sung, C., Dhamecha, T.I., Mukhi, N.: Improving short answer grading using transformer-based pre-training. In: Isotani, S., Mill'an, E., Ogan, A., Hatings, P., McLaren, B., Luckin, R. (eds.) Artificial Intelligence in Education (AIED 2019). LNAI (LNAI), vol. 11626, pp. 469–481 (2019)
29. Taghipour, K., Ng, H.T.: A neural approach to automated essay scoring. In: Proceedings of the 2016 Conference on Empirical Methods in Natural Language Processing, pp. 1882–1891 (2016)
30. Trehan, S., Sanzgiri, J., Li, C., Wang, R., Joshi, R.M.: Critical discussions on the massive open online course (MOOC) in India and China. Int. J. Educ. Dev. Using Inf. Commun. Technol. **13**(2), 141–165 (2017)
31. Uto, M.: A review of deep-neural automated essay scoring models. Behaviormetrika **48**, 459–484 (2021)
32. Uto, M., Louvigné, S., Kato, Y., Ishii, T., Miyazawa, Y.: Diverse reports recommendation system based on Latent Dirichlet allocation. Behaviormetrika **44**, 425–444 (2017)
33. Uto, M., Okano, M.: Learning automated essay scoring models using item-response-theory-based scores to decrease effects of rater biases. IEEE Trans. Learn. Technol. **14**(6), 763–776 (2021)
34. Uto, M., Xie, Y., Ueno, M.: Neural automated essay scoring incorporating hand-crafted features. In: Proceedings of 28th International Conference on Computational Linguistics, pp. 6077–6088 (2020)
35. Utz, S., Schultz, F., Glocka, S.: Crisis communication online: how medium, crisis type and emotions affected public reactions in the Fukushima Daiichi nuclear disaster. Publ. Relat. Rev. **39**, 40–46 (2013)
36. Vaswani, A., et al.: Attention is all you need. In: Proceedings of the 31st Conference on Neural Information Processing System (NIPS 2017), pp. 1–11 (2017)

Proposal of an Online Strength-Based CBT Intervention Model in Hospitalized Patients with COVID-19: Promotion of Psychological Well-Being and Prevention of Post-COVID Emotional Symptoms in Italian Medical Setting

Melania Severo[1(✉)], Antonella Calvio[2], Melania Rita Difino[1], Annalisa Zaffino[1], Salvatore Iuso[1], Donato Lacedonia[3], and Annamaria Petito[1]

[1] Department of Clinical and Experimental Medicine, University of Foggia, Foggia, Italy
melania.severo93@gmail.com
[2] Department of Humanistic Studies, University of Foggia, Foggia, Italy
[3] Department of Medical and Surgical Sciences, Institute of Respiratory Diseases, University of Foggia, "Policlinico Riuniti" University Hospital of Foggia, Foggia, Italy

Abstract. *Introduction:* Patients hospitalized with COVID-19 experience isolation, which contributes to their feelings of loneliness, anxiety, and fear. The present study aims to evaluate the outcomes of the strength-based CBT psychological intervention on patients hospitalized for COVID-19. The intervention consists of 8 online psychotherapy sessions carried out during the patients' hospitalization within the Pneumology Operating Unit. This intervention aims to reduce psychic symptomatology and to co-construct a personal model of resilience.

Methods: 7 hospitalized patients with COVID-19 who did not require intubation, 3 males and 4 females with long hospital stays were enrolled. Distress caused by traumatic events was assessed by Impact of Event Scale-Revised (IES- R), while the Clinical Outcomes in Routine Evaluation - Outcome Measure (CORE-OM) was used to evaluate the effectiveness of Strength Based CBT psychological intervention. Data were collected at the beginning of treatment (T0), at the end of treatment (T1), and at follow-up 6 months after the end (T2). The data were analyzed by ANOVA.

Results: Statistical analysis conducted shows a statistically significant decrease for posttraumatic symptoms (0.057) assessed by IES-R, specifically for hyperarousal reaction (0.0346) at T1 and T2. In addition, improvements are shown in the analyses conducted for the assessment of effectiveness of psycho-logical intervention as measured by CORE-OM.

Conclusions003A Although the sample size is a limitation of our study, it incentivizes us to use a strengths-based online CBT psychotherapy intervention for hospitalized patients with COVID-19, confirming the importance of psychological treatment to reduce the risk of developing PTSD in the most vulnerable patients.

Keywords: COVID-19 · resilience · e-therapy · well-being · digital setting

1 Introduction

Severe acute respiratory syndrome coronavirus 2 (SARS-CoV-2) is a new strain of coronavirus appeared at the end of 2019 in Cina and then quickly spread around the world. Symptoms and disease caused by SARS-CoV-2 has been subsequently named COVID-19. As of September 27, 2022, there have been over 612.724.171 million cases of coronavirus (COVID-19) in worldwide and 22.313.612 million in Italy (WHO, 2022). Italy was the first European country affected by the coronavirus. Since March 11th, jobs and schools were converted to smart-working and the lockdown was ex- tended to limits the diffusion of virus. There were immediate negative psychological effects of the pandemic and lockdown on population (Passavanti et al., 2021; Casagrande et al., 2020; Rossi et al, 2020). COVID-19 represents a threat to one's own safety that with its rapid spread has exacerbated population anxiety leading to hyper-arousal, hypervigilance, insomnia, intrusive thoughts, depression, and pain (Ran et al., 2020; Hou et al., 2021). COVID-19 may exacerbate anxiety, depression, and post-traumatic stress symptoms (Salari et al., 2020) particularly among quarantined individuals (Casagrande et al., 2020; Bonati et al., 2021). A recent systematic review and meta- analysis (Salari et al., 2020) shows that the prevalences rates of stress, anxiety, and depression due to the pandemic are 29.6, 31.9 and 33.7% respectively in the general population. Recent literature suggests that female gender and younger adults in Italian community sample are more vulnerable to psychological reactions to COVID-19 showing more trait anxiety and stress (Prete et al., 2020). Mazza and colleagues (2020) high- light an association between a history of stressful situations and higher level of anxiety and depression during COVID-19 pandemic. People who live stressing and traumatic experience of SARS-CoV-2 infection and symptoms manifestation of COVID-19 dis- ease, have to face up with sensation of uncertainty and emotion like anxiety and fear for a long period, from the moment they understand about the infection to their recovery. Loneliness and isolation due to social distancing, fear of stigma, anxiety for own life, deaths of other individuals and/or family members, fear and anger related to the risk of infecting others are some of reaction linked to infection by COVID-19 (Troyer et al., 2020; Brooks et al., 2020; Carvalho et al., 2020; Holmes et al., 2020). Further- more, emotions of higher bewilderment caused by an unprecedented dramatic health crisis experience and by persistent fear for our own surviving are added for individuals in which has been necessary the hospitalization (Bonazza et al., 2021). COVID-19 hospitalized patients experience isolation and the impossibility to receive closeness, con- solation, reassurance and support from their own parents or friends in this life period characterized by psychophysics distress. These conditions increase their emotional vulnerability, leading them to psychological diseases and sometimes psychiatric syndromes (Sun et al., 2021). Recent studies on patients with COVID-19 have shown a risk of developing psychopathologies (Tomasoni et al., 2021; Bo et al., 2021), because they may experience the infection and the hospitalization as trauma. Individuals hospitalized for COVID-19 faced several stressors: lack of knowledge about the virus, isolation, and fear for their health and survival. Also, patients who have undergone more intensive care may develop post-traumatic reactions, in fact, especially patients who have undergone an intensive care unit (ICU) admission may have experienced this event as traumatic, being exposed to invasive procedures and a reduction in their autonomy

(Davydow et al., 2008). Authors (Rogers et al., 2020) indicate that anxiety and depression may also persist in recovering patients. For instance, 30% of a sample of Italian patients reported anxiety or depressive symptoms 1-3 months after recovery (Tomasoni et al., 2021), 28% of them showed anxiety symptoms, 16% depressive symptoms and more than 36% post-traumatic stress symptoms within 2 months after hospital discharge. In a study sample of Chieffo et al. (2020) more than 80% of COVID-19 patients, presented mild-severe psychological distress and clinical symptoms such as sleep disorders, depression, anxiety, somatization and obsessive compulsion. Additionally, the Authors (Chieffo et al., 2020) reported that although sleep disturbances decrease after hospitalization, depression, somatization, and obsessive compulsivity symptoms persist and anxiety symptoms increase. These findings suggest that individuals who recovered from COVID-19 faced an extremely stressful experience. Rapid implementation of psychological intervention is essential to ensure the protection of patients from the psychological impact of COVID-19 (Cullen, Gulati, & Kelly, 2020) and to reduce the risk of developing post-COVID Syndrome, which is characterized by a wide range of manifestations and conditions recorded in approximately 90% of re- covered patients ranging from headache, muscle weakness, pain, fatigue, depression, anxiety to pulmonary function impairment, stroke and renal failure (Kamal et al., 2021, Klok et al., 2020). Cognitive behavioral therapy (CBT) is an evidence-based psycho- therapy widely used in the treatment and prevention of physical and psychological dis- tress to help individuals back to their normal psychological and social life (Hofmann et al., 2012; Ólason et al., 2018), also with internet-based activity (Schure et al., 2019). This approach offers treatment protocol focused to afford psychological symptoms consequently to stress and traumatic situations with specifics and evidence-based intervention. Fundamentally this therapy identifies cognitive bias, really important to increase consciousness about risks factor for psychological health. CBT is based on relation between emotions, beliefs and behaviours, and is characterized by a series of methods, including cognitive reconstruction, behavioral change and social support with aims to enhance identification of stress levels and modification of negative cognitive beliefs and behaviors (Beck, 1979). A Review of Meta-analyses conducted by Hofmann et al. (2012) on efficacy of this approach highlights that CBT is the most effective psychotherapy in treatment of anxiety disorders, somatoform disorders, bulimia, anger control problems, and general stress (Hofmann et al., 2012). Other studies shows efficacy of CBT in reduction of depression, insomnia and physical fatigue (Hollon et al., 2006; Ma et al., 2018; Worm-Smeitink et al., 2019). Recently, Li et al. (2020) demonstrate the effectiveness of CBT intervention in improving psychological health for hospitalized patients with COVID-19, reducing depression, anxiety, and stress symptoms. Authors (Li et al., 2020) suggests that the CBT intervention needs to be particularly focused on patients with COVID-19 who had a longer hospitalization. Useful is to implement standard CBT with CBT strength-based model (Padesky & Mooney, 2012) because it considers even protection factor based on strengths and individual resilience. Padesky e Mooney (2012) model includes four steps to resilience: search for strengths, construct a personal model of resilience (PMR), apply the PMR to areas of life difficulty, and practise resilience. The CBT based on strength points is useful be- cause after they have been exposed to a strong vulnerability, patients affect by COVID- 19 have to rebuild their own resilience starting from strengths and applying competence and capacities facing new challenges they have to afford. Cognitive, emotional, and interpersonal skills may foster adaptive coping responses and contribute to a personal resilience plan in individuals affected by mass stressful events. In Italy, several studies have explored COVID-19 impact to the psychophysics health of general population (Signorelli et al., 2020; Rossi et al., 2020), health care workers (Conti et al., 2020; Felice et al., 2020; Lasalvia et al., 2020) and affected patient (Chieffo et al., 2020), however, to our best knowledge, our study is the first in Italy to evaluate the effectiveness of CBT on psychological health of hospitalized patients with COVID-19 admitted in Pneumology Department. Focus on the psychological impact of COVID-19 on affected patients seems to be fundamental in the observation and assessment of the possible long-term effects of this new coronavirus. It would be desirable to consider risk factors such as anxiety-depressive syndrome which could also result in a PTSD, including individual protective factors such as adaptive coping, resilience and patient strengths. This study aims to investigate the effectiveness of standard CBT combined with strength-based intervention on hospitalized COVID-19 patients, considering both the remission of psychological symptoms of distress, and the acquisition of a personal model of resilience, in order to reduce future risk of PTSD. A secondary goal of the study was to reduce disease-related impairment after recovery, as one of the main dangers is the development of post-COVID syndrome. Finally, another purpose of our study was to evaluate psychological intervention feasibility as part of the standard care setting provided by the National Health System (NHS).

2 Materials and Methods

2.1 Study Design

The study was conducted at the University Pneumology Department of the University Hospital "Policlinico Riuniti" of Foggia. This study was designed as part of the "United and never alone" project (direttiva n. 133/2020 emergenza COVID-19. Istituzione Servizio Welfare COVID-19 Ospedaliero) in the first pandemic period. It was carried out in accordance with the World Medical Association Declaration of Helsinki and its subsequent revisions (WMA, 2013). The intervention was performed by CBT psychotherapists in training who received further professional training in strength-based CBT (Padesky and Mooney, 2012). Psychological characteristics have been assessed through different questionnaires at baseline before the intervention (t0), after the end of treatment (t1), and at 6-month follow up after the end of intervention (t2).

2.2 Study Sample

All the participants were hospitalized patients with COVID-19, they were reported by a Pulmonologist to the University Clinical Psychology Service of the University Hospital "Policlinico Riuniti" of Foggia. All participants expressed their willingness to participate in the study during the period from May 1 to June 10, 2020. The range of hospitalization was between 30 and 60 days. A total of 22 patients participated in a clinical interview with a qualified clinical psychologist, of these 22 only 7 were eligible and included in the intervention. The inclusion criteria were past positivity for COVID- 19, attending an outpatient clinic dedicated to Post-COVID-19 follow-up and had good communication and understanding of Italian. The exclusion criteria were previous diagnoses of psychiatric disorders, previous cognitive impairment, and to be transferred to the intensive care unit (ICU) if hospitalized. Based on the exclusion criteria, 15 patients were excluded. Before the beginning of intervention, an online survey was com- piled and completed. The ethical committee of University Hospitals approved the general study protocol (n. 145/CE/2020). The study was conducted following the Helsinki Declaration. All participants were informed of the purpose of the study, of their ability to withdraw from the study at any time, and that the study results would be used for scientific purposes. All provided participants signed an online informed consent to participate in the study.

2.3 Measurements

Sociodemographic and Psychosocial Features
Online survey included information on socio-demographic and clinical characteristics, such as age, gender, education, job condition, marital status, past and/or current psychopathology, use of medication, experiences with psychotherapy, and recent stressful events.

Post-traumatic Stress Symptoms
The Impact of Event Scale – Revised (IES-R; Weiss & Marmar, 1997) was used to evaluate psychological impact of recent and specific traumatic events. IES-R was used as a measure of post-traumatic stress symptoms due to the psychological impact of the COVID-19 pandemic. It has 22 items on a 5-point scale ranging from 0 ("not at all") to 4 ("extremely"). The results consist in a total score ranging from 0 to 88 with scores of 33 as probable post traumatic symptoms and in separates scores for three subscales: The Avoidance Scale, Intrusion Scale, and the Hyperarousal Scale.

Clinical Outcomes
The Clinical Outcomes in Routine Evaluation – Outcome Measure (CORE-OM; Palmieri et al., 2009) is a self-report questionnaire designed to be administered before and after psychotherapy to evaluate change in some domains. CORE-OM is composed by 34 items on 5-point scale ranging from 'not at all' to 'most or all of the time'. The 34 items of the measure cover four dimensions: Subjective well-being, Problems/symptoms, Life functioning and Risk/harm. The scale is administrated at the beginning of treatment and is repeated after the last session of psychotherapy to evaluate a measure of clinical outcome. CORE-OM has been validated with samples from the general population, NHS primary and secondary care, and in older adults.

Procedure and Phases of Intervention
Moving towards a conceptualization of resilience as a process, and not as a trait, the basic idea of Padesky and Mooney's (2012) protocol is that psychotherapeutic techniques could be applied to relieve symptoms in psychopathological conditions and to encourage quality, resources or strengths of an individual, in order to promote adaptation and self-care processes. The CBT strengths-based model for resilience develops the idea

that there could be many ways to develop abilities and resilient skills and that, in most cases, it is not necessary for the patient to develop new skills, rather the therapist can help patient to identify strengths point he already possesses and to construct a pattern of resilience from them. Strengths discovered are more likely to be unrelated to maladaptive cognitive or behavioral distortions. In the search for strengths, the clinician must move within the activities that the person regularly carries out, preferably circumscribing something they are passionate about, exploring hobbies, creative, artistic or daily activities in which they demonstrate particular competence or fun. Our proposed protocol was a combination of standard and strength-based CBT composed by eight online sessions of psychotherapy. This CBT treatment allows to act on the ability to cope and adapt in the face of adversity and restore positive functioning when stressors become overwhelming. The study sample consists of 7 hospitalized patients with COVID-19 who did not need intubation, 3 males and 4 females (average age of 44 years) with long hospital stays. The sample was evaluated at the beginning of the treatment (T0), at the end (T1) and in a follow-up 6 months after the end of treatment (T2). The clinical intervention was performed online. Psychosocial Index (PSI) was used to assess stress, well-being, distress, illness behaviour, and quality of life; the distress caused by traumatic events was evaluated with the Impact of Event Scale – Revised (IES-R); resilience was measured with the Connor- Davidson resilience scale (CD RISC) and CORE-OM was used to evaluate the efficacy of treatment. Data were analysed using descriptive methods and ANOVA. Each sessions lasted about 1 h and were carried out online. Patients were provided with a tablet to facilitate connection with the psychotherapist. For all patients, the operation began during hospitalization and ended at home, following discharge. The 8 sessions include the 4 phases described by the model of Padesky and Mooney (2012) integrated with the interventions of classical CBT. The sessions can be summarized as follows.

I Session
In the first session, the therapist checks the patient's general condition and introduces the goal and methods of the intervention (eight sessions of online psychotherapy). The therapist explores the patient's life areas and experiences through the ABC technique and uses different techniques: emotional psychoeducation, validation, normalization, restitution and homeworks.

II Session
In the second session, the therapist checks the patient's general condition, explores his life areas and experiences, and presents him with Lazarus and Folkman's (1984) stress-vulnerability model. In addition, the therapist shares with the patient the risk factors and protective factors that have emerged and assigns homeworks.

III Session
During this session, the therapist presents the strength-based cbt model for resilience (Step 1 strength-based cbt model: search for strengths by Padesky and Mooney): the therapist co-constructs with the patient a list of the patient's strengths (for example emotional, cognitive, spiritual skills, hobbies, abilities, interests), makes an analysis of the obstacles the patient encounters, draws up the list of thoughts/behaviors that can help overcome the obstacles, and assigns homeworks.

IV Session
The fourth session corresponds to the second phase of the model (Step 2: construct PMR). The therapist introduces the concept of resilience to the patient (Connor and Davidson, 2003; Atkinson et al., 2009), co-constructs the personal model of resilience (PMR) together with the patient based on the strengths identified in the research phase (the therapist sticks to the patient's own words, metaphors, images, thoughts in drafting the PMR in order to be easily retrieved). Next, the strengths are used for planning functional strategies and homeworks are assigned.

V Session
In this session, the therapist and patient co-construct a personal coping style through an assessment of functional coping strategies. Differences between coping and resilience are analyzed and homeworks are assigned

VI Session
The sixth session corresponds to phase three of the model (Step 3: Apply PMR): the therapist identifies the most vulnerable areas of life, writes down problem areas, and persists and helps the patient cope with obstacles that cannot be changed (functional coping style, ACT acceptance techniques), focusing on resilience and not on outcomes.

VII Session
The seventh session coincides with Step 4 (Practice Resilience). Behavioral resilience experiments are constructed to test the usefulness and quality of patient PMR.

VIII Session
In the eighth session there is searching for spontaneous opportunities to practice resilience in everyday situations: once patients have experience in using their PMR in planned experiments, the therapy shifts to searching for spontaneous opportunities to practice resilience in everyday situations. The focus is on acceptance of difficulties as a challenge to train resilience.

Statistical Analysis
Descriptive statistics related to age and mean scores of all psychological construct were calculated. To test the hypotheses that post-traumatic symptoms would decrease because of intervention one way ANOVA test was performed. Particularly, IES-R and CORE-OM were administered at T0 (baseline), T1 (after the end of treatment) and T2 (after 6 months at the end treatment). Differences in resilience and post-traumatic impact of event across time points (T0, T1, and T2) were analyzed by repeated measures ANOVA. The mean scores obtained in evaluations by IES-R and CORE-OM at T0, T1 and T2 have been compared by ANOVA for repeated measures in a single experimental group with "time" as factor with- in two levels (pre- and post-treatment). Analyses were conducted using the statistical software Grand Prism 5 (San Diego, CA, USA).

3 Results

The study sample consists of 7 hospitalized patients with COVID-19 who did not need intubation, 3 males and 4 females with long hospital stays, admitted in Pneumology Department. The participants average age was 44 (SD = 15.84), ranged within 24–64 years. The mean score of post-traumatic stress symptoms in our sample was 60.57. ANOVA analysis revealed that the only statistically significant decreases were found for post traumatic symptoms (0.057) evaluated by IES-R, especially for iperarousal reaction (0.0346) at T1 and T2. We can also point out an improvement trend in T1 and T2 evaluations for psychological distress evaluated by PSI and for general psychological outcome measured by CORE-OM. Results seem to indicate a positive impact of treatment on psychological condition.

4 Discussion

Our results, even if in a small sample, encourage the online used of Strengths-based CBT among hospitalized patients with COVID-19, confirming the importance of psychological interventions to reduce the risk of developing PTSD in the most exposed patients. Psychological intervention studies are rare or even inexistent to COVID-19 patients inside pneumology department. Hawke et al. (2022) showed that although a body of research is emerging to test interventions for health, cognition, and psychological well-being in long-term COVID, the breadth and scope of research remains limited. Further research on current interventions is needed to generate high- quality evidence on a wide range of candidate interventions for different patient populations with long-term COVID. In a recent review, D'Onofrio et al. (2022) showed that online psychological interventions can be a feasible and useful way to pro- vide support to people during the COVID-19 pandemic. Another advantage of such interventions is that they are more accessible, independent of time and place, with a high level of autonomy and privacy, and with lower costs. The authors highlight the usability and functionality of the online solution by technological tools, reporting high levels of user satisfaction with online health services. In other study, after a multidisciplinary programme integrating exercise and CBT addressed to long-COVID patients, Compagno et al. (2022) showed high improvements in levels of self-reported anxiety and depression. The Author conclude that the synergy between psychological treatment, multidisciplinary counselling and exercise also played an important role in improving upper and lower limb muscle strength, cardiopulmonary parameters, perceived physical and mental health, depression and anxiety. Therefore, CBT was effective in the treatment of patients with post-COVID syndrome. CBT is an evidence-based psychotherapy widely used to prevent and reduce psychophysical distress in the general population through online interventions (Schure et al., 2019) and also among inpatients (Ólason et al., 2018). According to the literature, CBT is the most effective and efficient psychotherapeutic approach to alleviate psychological distress and related symptoms, such as insomnia and physical fatigue (Ferrario, 2021) even when using brief programmes. Regardless of the specific symptomatology, the CBT intervention aimed to help in-patients identify their psychological stress levels and modify their cognitive beliefs, emotions, and dysfunctional behaviour, thus reducing their symptoms and psychological distress. In our study, combining standard CBT with the strengths-based CBT model (Padesky & Mooney, 2012), we worked on strengths-based protective factors and individual resilience. Thus, the aim of our study was not only to achieve remission of symptoms, but also to improve the impaired functioning of the disease after acute phase, where one of the major pitfalls was the development of post-COVID syndrome. Our results could have important implications inside clinical practice for the psychological well-being and mental health inside the COVID-19 pandemic context. Some limitations of the study must be considered, potentially influencing its results. The sample size is very small, since it was selected from a not large general population of inpatients meeting the inclusion criteria. The small sample size has certainly limited the possibilities of the statistical analysis, whether this study has made relevant data from the clinical point of view. There wasn't possibility to have any control sample. However, it doesn't reduce significatively data group and their significance relation with the meaning of clinical aspects. Finally, due to these limits, further research is needed to support our findings.

References

Atkinson, P.A., Martin, C.R., Rankin, J.: Resilience revisited. J. Psychiatr. Mental Health Nurs. **16**(2), 137–145 (2009). https://doi.org/10.1111/j.1365-2850.2008.01341.x

Beck, A.T. (ed.): Cognitive Therapy of Depression. Guilford Press, New York (1979)

Bo, H.X., et al.: Posttraumatic stress symptoms and attitude toward crisis mental health services among clinically stable patients with COVID-19 in China. Psychol. Med. **51**(6), 1052–1053 (2021). https://doi.org/10.1017/S0033291720000999

Bonati, M., et al.: Psychological distress among Italians during the 2019 coronavirus disease (COVID- 19) quarantine. BMC Psychiatry **21**(1), 20 (2021). https://doi.org/10.1186/s12888-020-03027-8

Bonazza, F., et al.: Psychological outcomes after hospitalization for COVID-19: data from a multidisciplinary follow-up screening program for recovered patients. Res. Psychother. (Milano) **23**(3), 491 (2021). https://doi.org/10.4081/ripppo.2020.491

Brooks, S.K., et al.: The psychological impact of quarantine and how to reduce it: rapid review of the evidence. Lancet (London, England) **395**(10227), 912–920 (2020). https://doi.org/10.1016/S0140-6736(20)30460-8

Carvalho, P., Moreira, M.M., de Oliveira, M., Landim, J., Neto, M.: The psychiatric impact of the novel coronavirus outbreak. Psychiatry Res. **286**, 112902. Advance online publication (2020). https://doi.org/10.1016/j.psychres.2020.112902

Casagrande, M., Favieri, F., Tambelli, R., Forte, G.: The enemy who sealed the world: effects quarantine due to the COVID-19 on sleep quality, anxiety, and psychological distress in the Italian population. Sleep Med. **75**, 12–20 (2020). https://doi.org/10.1016/j.sleep.2020.05.011

Chan, P., et al.: Characteristics of cognitive behavioral therapy for older adults living in residential care: protocol for a systematic review. JMIR Res. Protocols **7**(7), e164 (2018). https://doi.org/10.2196/resprot.9902

Chieffo, D.P.R., et al.: Psychopathological profile in COVID-19 patients including healthcare workers: the implications. Eur. Rev. Med. Pharmacol. Sci. **24**(22), 11964–11970 (2020). https://doi.org/10.26355/eurrev_202011_23858

Compagno, S., et al.: Physical and psychological reconditioning in long COVID syndrome: results of an out-of-hospital exercise and psychological - based rehabilitation program. Int. J. Cardiol. Heart Vasculature **41**, 101080 (2022). https://doi.org/10.1016/j.ijcha.2022.101080

Connor, K.M., Davidson, J.R.: Development of a new resilience scale: the Connor-Davidson Resilience Scale (CD-RISC). Depress. Anxiety **18**(2), 76–82 (2003). https://doi.org/10.1002/da.10113

Conti, C., Fontanesi, L., Lanzara, R., Rosa, I., Porcelli, P.: Fragile heroes. The psychological impact of the COVID-19 pandemic on health-care workers in Italy. PloS ONE **15**(11), e0242538 (2020). https://doi.org/10.1371/journal.pone.0242538

Cullen, W., Gulati, G., Kelly, B.D.: Mental health in the COVID-19 pandemic. QJM: Mon. J. Assoc. Phys. **113**(5), 311–312 (2020). https://doi.org/10.1093/qjmed/hcaa110

Davydow, D.S., Gifford, J.M., Desai, S.V., Needham, D.M., Bienvenu, O.J.: Posttraumatic stress disorder in general intensive care unit survivors: a systematic review. General Hosp. Psychiatry **30**(5), 421–434 (2008). https://doi.org/10.1016/j.genhosppsych.2008.05.006

D'Onofrio, G., et al.: Internet-based psychological interventions during SARS-CoV-2 pandemic: an experience in South of Italy. Int. J. Environ. Res. Publ. Health **19**(9), 5425 (2022). https://doi.org/10.3390/ijerph19095425

Felice, C., Di Tanna, G.L., Zanus, G., Grossi, U.: Impact of COVID-19 outbreak on healthcare workers in Italy: results from a national e-survey. J. Community Health **45**(4), 675–683 (2020). https://doi.org/10.1007/s10900-020-00845-5

Hartley, S., et al.: Self-referral to group cognitive behavioural therapy: is it effective for treating chronic insomnia?. L'Encephale **42**(5), 395–401 (2016). https://doi.org/10.1016/j.en-cep.2016.08.013

Hawke, L.D., Nguyen, A., Ski, C.F., Thompson, D.R., Ma, C., Castle, D.: Interventions for mental health, cognition, and psychological wellbeing in long COVID: a systematic review of registered trials. Psychol. Med. 1–15. Advance Online Publication (2022). https://doi.org/10.1017/S0033291722002203

Hofmann, S.G., Asnaani, A., Vonk, I.J., Sawyer, A.T., Fang, A.: The efficacy of cognitive behavioral therapy: a review of meta-analyses. Cogn. Therapy Res. **36**(5), 427–440 (2012). https://doi.org/10.1007/s10608-012-9476-1

Hollon, S.D., Stewart, M.O., Strunk, D.: Enduring effects for cognitive behavior therapy in the treatment of depression and anxiety. Annu. Rev. Psychol. **57**, 285–315 (2006). https://doi.org/10.1146/annurev.psych.57.102904.190044

Holmes, E.A., et al.: Multidisciplinary research priorities for the COVID-19 pandemic: a call for action for mental health science. Lancet. Psychiatry **7**(6), 547–560 (2020). https://doi.org/10.1016/S2215-0366(20)30168-1

Hou, W.K., et al.: Probable anxiety and components of psychological resilience amid COVID-19: a population-based study. J. Affect. Disord. **282**, 594–601 (2021). https://doi.org/10.1016/j.jad.2020.12.127

Kamal, M., Abo Omirah, M., Hussein, A., Saeed, H.: Assessment and characterisation of post-COVID-19 manifestations. Int. J. Clin. Pract. **75**(3), e13746 (2021). https://doi.org/10.1111/ijcp.13746

Klok, F.A., et al.: The Post-COVID-19 Functional Status scale: a tool to measure functional status over time after COVID-19. Eur. Respir. J. **56**(1), 2001494 (2020). https://doi.org/10.1183/13993003.01494-2020

Lasalvia, A., et al.: Psychological impact of COVID-19 pandemic on healthcare workers in a highly burdened area of north-east Italy. Epidemiol. Psychiatr. Sci. **30**, e1 (2020). https://doi.org/10.1017/S2045796020001158

Lazarus, R.S., Folkman, S.: Stress, Appraisal, and Coping. Springer, Cham (1984)

Lv, J., et al.: Influence of cognitive behavioral therapy on mood and quality of life after stent implantation in young and middle-aged patients with coronary heart disease. Int. Heart J. **57**(2), 167–172 (2016). https://doi.org/10.1536/ihj.15-259

Ma, Z.R., Shi, L.J., Deng, M.H.: Efficacy of cognitive behavioral therapy in children and adolescents with insomnia: a systematic review and meta-analysis. Brazil. J. Med. Biol. Res. = Revista brasileira de pesquisas medicas e biologicas **51**(6), e7070 (2018). https://doi.org/10.1590/1414-431x20187070

Mazza, C., et al.: A nationwide survey of psychological distress among Italian people during the COVID-19 pandemic: immediate psychological responses and associated factors. Int. J. Environ. Res. Publ. Health **17**(9), 3165 (2020). https://doi.org/10.3390/ijerph17093165

Ólason, M., Andrason, R.H., Jónsdóttir, I.H., Kristbergsdóttir, H., Jensen, M.P.: Cognitive behavioral therapy for depression and anxiety in an interdisciplinary rehabilitation program for chronic pain: a randomized controlled trial with a 3-Year Followup. Int. J. Behav. Med. **25**(1), 55–66 (2018). https://doi.org/10.1007/s12529-017-9690-z

Orrù, G., Ciacchini, R., Gemignani, A., Conversano, C.: Psychological intervention measures during the COVID-19 pandemic. Clin. Neuropsychiatry **17**(2), 76–79 (2020). https://doi.org/10.36131/CN20200208

Padesky, C.A., Mooney, K.A.: Strengths-based cognitive-behavioural therapy: a four-step model to build resilience. Clin. Psychol. Psychother. **19**(4), 283–290 (2012). https://doi.org/10.1002/cpp.1795

Palmieri, G., et al.: Validation of the Italian version of the clinical outcomes in routine evaluation outcome measure (CORE-OM). Clin. Psychol. Psychother. **16**(5), 444–449 (2009). https://doi.org/10.1002/cpp.646

Passavanti, M., et al.: The psychological impact of COVID-19 and restrictive measures in the world. J. Affect. Disord. **283**, 36–51 (2021). https://doi.org/10.1016/j.jad.2021.01.020

Prete, G., Fontanesi, L., Porcelli, P., Tommasi, L.: The psychological impact of COVID-19 in Italy: worry leads to protective behavior, but at the cost of anxiety. Front. Psychol. **11**, 566659 (2020). https://doi.org/10.3389/fpsyg.2020.566659

Que, J., et al.: Psychological impact of the COVID-19 pandemic on healthcare workers: a cross-sectional study in China. General psychiatry **33**(3), e100259 (2020). https://doi.org/10.1136/gpsych-2020-100259

Ran, L., Wang, W., Ai, M., Kong, Y., Chen, J., Kuang, L.: Psychological resilience, depression, anxiety, and somatization symptoms in response to COVID-19: a study of the general population in China at the peak of its epidemic. Soc. Sci. Med. (1982), **262**, 113261 (2020). https://doi.org/10.1016/j.socscimed.2020.113261

Rogers, J.P., et al.: Psychiatric and neuropsychiatric presentations associated with severe coronavirus infections: a systematic review and meta-analysis with comparison to the COVID-19 pandemic. Lancet. Psychiatr. **7**(7), 611–627 (2020). https://doi.org/10.1016/S2215-0366(20)30203-0

Rossi Ferrario, S., Panzeri, A., Cerutti, P., Sacco, D.: The psychological experience and intervention in post-acute COVID-19 inpatients. Neuropsychiatr. Dis. Treat. **17**, 413–422 (2021). https://doi.org/10.2147/NDT.S283558

Rossi, R., et al.: COVID-19 pandemic and lockdown measures impact on mental health among the general population in Italy. Front. Psychiatr. **11**, 790 (2020). https://doi.org/10.3389/fpsyt.2020.00790

Salari, N., et al.: Prevalence of stress, anxiety, depression among the general population during the COVID-19 pandemic: a systematic review and meta-analysis. Glob. Health **16**(1), 57 (2020). https://doi.org/10.1186/s12992-020-00589-w

Schure, M.B., et al.: Use of a fully automated internet-based cognitive behavior therapy intervention in a community population of adults with depression symptoms: randomized controlled trial. J. Med. Internet Res. **21**(11), e14754 (2019). https://doi.org/10.2196/14754

Signorelli, C., Scognamiglio, T., Odone, A.: COVID-19 in Italy: impact of containment measures and prevalence estimates of infection in the general population. Acta biomedica: Atenei Parmensis **91**(3-S), 175–179 (2020). https://doi.org/10.23750/abm.v91i3-S.9511

Sun, N., et al.: Qualitative study of the psychological experience of COVID-19 patients during hospitalization. J. Affect. Disord. **278**, 15–22 (2021). https://doi.org/10.1016/j.jad.2020.08.040

Tang, W., Kreindler, D.: Supporting homework compliance in cognitive behavioural therapy: essential features of mobile apps. JMIR Mental Health **4**(2), e20 (2017). https://doi.org/10.2196/mental.5283

Tomasoni, D., et al.: Anxiety and depression symptoms after virological clearance of COVID-19: a cross-sectional study in Milan, Italy. J. Med. Virol. **93**(2), 1175–1179 (2021). https://doi.org/10.1002/jmv.26459

Troyer, E.A., Kohn, J.N., Hong, S.: Are we facing a crashing wave of neuropsychiatric sequelae of COVID-19? Neuropsychiatric symptoms and potential immunologic mechanisms. Brain Behav. Immun. **87**, 34–39 (2020). https://doi.org/10.1016/j.bbi.2020.04.027

WHO COVID-19 Dashboard. Geneva: World Health Organization (2020). https://COVID19.who.int/. Accessed 26 Sept 202

World Medical Association Inc.: Declaration of Helsinki. Ethical principles for medical research involving human subjects. J. Indian Med. Assoc. **107**(6), 403–405 (2009)

Worm-Smeitink, M., et al.: Internet-based cognitive behavioral therapy in stepped care for chronic fatigue syndrome: randomized noninferiority trial. J. Med. Internet Res. **21**(3), e11276 (2019). https://doi.org/10.2196/11276

The Relationship Between Fluid Intelligence and Memory and How to Measure it with Technological Tools

Fulvia Francesca Campo[1,2], Francesco Carlomagno[1,2], and Elvira Brattico[1,2(✉)]

[1] Department of Education, Psychology, Communication, University of Bari Aldo Moro, Bari, Italy
elvira.brattico@uniba.it
[2] Department of Clinical Medicine, Center for Music in the Brain, Aarhus University and The Royal Academy of Music, Aarhus/Aalborg, Denmark

Abstract. General fluid intelligence (gF) is a key cognitive ability allowing us to flexibly adapt to the environment through its preferential linkage to several cognitive abilities, including working memory (WM) and long-term memory. In neuroimaging studies, we demonstrated the relation between WM abilities and sensory memory cortical processes, indexed by the mismatch negativity (MMN) response, that statistically predict the environment based on prior experience. We further examined whether neural sensory memory processes are linked to gF (besides WM), and obtained positive findings with enhanced MMN for higher gF and WM skills. Typical in such studies, sophisticated neuroimaging methods are combined with paper and pencil tests for assessing WM and gF in experimental sessions lasting several hours and requiring the presence of licensed psychologists. The capillary diffusion of computers and the internet permits a different approach to cognitive assessment, adopted thus far mainly in behavioral research. We illustrate ongoing studies using digital self-administered assessment of cognitive abilities and other individual differences in a school setting, allowing a fun, human-error-free, time- and cost-efficient quantification of gF and WM. However, administering such tests via PC and online is not totally problem-free and studies of reliability are still scarce. Future research should deepen the psychometric properties of self-administered digital psychological tests for a successful application to neuroimaging studies investigating the neural bases of individual differences in cognition and emotion.

Keywords: Intelligence · working memory (WM) · IQ · gF · individual differences · online tests

1 Introduction

A key aspect of the human brain is its ability to flexibly adapt to the environment in a variety of ways, through a wide range of cognitive and emotional abilities, determining wide individual differences in our reactions to environmental stimuli and conditions

(Ashton et al., 2000; Barbey et al., 2013; Goldstein and Naglieri, 2014). Intelligence is maybe one of the most fascinating sources of individual differences, attracting the interest of scientists from various fields (Cattell, 1963; Clarke and Sternberg, 1986; Gardner and Hatch, 1989; Gray et al., 2003; Schneider et al., 2014). The first who introduced the concept of general intelligence was Charles Spearman, observing that performance was correlated across a spectrum and proposing a general g factor that accounts for performance correlations among all cognitive tasks, with residual differences across tasks reflecting task-specific factors (Spearman, 1904). Subsequently, an attempt was made to measure the *g factor* through tests that generate an intelligence quotient (IQ), which correlates with gender (Irwing and Lynn, 2005; Johnson et al., 2008; Lynn, 1999) and socioeconomic status (Burt, 1959, 1961; McManus, 2004).

What has emerged is that individual differences in intelligence in the population generally follow a normal distribution, with the exception of a slight excess at the lower end of the distribution due to the existence of severe disorders that may involve impaired cognitive abilities (Deary et al., 2010). Males have a somewhat broader but consistent distribution than females at both ends of the range (Johnson et al., 2008). Individual differences in human intelligence are today a well-established fact, with a high stability in rank order throughout development (Moffitt et al., 1993), and even over large time periods: indeed, a single 45-min IQ test had a correlation of 0.63 (0.73 when deattenuated for range limitations) in people tested twice, at ages 11 and then at ages 79 (Deary et al, 2000). IQ differences are also strongly predictive of school achievement (Johnson et al., 2006), occupational attainment, social mobility (Strenze, 2007) and job performance (Gottfredson, 1997).

In a controversial theory by Charlton (2009), however, it has been proposed that high-IQ people tend to be deficient in common sense (i.e., "clever sillies"), holding counter-intuitive views on social phenomena due to the cognitive stratification of modern societies that restricts communication between individuals on the basis of IQ and that amplifies random 'silliness', generating opinions and behaviors among the highest IQ people "which are not just lacking in common sense, but (are) perversely wrong" (Charlton, 2009, p. 867). Along the same lines, Gross (1993) has already stated that children who are intellectually gifted differ from their peers not only in terms of their intellectual and academic abilities but also in terms of their social and emotional development. Moreover, numerous reports of stress, anxiety, loneliness, and depression in intellectually gifted people (Persson, 2007) have led Fiedler (1999) to draw the probably overly broad conclusion that giftedness is a condition that almost always results in adjustment problems. On the contrary, Freeman (1991; 2013) makes the opposing case, contending that there is no solid scientific evidence linking exceptionally high ability per se to emotional issues. On the contrary, she found participants of her study to be extremely sensitive, arguing that the many gifted children's supersensitivity means that they can not only take modest criticism extremely personally, but they can also react to a wider range of subtleties, speculating that it may be this high level of sensitivity in infants which itself enables giftedness to develop (Freeman, 1991). Persson (2007) seek for a compromise between these two positions, affirming that the higher the IQ score, the greater the dynamic range and intensity of the individual. Extremely intellectually gifted people are quicker, seem to react more profoundly, feel more, understand more, do more and need and want more. They typically do not fit into society not because they lack empathy, social skills, societal concern, or interest. Instead, their social context finds it difficult to accept them because they cannot relate to them, which frequently leads to isolation and alienation (Persson, 2007).

Nevertheless, people with higher IQ in childhood or adolescence tend to have better health in later stages of life (Batty et al., 2007): among one million men followed for approximately 20 years after taking IQ tests at about the age of 20, an advantage in IQ of one standard deviation was associated with a 32% reduction in mortality (Batty et al., 2009).

Over the last century, anyway, there has been substantial debate over whether general intelligence is unitary or constituted of multiple factors (Carroll, 1993; Cattell, 1949; Cattell and Horn, 1978; Johnson and Bouchard, 2005). This debate is driven by the observation that test measures tend to form distinctive clusters, as if a more complex set of factors contribute to correlations in performance (Carroll, 1993). In this context, the psychological construct of emotional intelligence has been put forward to describe individual differences in how we identify, express and regulate emotions (Salovey and Mayer, 1990). Overall, the research on the multifactorial aspects of intelligence remains timely.

2 The Neural Correlates of Intelligence

The heritability and, hence, the genetic component of intelligence is a well-established fact (Plomin et al., 2008), with a total variance in general intelligence that can be attributed to genetic influences ranging from 30 up to 80% (Deary et al., 2010). Broad categories of cognitive abilities, such as verbal and perceptual, typically show comparable levels of genetic influence (Johnson et al., 2007; Posthuma et al., 2003; Posthuma et al., 2001; Rijsdijk et al., 2002), whereas the genetic influence on memory tends to be slightly smaller (Johnson et al., 2007; Posthuma et al., 2001; Posthuma et al., 2003; Rijsdijk et al., 2002; Finkel et al., 1995). The genetic influences on general intelligence, with which these domains have a strong correlation, are responsible for a large portion of the heritability of these traits, increasing with age (McCartney et al., 1990; McGue et al., 1993; Wilson, 1978), from about 30% in early childhood (Spinath et al., 2003) to as much as 70–80% in adulthood (Edmonds et al., 2008; Jacobs et al., 2007; Johnson et al., 2007).

The development of neuroimaging techniques made it possible to extend the investigation of intelligence-size relationships to specific in vivo brain regions, by combining paper and pencil tests with sophisticated neuroimaging techniques such as functional magnetic resonance (fMRI), electroencephalography (EEG) and magnetoencephalography (MEG). Specifically, the fMRI measures the blood oxygenation level in the brain areas, reflecting their activations; the EEG measures the electrical activity on the scalp, allowing to obtain macroscopic representations of brain activity, while the MEG is a functional neuroimaging technique that measures and records the magnetic fields produced by the electrical activity of the brain allowing to obtain greater spatial and temporal precision compared to the EEG.

Neuroimaging studies found relationships between intelligence and frontal, parietal, temporal, and hippocampus volumes, all of which were rarely larger than $r = 0.25$.

(Andreasen et al., 1993; Flashman et al., 1997; MacLullich et al., 2002; McDaniel, 2005; Witelson et al., 2006). Jung and Haier (2007) proposed that individual differences in general intelligence are correlated with a network of brain regions, including those in the dorsolateral prefrontal cortex, parietal lobe, anterior cingulate cortex, and specific regions of the temporal and occipital lobes. According to their Parieto-Frontal Integration Theory of Intelligence (P-FIT, Colom et al., 2009; Jung and Haier, 2007), cognitive function results from a hierarchical chain of subsequent brain processes that begins in the temporal and occipital areas of the brain, where sensory information is first elaborated, and moves on to the frontal areas of the brain, where it is integrated and abstracted.

Limit of the P-FIT theory, however, is that it localizes the primary brain regions involved in cognitive processing rather than directly considering the brain as a dynamic network in which the resolution of complex tasks would be the result of a constant communication across the entire brain. Indeed, recent research suggests that the brain should be considered as a dynamic network and its properties studied as such (Deco et al., 2015; Rubinov and Sporns, 2010).

More recently, a mathematically-based theory of neural function, the predictive coding theory (PCT), has been put forward to explain how the brain shares and integrates information (Friston, 2002, 2005). The theory states that the brain uses a Bayesian inference to predict the causes and sources of its internal states from the actual sensory input and compares it to prior "knowledge" that has been accumulated through experience. Hence, according to PCT, the brain functions as a "hypothesis-tester" that aims to "explain away" prediction error by modifying its a priori predictions (Friston, 2005; Vuust and Witek, 2014). In order for this to occur, PCT postulates a multi-level cascade of neural processing at different time-scales, with each level attempting to predict the activity at the level below it through backward connections. According to Roepstorff et al. (2010), culture and past experiences both have an impact on higher-level predictions (the "hyper-priors"; Friston et al., 2008) which serve as priors for lower-level processing, or "empirical Bayes," (Robbins, 1956). Even short-term priors may influence predictions made on a moment-to-moment basis, demonstrating that the process is influenced by more than just lifetime events (Vuust and Witek, 2014): for instance, a metrically complex rhythmic pattern may be perceived differently depending on whether you have heard (Kalender et al., 2013) or played (Vuust et al., 2012) it before. It may also be perceived differently depending on how frequently the pattern is present in the current musical context (Huron, 2008).

PCT has largely been shown to be able to explain in great detail a wide variety of low-level perceptual processes, but it is also widely believed that PCT can account for high-level prefrontal cognitive abilities, such as categorisation, the influence of abstract knowledge on perception, recall and reasoning about conceptual knowledge, context-dependent behavioral control, naive physics and even language (Alexander and Brown, 2018; Lupyan and Clark, 2015; Spratling, 2016).

A neurophysiological probe of PCT is the auditory evoked response known as the "mismatch negativity response" (MMN), since it is produced when these predictive models and the sensory input (a deviant sound feature in a stream of repetitive sounds) mismatch. Hence, MMN (Näätänen et al., 1978) is considered a prediction error signal of the error minimization process that is described by PCT (Friston, 2005). MMN peaks frontally 150–200 ms after the onset of the stimulus (Näätänen et al., 1978; Picton et al., 2000; Sams et al., 1985). Even abstract errors, such as the violation of basic rules in tone patterns or combinations, can elicit the MMN prediction error signal (Saarinen et al., 1992; Virtala et al., 2011). MMN is, thus, considered a reliable neurophysiological index of sensory memory formation and predictive processes in the brain (Atienza et al., 2002; Cheour et al., 2000, Ruzzoli et al., 2012; Winkler and Czigler, 2012).

3 The Traditional Assessment of Intelligence

The primary driver for developing an intelligence test specifically for educational selection came from France in 1904, when the minister of public instruction in Paris formed a committee to find a way to identify kids with learning difficulties. The first version of the Binet–Simon Scale was then published in 1905, and an updated version followed in 1908 with the introduction of the concept of "mental age", which was the age for which a child's score was most typical, regardless of their chronological age. The potential of intelligence testing and IQ scores to identify intellectual capacity in adults as well as children was soon recognized, and the First World War saw the introduction in the US army. Following the popularity and success of the army tests, the US College Board began conducting IQ mass testing in 1926 with the introduction of the Scholastic Aptitude Test (SAT), which was created to ease entry into US colleges (Rust and Golombok, 2014).

Nowadays, intelligence tests are conceptualized more broadly and put a greater emphasis on a variety of different cognitive domains such as reasoning, memory, processing speed, spatial ability and, in general, executive functions (Deary et al., 2010), allowing everyone to identify both their areas of strength and those that they are most likely to find difficult. Assessments of specific forms of intelligence, such as verbal, numerical, and critical thinking abilities, remain to be crucial for admission to programs of professional training that require these abilities. Additionally, broad-spectrum evaluations of the numerous fundamental cognitive abilities that support key learning processes play an increasingly important role in determining which individuals most require remedial learning programs (Rust and Golombok, 2014).

Although cognitive domains are commonly thought to be independent, differential psychology has firmly proven that they are not: people who perform well in one domain also tend to perform well in the others (Deary, 2000; Deary et al., 2001; Jensen, 1987, Jensen, 2006, Neubauer and Bucik, 1996, Vernon, 1990). This is recognized in the term "general fluid intelligence" (gF), a major dimension of individual differences and that refers to reasoning and novel problem-solving ability (Cattell, 1971). Some individual tests, such as Raven's Progressive Matrices, which is used to assess non-verbal reasoning, are good indicators of gF (Deary et al., 2010). A g factor almost always accounts for 40% or more of the total variance in test batteries that typically contain 10–15 different cognitive tasks involving a variety of materials and content (Deary et al., 2010). If we look at batteries that cover all cognitive domains, instead, the Wechsler tests are probably the most comprehensive clinical tests sampling skills in verbal and non-verbal areas of intellectual functioning, with the Wechsler Adult intelligence Scale 4th Edition (WAIS-IV) representing the gold-standard in the adult IQ measurement (Hartman, 2009).

Another kind of intelligence tests are those who aim to assess social or emotional intelligence (EI), such as the Mayer–Salovey–Caruso Emotional Intelligence Test (MSCEIT; Mayer et al., 2003), the Emotional Competence Inventory (ECI; Boyatzis and Sala, 2004) or the Bar-On Emotional Quotient Inventory (EQ-i; Bar-On, 2000). However, different definitions of the EI construct were used by the creators of EI measures, which led to different types and numbers of dimensions for the various measures (Gowing, 2001). Few studies have examined the overlap between trait and ability-based EI measures among different tests and scales (e.g., Brackett and Mayer, 2003; Mayer et al., 2000) and the weak correlation emerged raises serious questions about whether they are all actually measuring the same construct (Conte, 2005; Matthews et al., 2004).

Tests and batteries assessing the multifactorial nature of intelligence have the advantage of being easily administered in various settings and over a wide range of population and even in naturalistic settings, combining increasingly selective and specific research questions. However, they typically require paper, pencil and a chronometer, plus the presence of a licensed psychologist which administers the performance tests to the individual. The scoring of the test is conducted by first transposing the paper responses into a digital platform (e.g., Microsoft Excel) and then confronting those scores with the norms from the published paper manual (e.g., WAIS-IV manual) in a subsequent phase. The administration and scoring phases are not free of measurement errors although psychologists typically attend several hours of dedicated training and internship.

4 The Neural Relationship Between Cognitive Abilities: Intelligence and Memory

Several studies have evidenced a relationship between gF and other cognitive abilities, specifically working memory (WM), although they remain two separate constructs (De Abreu and Gathercole, 2010; Unsworth, 2010; Unsworth et al., 2014). WM is a limited-capacity attention-controlled cognitive system that is responsible for the transient holding, processing, and manipulation of information, and thus it plays an important role in several cognitive processes such as reasoning and decision making (Baddeley, 1992; Förstl et al., 2006; Engle et al., 1999). Many scholars have posited that WM is an essential component of intelligence (Schweizer and Moosbrugger, 2004). Indeed, WM is responsible for errors to happen in intelligence tests (e.g., Jensen, 1992; Schweizer, 2000; Schweizer and Koch, 2001). The relationship between gF and WM is most evident during unspeed tasks (Chuderski, 2013) and attentional control (Conway et al., 2002, Cowan et al., 2006; Kane and Engle, 2002), given that behavioral measures requiring attentional control are where differences in gF are most noticeable (Kane and Engle, 2002; Conway et al., 2002).

Moreover, gF is linked even with semantic memory (Zajenkowski and Szymanik, 2013), and it was shown that the contribution of intelligence and WM to various linguistic structures depends on the syntactic complexity of the verbal material (Daneman and Merikle, 1996).

In further support of the association between gF and WM are studies demonstrating that they share neural foundations. Already the P-FIT theory (Colom et al., 2009; Jung and Haier, 2007) postulated the hierarchical succession of neural activity in WM-related areas (such as the dorsolateral prefrontal regions) for the integration, abstraction and reasoning processes that constitute intelligence construct. Other neuroimaging findings have evidenced a partial overlap between gF and WM (e.g., Burgess et al., 2011, Magnuson et al., 2015), and some of these highlight a correlation between individual differences in frontal and parietal activation during n-back tasks and the gF (Tang et al., 2010), even if the result is not confirmed by other authors (Waiter et al., 2009).

A further aspect to be taken into consideration within the research on cognitive abilities is the relationship they have not only with short-term memory and WM, but even with sensory memory. Indeed, participants performing better in WM tests, taken from Wechsler Memory Scale (WMS-III), showed a stronger MMN (measured with MEG) in frontal regions in response to violated predictions of auditory sequences (Bonetti, et al., 2018). These results were extended in another MEG study by Campo et al. (2022), evidencing the relationship between MMN strength in fronto-temporal brain areas and WM scores, as obtained, this time, with the Digit Span task of WAIS-IV. Therefore, these results suggest that intelligence is related to predictive processes occurring at the pre-attentional sensory memory level.

Individual differences in fluid intelligence are, thus, related to differences in sensory and working memory abilities, with higher IQ in individuals showing better sensory memory neural mechanisms and performing better in WM tests. However, the opposite does not seem to be true based on the latest studies and even reviews. For instance, several reviews highlight the absence of clear effects of WM training on other cognitive skills classically linked to intelligence, such as verbal or non-verbal reasoning (Melby-Lervåg et al., 2016; Sala et al., 2019; Sala and Gobet, 2017; 2020), although other studies show discordant evidence (Smithers et al., 2018).

5 A Further Link Between Intelligence and Memory Found in Sleep

An explanation of the elective link between intelligence and memory has been found in recent years in the analysis of sleep-dependent memory consolidation processes. In fact, sleep has long been recognized as one of the biological conditions required for effective memory consolidation (Helmuth, 2000), which is the process of turning a fresh, labile memory into a lasting long-term memory.

There is a compelling body of evidence linking rapid eye movement (REM) sleep and memory, both in human (Smith, 1985, Smith, 1995, Stickgold and Walker, 2007) and animal (Hennevin et al., 1995, Smith, 2003) studies, although an implication of nREM sleep in consolidation of new learning has emerged as well (Buzsáki, 1984, Buzsáki, 1989, Gais and Born, 2004, Nader and Smith, 2003, Smith and MacNeill, 1994). In particular, Stage 2 of nREM sleep is characterized by "sleep spindles", EEG events that reflect, at the electrophysiological level, a mechanism involved in the consolidation of memory during sleep. Moreover, recent studies have shown that sleep spindles may act as a physiological indicator of intelligence and reflect intellectual ability as measured by aptitude batteries, including IQ tests (Fogel and Smith, 2011), with lower sleep spindle frequency associated with better performance on the perceptual reasoning and WM (Gruber et al., 2013) and the number of sleep spindles positively and highly correlated with general intellectual abilities including Full-scale IQ and Performance IQ (Nader and Smith 2001, 2003).

6 Looking at the Future: Using Technology for the Assessment of Individual Differences

In the last few years, the fields of computing and telecommunications have experienced rapid development. This has rapidly affected the way individual differences in cognitive, affective and social skills are assessed in different kinds of settings. For instance, several publishers and laboratories have developed and validated on a normative population a variety of computerized tests, especially for children, or implemented automatic scoring based on button press responses on a PC keyboard, including for the assessment of emotional intelligence (e.g., www.giuntitesting.com).

Administering psychological tests for assessing individual differences in cognitive and other skills via PC has the undoubted advantage of being able to standardize the setting even during a group administration. This digital approach is, furthermore, time- and cost-efficient. Indeed, the administration and scoring via computers of tests such as for assessing IQ or emotional intelligence saves the time of transcription from paper to Excel tables and manual calculation of the scores. Another benefit of using computers in psychological testing is their scoring accuracy because they are less prone to human error, providing a more objective and less biased interpretation by minimizing the possibility of selective interpretation of data (Nezami and Butcher, 2000).

Moreover, the "opening up" of the Internet, which has quickly become a commonplace and integral part of daily life, has had profound implications for the working practices of many people, including psychologists. The massive use of the internet has made it natural to delegate part of the psychological assessment through various technological media. In the years of Covid-19 pandemic, the strong limitation of physical contact often made the use of online psychological assessment the only solution for completing therapeutic programs or research examinations.

Although there has been an inevitable increase in the pandemic years, digital online assessments have been widely conducted for some time. When VandenBos and Williams (2000) investigated the extent to which psychologists were offering different services via a variety of technologies, they discovered that 15.1% of their respondents had mentioned offering "psychological or neuropsychological assessment" via "Other: Facsimiles, E-mail, etc."

A recent example of computerized psychological tests and questionnaires provided in a naturalistic setting, namely middle schools, is provided by the MiddleSchool project, reported in Lippolis et al. (2022c) and in two papers from this same issue (Lippolis et al., 2022a; Matarrelli et al., submitted). In this work, a computer battery of tests and questionnaires was adopted for assessing individual differences in a variety of cognitive, emotional and social skills on pre-adolescent children and how those were dependent on music curricular activities. Specifically, the tests measured visual-spatial working memory skills, fluid intelligence and perceptive and mnemonic skills related to music, using the LongGold Online Test Battery (www.longgold.org) (Fig. 1). In detail, the gF was measured using 8 matrix reasoning items based on similar rules followed by Raven's

Progressive Matrices; these items were taken from the public online platform ICAR (International Cognitive Ability Resource; www.icar-project.com). Each item consists of a box to be completed and 8 different distractors. After 120 s from the administration of the object, the box to be filled in was made to disappear, leaving available to the subject only the possible answers to be selected.

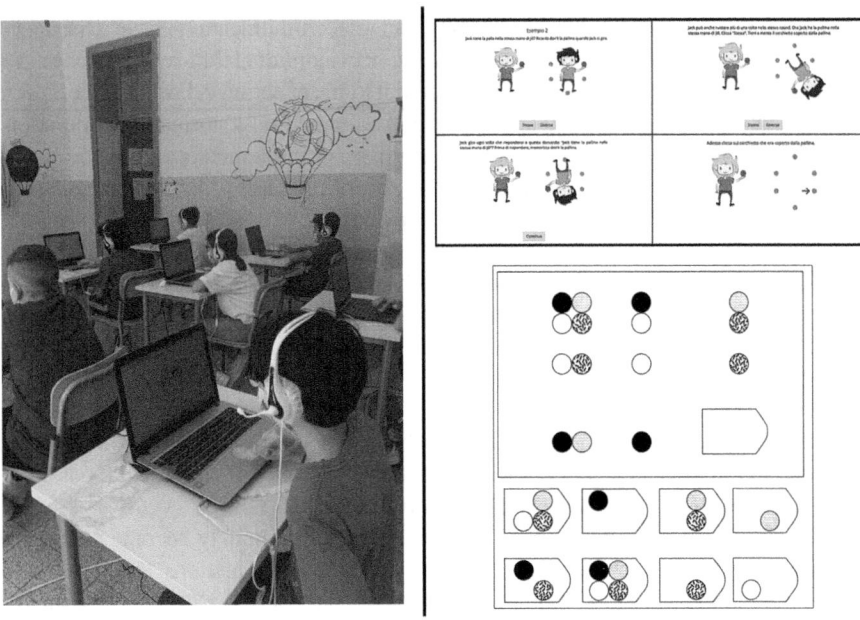

Fig. 1. Pre-adolescent children participating in the experiment with the different tests at their school classroom.

Within the MiddleSchool project, the preadolescent participants were asked also to fill in questionnaires that were presented either within the LongGold Online Test platform or within a Google form. These self-administered questionnaires assessed affective, relational and musical abilities (e.g., empathy, conduct problems, hope, musical reward sensitivity; Lippolis et al., 2022.b; Matarrelli et al. 2022). Overall, the experimental session conducted by kids in their classroom (see Fig. 1) or in the IT rooms of their schools lasted around one hour in total, and was very well tolerated and even fun for the participants.

Online tools designed to assess intelligence are quite scarce. An example of a test that exists both online and in paper-and-pencil version is the MSCEIT, a self-reported assessment tool which aims to evaluate the EI quotient, or the Raven's Progressive Matrices (Raven et al., 2018).

Another concrete example of digital assessment of cognitive abilities is the screening test conducted by the association MENSA - The High IQ Society, a non-profit organization that accepts participants with IQ scores in the 98th percentile or higher. Their online test is Raven's like (https://test.mensa.no/) and provides candidate members who

7 Limits of Technological Applications in IQ Testing

Even though computerized assessment of cognitive and other abilities has many benefits, this method is not totally problem-free. It is important to note that the differences between standard and computerized administration procedures can have a significant impact on the comparability of the two types of neuropsychological measures and the outcomes that are found. This idea is supported by French and Beaumont's (1990) research: they examined the validity of computerized versions of the Mill Hill Vocabulary Test as well as the Standard Progressive Matrices Test among patients who were administered computerized and standard versions of each instrument. On the Mill Hill Vocabulary Test, there were no appreciable score differences between the two versions; however, this was not the case for the Standard Progressive Matrices Test. On it, participants performed better on the computerized version in terms of scores on the standard version. The researchers came to the conclusion that it was not possible to use the two versions of this particular test interchangeably (French and Beaumont, 1990).

Apart from these few pieces of evidence, however, there is a scarcity of studies in the literature that investigate the reliability aspect of online assessment, especially when considering healthy participants. Importantly, the last generations are extremely familiar with technology, to watching screens and to playing computer games; hence, providing tests via technological tools might increase motivational engagement, in compliance with the gamification philosophy (Hamari, 2007), and, as a consequence, even results' reliability.

8 Conclusions

Intelligence, therefore, is a large and multifaceted construct which might even encompass emotional aspects, and its relationship with other cognitive functions is just starting to be widely investigated (Smid et al., 2020). Technology may be a useful tool that permits psychologists, researchers and participants to save time and resources, but more research should be conducted, comparing in presence to online assessment, in order to better understand the reliability and replicability of the digital vs. traditional tests.

Acknowledgements. The Center for Music in the Brain is funded by the Danish National Research Foundation (DNRF project number 117). We thank the Italian section of Mensa: The International High IQ Society for a grant awarded to Fulvia Francesca Campo.

References

Alexander, W.H., Brown, J.W.: Frontal cortex function as derived from hierarchical predictive coding. Sci. Rep. **8**(1), 1–11 (2018). https://doi.org/10.1038/s41598-018-21407-9

Andreasen, N.C., et al.: Intelligence and brain structure in normal individuals. Am. J. Psychiatr. **150**, 130–130 (1993). https://doi.org/10.1176/ajp.150.1.130

Ashton, M.C., Lee, K., Vernon, P.A., Jang, K.L.: Fluid intelligence, crystallized intelligence, and the openness/intellect factor. J. Res. Pers. **34**(2), 198–207 (2000). https://doi.org/10.1006/jrpe.1999.2276

Atienza, M., Cantero, J.L., Dominguez-Marin, E.: Mismatch negativity (MMN): an objective measure of sensory memory and long-lasting memories during sleep. Int. J. Psychophysiol. **46**(3), 215–225 (2002). https://doi.org/10.1016/S0167-8760(02)00113-7

Baddeley, A.: Working memory. Science **255**(5044), 556–559 (1992). https://doi.org/10.1126/science.1736359

Bar-On, R.: Emotional and Social Intelligence: Insights from the Emotional Quotient Inventory (2000)

Barbey, A.K., Koenigs, M., Grafman, J.: Dorsolateral prefrontal contributions to human working memory. Cortex **49**(5), 1195–1205 (2013). https://doi.org/10.1016/j.cortex.2012.05.022

Batty, G.D., Deary, I.J., Gottfredson, L.S.: Premorbid (early life) IQ and later mortality risk: systematic review. Ann. Epidemiol. **17**(4), 278–288 (2007). https://doi.org/10.1016/j.annepidem.2006.07.010

Batty, G.D., et al.: IQ in early adulthood and mortality by middle age: cohort study of 1 million Swedish men. Epidemiology, 100–109 (2009). https://doi.org/10.1097/EDE.0b013e31818ba076

Boyatzis, R.E., Sala, F.: The emotional competence inventory (ECI). In: Geher, G. (ed.) Measuring Emotional Intelligence: Common Ground and Controversy, pp. 147–180. Nova Science Publishers (2004)

Brackett, M.A., Mayer, J.D.: Convergent, discriminant, and incremental validity of competing measures of emotional intelligence. Pers. Soc. Psychol. Bull. **29**(9), 1147–1158 (2003). https://doi.org/10.1177/0146167203254596

Burgess, G.C., Gray, J.R., Conway, A.R., Braver, T.S.: Neural mechanisms of interference control underlie the relationship between fluid intelligence and working memory span. J. Exp. Psychol. Gen. **140**(4), 674 (2011). https://doi.org/10.1037/a0024695

Burt, C.: Class differences in general intelligence: III. Br. J. Stat. Psychol. **12**(1), 15–33 (1959). https://doi.org/10.1111/j.2044-8317.1959.tb00021.x

Buzsáki, G.: Long-term changes of hippocampal sharp-waves following high frequency afferent activation. Brain Res. **300**(1), 179–182 (1984). https://doi.org/10.1016/0006-8993(84)91356-8

Buzsáki, G.: Two-stage model of memory trace formation: a role for "noisy" brain states. Neuroscience **31**(3), 551–570 (1989). https://doi.org/10.1016/0306-4522(89)90423-5

Campo, F.F., et al.: Fluid intelligence and auditory predictive processing: associations between MMN parameters and performance scores [Unpublished manuscript]. Department of Education, Psychology, Communication. University of Bari Aldo Moro (2022)

Carroll, J.B.: Human Cognitive Abilities: A Survey of Factor-Analytic Studies (No. 1). Cambridge University Press, Cambridge (1993)

Cattell, R.B.: Abilities, Their Structure, Growth, and Action. Houghton Mifflin, Boston (1971)

Cattell, R.: Culture Free Intelligence Test, Scale 1, Handbook. Institute of Personality and Ability, Champaign (1949)

Cattell, R.B.: Theory of fluid and crystallized intelligence: a critical experiment. J. Educ. Psychol. **54**(1), 1 (1963). https://doi.org/10.1037/h0046743

Cattell, R.B., Horn, J.L.: A check on the theory of fluid and crystallized intelligence with description of new subtest designs. J. Educ. Meas. **15**(3), 139–164 (1978). https://doi.org/10.1111/j.1745-3984.1978.tb00065.x

Charlton, B.G.: Clever sillies: why high IQ people tend to be deficient in common sense. Med. Hypotheses **73**(6), 867–870 (2009). https://doi.org/10.1016/j.mehy.2009.08.016

Cheour, M., Leppänen, P.H., Kraus, N.: Mismatch negativity (MMN) as a tool for investigating auditory discrimination and sensory memory in infants and children. Clin. Neurophysiol. **111**(1), 4–16 (2000). https://doi.org/10.1016/S1388-2457(99)00191-1

Chuderski, A.: When are fluid intelligence and working memory isomorphic and when are they not? Intelligence **41**(4), 244–262 (2013). https://doi.org/10.1016/j.intell.2013.04.003

Clarke, A.M., Sternberg, R.J.: Beyond IQ: a triarchic theory of human intelligence. Br. J. Educ. Stud. (1986). https://doi.org/10.2307/3121332

Colom, R., et al.: Gray matter correlates of fluid, crystallized, and spatial intelligence: testing the P-FIT model. Intelligence **37**(2), 124–135 (2009). https://doi.org/10.1016/j.intell.2008.07.007

Conte, J.M.: A review and critique of emotional intelligence measures. J. Organ. Behav. **26**(4), 433–440 (2005). https://doi.org/10.1002/job.319

Conway, A.R.A., Cowan, N., Bunting, M.F., Therriault, D.J., Minkoff, S.R.B.: A latent variable analysis of working memory capacity, short-term memory capacity, processing speed, and general fluid intelligence. Intelligence **30**(2), 163–184 (2002). https://doi.org/10.1016/S0160-2896(01)00096-4

Cowan, N., Fristoe, N.M., Elliott, E.M., Brunner, R.P., Saults, J.S.: Scope of attention, control of attention, and intelligence in children and adults. Mem. Cognit. **34**(8), 1754–1768 (2006). https://doi.org/10.3758/BF03195936

Daneman, M., Merikle, P.M.: Working memory and language comprehension: a meta-analysis. Psychon. Bull. Rev. **3**(4), 422–433 (1996). https://doi.org/10.3758/BF03214546

De Abreu, P.M.E., Conway, A.R., Gathercole, S.E.: Working memory and fluid intelligence in young children. Intelligence **38**(6), 552–561 (2010). https://doi.org/10.1016/j.intell.2010.07.003

Deary, I.J.: Looking Down on Human Intelligence: From Psychometrics to the Brain. Oxford University Press, Oxford (2000). https://doi.org/10.1093/acprof:oso/9780198524175.001.0001

Deary, I.J., Der, G., Ford, G.: Reaction times and intelligence differences: a population-based cohort study. Intelligence **29**(5), 389–399 (2001). https://doi.org/10.1016/S0160-2896(01)00062-9

Deary, I.J., Penke, L., Johnson, W.: The neuroscience of human intelligence differences. Nat. Rev. Neurosci. **11**(3), 201–211 (2010). https://doi.org/10.1038/nrn2793

Deary, I.J., Whalley, L.J., Lemmon, H., Crawford, J.R., Starr, J.M.: The stability of individual differences in mental ability from childhood to old age: follow-up of the 1932 Scottish Mental Survey. Intelligence **28**(1), 49–55 (2000). https://doi.org/10.1016/S0160-2896(99)00031-8

Deco, G., Tononi, G., Boly, M., Kringelbach, M.L.: Rethinking segregation and integration: contributions of whole-brain modelling. Nat. Rev. Neurosci. **16**(7), 430–439 (2015). https://doi.org/10.1038/nrn3963

Edmonds, C.J., et al.: Inspection time and cognitive abilities in twins aged 7 to 17 years: age-related changes, heritability and genetic covariance. Intelligence **36**(3), 210–225 (2008). https://doi.org/10.1016/j.intell.2007.05.004

Engle, R.W., Tuholski, S.W., Laughlin, J.E., Conway, A.R.: Working memory, short-term memory, and general fluid intelligence: a latent-variable approach. J. Exp. Psychol. Gen. **128**(3), 309 (1999). https://doi.org/10.1037/0096-3445.128.3.309

Fiedler, E.D.: Gifted children: the promise of potential/the problems of potential. In: Handbook of Psychosocial Characteristics of Exceptional Children, pp. 401–441. Springer, Boston (1999). https://doi.org/10.1007/978-1-4757-5375-2_16

Finkel, D., Pedersen, N.L., McGue, M., McClearn, G.E.: Heritability of cognitive abilities in adult twins: comparison of Minnesota and Swedish data. Behav. Genet. (1995). https://doi.org/10.1007/BF02253371

Flashman, L.A., Andreasen, N.C., Flaum, M., Swayze, V.W., II.: Intelligence and regional brain volumes in normal controls. Intelligence **25**(3), 149–160 (1997). https://doi.org/10.1016/S0160-2896(97)90039-8

Fogel, S.M., Smith, C.T.: The function of the sleep spindle: a physiological index of intelligence and a mechanism for sleep-dependent memory consolidation. Neurosci. Biobehav. Rev. **35**(5), 1154–1165 (2011). https://doi.org/10.1016/j.neubiorev.2010.12.003

Förstl, H., Tulving, E., Craik, F.I.M.: The Oxford Handbook of Memory. Zeitschrift für Psychiatrie, Psychologie und Psychotherapie, vol. 54 (2006). https://doi.org/10.1024/1661-4747.54.1.68a

Freeman, J.: Gifted Children Growing Up. Cassel, London (1991)

Freeman, J.: Gifted Children Grown Up. David Fulton Publishers (2013). https://doi.org/10.4324/9780203065587

French, C.C., Beaumont, J.G.: A clinical study of the automated assessment of intelligence by the Mill Hill Vocabulary test and the Standard Progressive Matrices test. J. Clin. Psychol. **46**(2), 129–140 (1990). https://doi.org/10.1002/1097-4679(199003)46:2%3c129::AID-JCLP2270460203%3e3.0.CO;2-Y

Friston, K.: Beyond phrenology: what can neuroimaging tell us about distributed circuitry? Annu. Rev. Neurosci. **25**(1), 221–250 (2002). https://doi.org/10.1016/j.neunet.2003.06.005

Friston, K.: A theory of cortical responses. Philos. Trans. Roy. Soc. B: Biol. Sci. **360**(1456), 815–836 (2005). https://doi.org/10.1098/rstb.2005.1622

Friston, K., et al.: Multiple sparse priors for the M/EEG inverse problem. NeuroImage **39**(3), 1104–1120 (2008). https://doi.org/10.1016/j.neuroimage.2007.09.048

Gais, S., Born, J.: Declarative memory consolidation: mechanisms acting during human sleep. Learn. Mem. **11**(6), 679–685 (2004). https://doi.org/10.1101/lm.80504

Gardner, H., Hatch, T.: Educational implications of the theory of multiple intelligences. Educ. Res. **18**(8), 4–10 (1989). https://doi.org/10.3102/0013189X018008004

Goldstein, S., Naglieri, J.A.: Handbook of Executive Functioning (2014). https://doi.org/10.1007/978-1-4614-8106-5

Gottfredson, L.S.: Why g matters: the complexity of everyday life. Intelligence **24**(1), 79–132 (1997). https://doi.org/10.1016/S0160-2896(97)90014-3

Gowing, M.K.: Measurement of individual emotional competence. In: The Emotionally Intelligent Workplace: How to Select for, Measure, and Improve Emotional Intelligence in Individuals, Groups, and Organizations, pp. 83–131 (2001)

Gray, J.R., Chabris, C.F., Braver, T.S.: Neural mechanisms of general fluid intelligence. Nat. Neurosci. **6**(3), 316–322 (2003). https://doi.org/10.1038/nn1014

Gruber, R., et al.: The association between sleep spindles and IQ in healthy school-age children. Int. J. Psychophysiol. **89**(2), 229–240 (2013). https://doi.org/10.1016/j.ijpsycho.2013.03.018

Hamari, J.: Gamification. The Blackwell Encyclopedia of Sociology, pp. 1–3 (2007). https://doi.org/10.1002/9781405165518.wbeos1321

Hartman, D.E.: Wechsler adult intelligence scale IV (WAIS IV): return of the gold standard. Appl. Neuropsychol. **16**(1), 85–87 (2009). https://doi.org/10.1080/09084280802644466

Helmuth, L.: Video game images persist despite amnesia. Science **290** (2000). https://doi.org/10.1126/science.290.5490.247a

Hennevin, E., Hars, B., Maho, C., Bloch, V.: Processing of learned information in paradoxical sleep: relevance for memory. Behav. Brain Res. **69**(1–2), 125–135 (1995). https://doi.org/10.1016/0166-4328(95)00013-J

Huron, D.: Sweet Anticipation: Music and the Psychology of Expectation. MIT Press, Cambridge (2008)

Irwing, P., Lynn, R.: Sex differences in means and variability on the progressive matrices in university students: a meta-analysis. Br. J. Psychol. **96**(4), 505–524 (2005). https://doi.org/10.1348/000712605X53542

Jacobs, N., Van Os, J., Derom, C., Thiery, E.: Heritability of intelligence. Twin Res. Hum. Genet. **10**(S1), 11–14 (2007). https://doi.org/10.1375/twin.10.supp.11

Jensen, A.R.: Individual differences in the Hick paradigm (1987)

Jensen, A.R.: Relation between information processing time and right/wrong responses. Am. J. Ment. Retard. **97**(3), 290–292 (1992)

Jensen, A.R.: Clocking the mind: mental chronometry and individual differences. Elsevier (2006). https://doi.org/10.1016/j.intell.2014.09.006

Johnson, W., Bouchard, T.J., Jr.: The structure of human intelligence: It is verbal, perceptual, and image rotation (VPR), not fluid and crystallized. Intelligence **33**(4), 393–416 (2005). https://doi.org/10.1016/j.intell.2004.12.002

Johnson, W., et al.: Genetic and environmental influences on the Verbal-Perceptual-Image Rotation (VPR) model of the structure of mental abilities in the Minnesota study of twins reared apart. Intelligence **35**(6), 542–562 (2007). https://doi.org/10.1016/j.intell.2006.10.003

Johnson, W., Carothers, A., Deary, I.J.: Sex differences in variability in general intelligence: a new look at the old question. Perspect. Psychol. Sci. **3**(6), 518–531 (2008). https://doi.org/10.1111/j.1745-6924.2008.00096.x

Johnson, W., McGue, M., Iacono, W.G.: Genetic and environmental influences on academic achievement trajectories during adolescence. Dev. Psychol. **42**(3), 514 (2006). https://doi.org/10.1037/0012-1649.42.3.514

Jung, R.E., Haier, R.J.: The Parieto-Frontal Integration Theory (P-FIT) of intelligence: converging neuroimaging evidence. Behav. Brain Sci. **30**(2), 135–154 (2007). https://doi.org/10.1017/S0140525X07001185

Kane, M.J., Engle, R.W.: The role of prefrontal cortex in working-memory capacity, executive attention, and general fluid intelligence: an individual-differences perspective. Psychon. Bull. Rev. **9**(4), 637–671 (2002). https://doi.org/10.3758/bf03196323

Kalender, B., Trehub, S.E., Schellenberg, E.G.: Cross-cultural differences in meter perception. Psychol. Res. **77**(2), 196–203 (2013). https://doi.org/10.1007/s00426-012-0427-y

Lippolis, M., et al.: Sensitivity to social reward in music behavior changes after curricular music training in preadolescence [Unpublished manuscript]. Department of Education, Psychology, Communication. University of Bari Aldo Moro (2022a)

Lippolis, M., Matarrelli, B., Carraturo, G., Vuust, P., Brattico, E.: Musical sophistication predicts all empathy subscales except for personal distress in Italian and Spanish preadolescents [Unpublished manuscript]. Department of Education, Psychology, Communication. University of Bari Aldo Moro (2022b)

Lippolis, M., et al.: Learning to play a musical instrument in the middle school is associated with superior audiovisual working memory and fluid intelligence: a cross-sectional behavioral study. Front. Psychol. **13**, 982704 (2022). https://doi.org/10.3389/fpsyg.2022.982704

Lupyan, G., Clark, A.: Words and the world: predictive coding and the language-perception-cognition interface. Curr. Dir. Psychol. Sci. **24**(4), 279–284 (2015). https://doi.org/10.1177/0963721415570732

Lynn, J.: The effect of race and sex on physicians' recommendations for cardiac catheterization. J. Am. Geriatr. Soc. 1390 (1999)

MacLullich, A.M.J., Ferguson, K.J., Deary, I.J., Seckl, J.R., Starr, J.M., Wardlaw, J.M.: Intracranial capacity and brain volumes are associated with cognition in healthy elderly men. Neurology **59**(2), 169–174 (2002). https://doi.org/10.1212/WNL.59.2.169

Magnuson, M.E., et al.: Errors on interrupter tasks presented during spatial and verbal working memory performance are linearly linked to large-scale functional network connectivity in high temporal resolution resting state fMRI. Brain Imaging Behav. **9**(4), 854–867 (2015). https://doi.org/10.1016/j.intell.2008.09.008

Matarrelli, B., Lippolis, M., Vuust, P., Brattico, E.: An Italian validation of the Childre's Hope Scale: evaluating hope to promote flourishing and well-being in pre-adolescence. [Unpublished manuscript]. Department of Education, Psychology, Communication. University of Bari Aldo Moro (2022)

Matthews, G., Zeidner, M., Roberts, R.D.: Emotional Intelligence: Science and Myth. MIT Press, Cambridge (2004)

Mayer, J.D., Salovey, P., Caruso, D.R., Sternberg, R.J.: Models of Emotional Intelligence. JD Mayer (2000)

Mayer, J.D., Salovey, P., Caruso, D.R., Sitarenios, G.: Measuring emotional intelligence with the MSCEIT V2. 0. Emotion **3**(1), 97 (2003). https://doi.org/10.1037/1528-3542.3.1.97

McCartney, K., Harris, M.J., Bernieri, F.: Growing up and growing apart: a developmental meta-analysis of twin studies. Psychol. Bull. **107**(2), 226 (1990). https://doi.org/10.1037/0033-2909.107.2.226

McDaniel, M.A.: Big-brained people are smarter: a meta-analysis of the relationship between in vivo brain volume and intelligence. Intelligence **33**(4), 337–346 (2005). https://doi.org/10.1016/j.intell.2004.11.005

McGue, M., Bouchard, T.J., Iacono, W.G., Lykken, D.T., Plomin, R., McClearn, G.: Nature, Nurture, and Psychology (1993)

McManus, I.C.: Measuring participation in UK medical schools: social class data are problematic to interpret. BMJ **329**(7469), 800–801 (2004). https://doi.org/10.1136/bmj.329.7469.800-c

Melby-Lervåg, M., Redick, T.S., Hulme, C.: Working memory training does not improve performance on measures of intelligence or other measures of "far transfer" evidence from a meta-analytic review. Perspect. Psychol. Sci. **11**(4), 512–534 (2016). https://doi.org/10.1177/17456916166356

Moffitt, T.E., Caspi, A., Harkness, A.R., Silva, P.A.: The natural history of change in intellectual performance: who changes? How much? Is it meaningful? Child Psychol. Psychiatry. Allied Discip. **34**(4), 455–506 (1993)

Näätänen, R., Gaillard, A.W., Mäntysalo, S.: Early selective-attention effect on evoked potential reinterpreted. Acta Physiol. (Oxf) **42**(4), 313–329 (1978). https://doi.org/10.1016/0001-6918(78)90006-9

Nader, R.S., Smith, C.T.: The relationship between stage 2 sleep spindles and intelligence. In: Sleep, vol. 24, pp. A160–A160 (2001)

Nader, R., Smith, C.: A role for stage 2 sleep in memory processing. Sleep Brain Plastic. **1**(9), 87–99 (2003). https://doi.org/10.1093/acprof:oso/9780198574002.003.0005

Neubauer, A.C., Bucik, V.: The mental speed—IQ relationship: unitary or modular? Intelligence **22**(1), 23–48 (1996). https://doi.org/10.1016/S0160-2896(96)90019-7

Nezami, E., Butcher, J.N.: Pros and cons of computerized psychological assessment. In: Handbook of Psychological Assessment, 3rd edn (2000)

Persson, R.S.: The myth of the antisocial genius: a survey study of the socio-emotional aspects of high-IQ individuals. Gifted Talent. Int. **22**(2), 19–34 (2007). https://doi.org/10.1080/15332276.2007.11673492

Picton, T.W., Alain, C., Otten, L., Ritter, W., Achim, A.: Mismatch negativity: different water in the same river. Audiol. Neurotol. **5**(3–4), 111–139 (2000). https://doi.org/10.1159/000013875

Plomin, R., DeFries, J.C., McClearn, G.E.: Behavioral Genetics. Macmillan, New York (2008)

Posthuma, D., Baaré, W.F., Pol, H.E.H., Kahn, R.S., Boomsma, D.I., De Geus, E.J.: Genetic correlations between brain volumes and the WAIS-III dimensions of verbal comprehension, working memory, perceptual organization, and processing speed. Twin Res. Hum. Genet. **6**(2), 131–139 (2003). https://doi.org/10.1375/twin.6.2.131

Posthuma, D., De Geus, E.J.C., Boomsma, D.I.: Perceptual speed and IQ are associated through common genetic factors. Behav. Genet. **31**(6), 593–602 (2001). https://doi.org/10.1023/A:1013349512683

Raven, J.C., Rust, J., Chan, F., Zhou, X.: Raven's Progressive Matrices 2, Clinical Edition (Raven's 2) (2018)

Rijsdijk, F.V., Vernon, P.A., Boomsma, D.I.: Application of hierarchical genetic models to Raven and WAIS subtests: a Dutch twin study. Behav. Genet. **32**(3), 199–210 (2002). https://doi.org/10.1023/A:1016021128949

Rubinov, M., Sporns, O.: Complex network measures of brain connectivity: uses and interpretations. Neuroimage **52**(3), 1059–1069 (2010). https://doi.org/10.1016/j.neuroimage.2009.10.003

Rust, J., Golombok, S.: Modern Psychometrics: The Science of Psychological Assessment. Routledge, London (2014)

Ruzzoli, M., Pirulli, C., Brignani, D., Maioli, C., Miniussi, C.: Sensory memory during physiological aging indexed by mismatch negativity (MMN). Neurobiol. Aging **33**(3), 625-e21 (2012). https://doi.org/10.1016/j.neurobiolaging.2011.03.021

Saarinen, J., Paavilainen, P., Schöger, E., Tervaniemi, M., Näätänen, R.: Representation of abstract attributes of auditory stimuli in the human brain. NeuroReport **3**(12), 1149–1151 (1992). https://doi.org/10.1097/00001756-199212000-00030

Sala, G., Aksayli, N.D., Tatlidil, K.S., Gondo, Y., Gobet, F.: Working memory training does not enhance older adults' cognitive skills: a comprehensive meta-analysis. Intelligence **77**, 101386 (2019). https://doi.org/10.1016/j.intell.2019.101386

Sala, G., Gobet, F.: Working memory training in typically developing children: a meta-analysis of the available evidence. Dev. Psychol. **53**(4), 671 (2017). https://doi.org/10.1037/dev0000265

Sala, G., Gobet, F.: Working memory training in typically developing children: a multilevel meta-analysis. Psychon. Bull. Rev. **27**(3), 423–434 (2020). https://doi.org/10.3758/s13423-019-01681-y

Salovey, P., Mayer, J.D.: Emotional intelligence. Imagin. Cogn. Pers. **9**(3), 185–211 (1990). https://doi.org/10.2190/DUGG-P24E-52WK-6CDG

Sams, M., Paavilainen, P., Alho, K., Näätänen, R.: Auditory frequency discrimination and event-related potentials. Electroencephalogr. Clin. Neurophysiol./Evoked Potent. Sect. **62**(6), 437–448 (1985). https://doi.org/10.1016/0168-5597(85)90054-1

Schneider, W., Niklas, F., Schmiedeler, S.: Intellectual development from early childhood to early adulthood: the impact of early IQ differences on stability and change over time. Learn. Individ. Differ. **32**, 156–162 (2014). https://doi.org/10.1016/j.lindif.2014.02.001

Schweizer, K.: Cognitive mechanisms at the core of success and failure in intelligence testing. Psychol. Test Assess. Model. **42**(2), 190 (2000)

Schweizer, K., Koch, W.: Kapazitätslimitierung und intellektuelle leistungsfähigkeit [Capacity limitation and intellectual ability]. Z. Exp. Psychol. **48**(1), 1–19 (2001). https://doi.org/10.1026/0949-3946.48

Schweizer, K., Moosbrugger, H.: Attention and working memory as predictors of intelligence. Intelligence **32**(4), 329–347 (2004). https://doi.org/10.1016/j.intell.2004.06.006

Smid, C.R., Karbach, J., Steinbeis, N.: Toward a science of effective cognitive training. Curr. Dir. Psychol. Sci. **29**(6), 531–537 (2020). https://doi.org/10.1177/0963721420951599

Smith, C.: Sleep states and learning: a review of the animal literature. Neurosci. Biobehav. Rev. **9**(2), 157–168 (1985). https://doi.org/10.1016/0149-7634(85)90042-9

Smith, C.: Sleep states and memory processes. Behav. Brain Res. **69**(1–2), 137–145 (1995). https://doi.org/10.1016/0166-4328(95)00024-N

Smith, C.: The REM sleep window and memory processing. Sleep Brain Plastic. 117–133 (2003)

Smith, C., MacNeill, C.: Impaired motor memory for a pursuit rotor task following Stage 2 sleep loss in college students. J. Sleep Res. **3**(4), 206–213 (1994). https://doi.org/10.1111/j.1365-2869.1994.tb00133.x

Smithers, L.G., Sawyer, A.C.P., Chittleborough, C.R., Davies, N., Smith, G.D., Lynch, J.: A systematic review and meta-analysis of effects of early life non-cognitive skills on academic, psychosocial, cognitive and health outcomes. Nat. Hum. Behav. **2**, 867–880 (2018). https://doi.org/10.1038/s41562-018-0461-x

Spearman, C.: "General Intelligence" objectively determined and measured. Am. J. Psychol. **15**, 201–293 (1904)

Spinath, F.M., Ronald, A., Harlaar, N., Price, T.S., Plomin, R.: Phenotypic g early in life: On the etiology of general cognitive ability in a large population sample of twin children aged 2–4 years. Intelligence **31**(2), 195–210 (2003). https://doi.org/10.1016/S0160-2896(02)00110-1

Spratling, M.W.: Predictive coding as a model of cognition. Cogn. Process. **17**(3), 279–305 (2016). https://doi.org/10.1007/s10339-016-0765-6

Stickgold, R., Walker, M.P.: Sleep-dependent memory consolidation and reconsolidation. Sleep Med. **8**(4), 331–343 (2007). https://doi.org/10.1016/j.sleep.2007.03.011

Strenze, T.: Intelligence and socioeconomic success: a meta-analytic review of longitudinal research. Intelligence **35**(5), 401–426 (2007). https://doi.org/10.1016/j.intell.2006.09.004

Tang, C.Y., et al.: Brain networks for working memory and factors of intelligence assessed in males and females with fMRI and DTI. Intelligence **38**(3), 293–303 (2010). https://doi.org/10.1016/j.intell.2010.03.003

Unsworth, N.: On the division of working memory and long-term memory and their relation to intelligence: a latent variable approach. Acta Physiol. (Oxf) **134**(1), 16–28 (2010). https://doi.org/10.1016/j.actpsy.2009.11.010

Unsworth, N., Fukuda, K., Awh, E., Vogel, E.K.: Working memory and fluid intelligence: capacity, attention control, and secondary memory retrieval. Cogn. Psychol. **71**, 1–26 (2014). https://doi.org/10.1016/j.cogpsych.2014.01.003

VandenBos, G.R., Williams, S.: The Internet versus the telephone: what is telehealth anyway? Prof. Psychol. Res. Pract. **31**(5), 490 (2000). https://doi.org/10.1037/0735-7028.31.5.490

Vernon, P.A.: An overview of chronometric measures of intelligence. Sch. Psychol. Rev. **19**(4), 399–410 (1990). https://doi.org/10.1080/02796015.1990.12087347

Virtala, P., et al.: The preattentive processing of major vs. minor chords in the human brain: an event-related potential study. Neurosci. Lett. **487**(3), 406–410 (2011). https://doi.org/10.1016/j.neulet.2010.10.066

Vuust, P., Brattico, E., Seppänen, M., Näätänen, R., Tervaniemi, M.: The sound of music: differentiating musicians using a fast, musical multi-feature mismatch negativity paradigm. Neuropsychologia **50**(7), 1432–1443 (2012). https://doi.org/10.1016/j.neuropsychologia.2012.02.028

Vuust, P., Witek, M.A.: Rhythmic complexity and predictive coding: a novel approach to modeling rhythm and meter perception in music. Front. Psychol. **5**, 1111 (2014). https://doi.org/10.3389/fpsyg.2014.01111

Waiter, G.D., et al.: Exploring possible neural mechanisms of intelligence differences using processing speed and working memory tasks: an fMRI study. Intelligence **37**(2), 199–206 (2009). https://doi.org/10.1016/j.intell.2008.09.008

Wilson, R.S.: Synchronies in mental development: an epigenetic perspective: early mental development of twins and siblings is analyzed within the framework of evolutionary theory. Science **202**(4371), 939–948 (1978). https://doi.org/10.1126/science.568822

Winkler, I., Czigler, I.: Evidence from auditory and visual event-related potential (ERP) studies of deviance detection (MMN and vMMN) linking predictive coding theories and perceptual object representations. Int. J. Psychophysiol. **83**(2), 132–143 (2012). https://doi.org/10.1016/j.ijpsycho.2011.10.001

Witelson, S.F., Beresh, H., Kigar, D.L.: Intelligence and brain size in 100 postmortem brains: sex, lateralization and age factors. Brain **129**(2), 386–398 (2006). https://doi.org/10.1093/brain/awh730

Zajenkowski, M., Szymanik, J.: Most intelligent people are accurate and some fast people are intelligent: intelligence, working memory, and semantic processing of quantifiers from a computational perspective. Intelligence **41**(5), 456–466 (2013). https://doi.org/10.1016/j.intell.2013.06.020

New Digital Technologies for Psychotherapy

Giusi Antonia Toto(✉) and Pierpaolo Limone

Learning Science Hub, University of Foggia, Via Arpi 176, Foggia, Italy
`giusi.toto@umifg.it`

Abstract. What will happen when an artificial intelligence entity has access to all of the information saved about me online, together with the ability to handle my information in an efficient and error-free manner? Is it possible that such a person could not serve as my ideal therapist? Would there ever be a time when you would feel comfortable confiding in an all-knowing, all-perceiving and highly intelligent robot therapist? This is the point in time when technological singularity will occur for psychotherapy; there is a horizon beyond which we cannot sight nor even begin to conceive what is beyond it. If it is possible for human intelligence to develop artificial intelligence that is more advanced than that of its creators, then it is also possible for artificial intelligence to create a subsequent generation of intellect that is even more advanced. An unavoidable cycle of positive feedback would eventually result in an intelligence growth rate that was exponential. The term "Therapist Panopto's" is presented in this article as a working hypothesis to investigate the implications for psychotherapy of an artificial therapeutic agent. This agent would ben access all available data for a potential client and process these with an intelligence that is unimaginably more advanced than human beings currently possess. The delicate dependence of complex techno-social systems on their starting conditions makes it hard to make any kind of prediction, even though this opens up a new viewpoint on the potential of psychotherapy in the future. Both humans and artificial intelligence come together to form a biotechnological system. The evolution of the participating actors in this complex superorganism is dependent not only on the individual actions of each actor but also on the fact that each actor is a coevolving part of a self-organized whole.

Keywords: Psychotherapy · New Digital Technologies · Artificial Intelligence

1 Introduction

Back in the 1960s, psychological approaches to the treatment of mental health issues were only beginning to undergo a fundamental transformation. The research methodologies of experimental psychology and experimental clinical medicine first started to be applied to the process of developing and evaluating psychological treatments. Currently, psychological treatments are starting to undergo a new phase driven by the ubiquitous availability of digital technology. Fairburn and Patel [1] provided a much-needed narrative review of the digital interventions to date (i.e., mobile apps, internet-based interventions, computerized cognitive training), those in the pipeline, and their likely impact on clinical practice and the global dissemination of psychological treatments [2]. They did this by taking stock of the current tech revolution occurring in clinical psychology.

Individuals can take advantage of a large number of services that are part of the expansive field of healthcare and welfare, many of which are designed to improve both an individual's physical and mental wellness, and although the setting and target people may vary, the professionals use a number of the same solutions that frequently involve face-to-face communication. However, digital technologies also have the potential to assist these service offerings, either on their own or in conjunction with other services already being provided. The use of new technologies may enable better flexibility, to provide interventions in their natural settings, to reach a bigger population without the risk of stigmatization, and to reduce the overall cost of providing services in comparison to how they are now provided. Research is increasingly demonstrating how the selective and targeted application of technology can have a significant impact on the quality of care as well as the role that users can play in the organization and delivery of services [3]. For instance, users may be able to exercise a greater degree of control over their medical care, which is particularly important in the setting of chronic illness. Despite this, there is a significant gap between what is technically feasible and the amount of study that has been carried out up to this point. As a direct consequence of this, there is an excessively large number of choices, which makes it difficult to get an overall picture. For this reason, there have already been efforts made to structure certain aspects of the field, such as for particular technologies, such as internet-based mental health interventions, and smartphone apps, or particular domains, such as emotion regulation in clinical psychology. These efforts have been made to address the issue. The purpose of this current overview of reviews is to build upon the work done previously by broadening the scope of the study to include all technologies that can be used in the overarching field of mental health and wellness.

The field of mental health is now experiencing the effects of the digital revolution. Examples such as the fast-expanding usage of mobile health apps, the incorporation of sophisticated machine learning or artificial intelligence for clinical decision support and automated therapy, and the use of virtual reality-based treatments are three prominent examples [4]. These various technologies have the potential to solve several significant issues that are currently present in the field of mental health care. Some of these issues include a lack of measurement, uneven access to clinicians, delays in receiving care, fragmentation of care, and unfavorable attitudes toward psychiatry. In this section, the writers provide a summary of the current condition of digital mental health, which is rapidly evolving. They explain what digital health can offer for evaluation, treatment, and care integration, and they describe some of the problems and some new prospects for breakthroughs in this sector. More specifically, they highlight the existing unmet needs that developing technologies may be able to answer. The assessment comes to a close with recommendations that physicians follow to incorporate digital technology into their line of work and to offer patients advice that is both responsible and helpful. It is not the purpose of this project to evaluate the efficacy of individual methods but rather to organize and structure the existing technologies and treatments that have been the subject of studies. We hope to further structure this domain by summarizing the large body of research that has been conducted to date and by highlighting both similarities and differences across approaches and settings. In doing so, we will also provide information regarding the research gaps that are currently still present.

2 Background

It is challenging to precisely date the development of psychotherapy as a distinct field of study. Could it have started when two friends got together regularly to chat about life, or when the first academic article on the topic was produced and published? Although the date and venue of first therapeutic discussions are unknown, there is historical evidence to highlight the development of psychotherapy (also called talk therapy) over the years. Psychotherapy refers to any approach taken to assist individuals coping with emotional, psychological, or behavioral difficulties.

The word "psycho" has its origins in Greek and can be translated as either "soul" or "mind." Today, the prefix "psycho" can be found in a wide variety of terms about mental health, as in "psychotherapy."

- People may seek psychotherapy for a variety of reasons, including the following:
- disagreement in a relationship
- professional obstacles to overcome
- personal concerns and apprehensions
- alterations in either behavior or mood
- having a hard time dealing with stress
- traumatic experiences
- occurrences from one's youth
- disordered states of the mind

Counseling may also help to maintain connection and keep lines of communication open, as certain individuals are regular at therapy because they find directed conversation helpful and not necessarily because they have persistent problems.

2.1 Origin of Psychotherapy

Alterations in one's mental health were seen as portents, curses, or messages from the gods in several ancient cultures. Conversely, it is commonly believed that ancient Greeks were the first to treat mental problems as medical conditions, and ancient Greek philosophers were among the first to investigate the relationship between psychological and physical well-being. The ancient Greek philosophers, Plato, Xenophon, and Aristotle, all showed an interest in the field that would later develop into psychotherapy, and eventually, medical practitioners of the time, such as Galen and Hippocrates, continued their research into the connection between mental health and medicine, disproving the notion that medical disorders were caused by influences from other worlds. The fall of the Roman Empire and the beginning of the Dark Ages brought about a reversal in the progress that had been made by the Greeks. During the Middle Ages, there was a resurgence of the widespread idea that the supernatural existed, and the old teachings that linked mental health and medicine were, for the most part, forgotten. Those who struggled with mental health disorders were frequently the victims of a general lack of comprehension, and possibly, individuals who struggled with their mental health were more likely to be thought of as "touched by witchcraft" compared to those who were living with a disorder in the past.

The practice of psychotherapy is always developing, as it did hundreds of years before, and research has provided support for a large number of theories and approaches to treatment; however, the procedures involved in addressing issues of mental health continue to develop. Previously, scientists and therapists did not have access to the vast amounts of empirical data and research that are readily available to mental health practitioners today. This research and data are supported by practice regulations and diagnostic standards. Midway through the 1920s, psychoanalysts in the United States were required to hold a medical degree, and at the end of the 1960s, groundbreaking diagnostic tools such as the Diagnostic and Statistical Manual of Mental Disorders (DSM) [5] was made available to psychoanalysts and clinicians, and since its publication in 1968, the DSM has provided diagnostic criteria for an extensive range of mental health problems.

In addition to the accumulation of knowledge and evidence that has occurred over time, contemporary psychotherapy may now reach a greater number of individuals through the use of online forms. Because of the internet, it is possible to:

- obtain information about the various diagnoses of mental disorders.
- seek support groups.
- access therapists and other mental health support services.
- participate in online sessions of psychotherapy.

2.2 How People Started the Adaption of Psychotherapy

According to Jim Haggerty [6], transfer of aggression among individuals has been ongoing for hundreds of years, although different from what is observable today. The history of therapy for mental disorders dates back to ancient times, and ancient Greeks were the first to classify what we now refer to as "mental disease" as a medical ailment rather than a symptom of possession by evil spirits. At first, they believed that hysteria only affected women because of their wacky uteruses, and their approach to treating mental illnesses was unusual, to say the least. Both bathing and bloodletting were common treatments for mental illnesses in the past, and the therapeutic significance of words of encouragement and support as well as words of consolation was ignored. People believed that supernatural forces caused mental disease during the Middle Ages, which followed the collapse of the Roman Empire, and torture was employed to extract admissions of possession by demons from the victims. It was in the sixth century during the time of that psychotherapy as a method of treating the mentally ill first came into existence.

In 1853, Walter Cooper Dendy was the first to use the phrase "psycho-therapeia." around the turn of the century, and Sigmund Freud developed psychoanalysis and made significant contributions to the field through his studies on infantile sexuality, use of dreams, description of the unconscious, and his model of the human mind. Freud is credited with developing the modern concept of the unconscious.

Freud theorized that the storage of memories or thoughts in one's unconscious mind was the root cause of mental disease and believed that the key to successful treatment was paying attention to the patient while also offering interpretations to jog their memory, as this would reduce the severity of the symptoms. Around 1950, the field of American psychology started to incorporate more active therapies like behavioral psychology as a means of treating emotional and behavioral issues. Also, cognitive behavioral therapy has become an important kind of treatment for a wide variety of psychiaric illnesses because it combines traditional talk therapy with an emphasis on the patient's ideas and feelings.

Carl Rogers [7] established the concept of unconditional positive regard in the 1940s, which refers to the transfer of warmth, authenticity, and acceptance from the therapist to the individual being treated. In the 1960s, more than 60 distinct styles of psychotherapy were developed with names like guided imagery and psychodrama among them. More condensed forms of treatment are being included in psychotherapy in response to the dual challenges of cost and availability of time, and the proliferation of managed care insurance plans and coverage caps are both contributing factors to the acceleration of this trend. Furthermore, people struggling to cope with certain issues might find assistance through a variety of different therapeutic modalities that all provide some form of short therapy.

3 Issues that the Proliferation of Digital Health Technologies May Help to Resolve in Future

Smartphones, virtual reality (VR), artificial intelligence (AI), and machine learning algorithms are only some of the digital technologies that are available to change psychiatry. However, the question that still has to be answered is how these technologies will be applied to make a difference for both patients and physicians. Within the confines of this structure, it may be beneficial to identify five broad challenges that have the potential to be addressed by digital mental health.

The lack of an objective or uniform means of measurement is the first problem that must be addressed. Although other medical fields such as oncology have integrated structured, standardized, and validated tools based on biological markers and objective signs to diagnose and guide treatment, analogous tools in psychiatry are either absent or, when available (for example, semi structured interviews for diagnosis), are rarely used outside of research settings. Conversely, other branches of medicine such as oncology have included systematic, standardized, and validated diagnostic methods that are based on biological markers and objective indicators. Furthermore, there is currently no approach for either the diagnosis or evaluation of outcomes that make use of objective, continuous, ecological assessments of emotion, cognition, and behavior, which is the case for both the diagnosis and the evaluation. Measurement-based care is a relatively new concept that has recently been offered as a foundation for improving the overall quality of mental health care as a whole. The accessibility of treatment options for mental illness is the focus of the second area of concern, and there are significant areas of the industrialized world as well as the vast majority of the developing world that do not have access to mental health care that is supported by evidence. The Substance Abuse and Mental Health Services Administration reports that in 55% of counties in the United

States, there are no mental health specialists present, and only about 2% of people diagnosed with major mental illnesses receive evidence-based treatments (such as supported employment, family psychoeducation, and assertive community treatment) according to the findings of a recent interagency study on the state of treatment for major mental illness [8].

Third, even for individuals who are successful in accessing treatment, there is generally a considerable amount of waiting time before commencement of treatment. This is not merely because there is an inadequate supply of treatment options but also due to the hesitancy of people to seek therapy. Patients in the United States who presented themselves at community clinics in need of assistance after suffering their first psychotic episode had an untreated phase of their condition that lasted for a median of 74 weeks, according to the study results, and this delay has significant repercussions on outcomes because it frequently results in patients receiving therapy for the first time after a significant amount of time spent battling psychosocial impairment. This makes it more difficult for patients to recover from their condition after receiving treatment.

Fourth, patients may find it challenging to navigate the complicated landscape of the mental healthcare system because the system is comprised of a range of professions, therapies, and even points of view, all of which combine to create a maze-like environment. Patients who suffer from both types of sickness are often treated in different silos, although psychological disorders (including drug use disorders) and physical medical ailments are highly comorbid. These silos have their medical records and utilize various sources of funding, and even the treatment of mental disease is typically delivered in fragments rather than continuously. In addition, only 52% of patients discharged from an emergency room following an incident of self-harm were seen the following month for an outpatient mental health follow-up session, and this percentage was lower than the national average of 73%. This is just one illustration among many.

The last concern, but certainly not the least, is the attitude barriers, which is tied to the first four concerns. These obstacles, which are more frequently referred to as stigma and consist of a variety of unfavorable attitudes—particularly negative perceptions about psychiatrists, diagnostic labels, and treatments—are what impede some people from seeking therapy or from adhering to treatment, respectively. For instance, according to the findings of the National Comorbidity Survey Replication, 55% of persons diagnosed with a mental problem do not receive treatment for their ailment despite the available effective treatment options. Although many people believed that the low rate of care was due to a lack of access, a surprising follow-up study to this report indicated that the cause for this low rate of care was more commonly "attitudinal barriers" rather than "structural hurdles." This finding came as a surprise because the original report suggested that the cause of this low rate of care was "structural hurdles".

Is it conceivable for digital technology to solve problems associated with measurement, access, delay, fragmentation, and negative attitudes? There is currently no mobile application that will make the treatment of mental illness more effectively. Despite this, however, there have been some exciting breakthroughs in diagnosis, treatment, and care integration that are already beginning to transform how patients and clinicians communicate with one another, and although there seems to be nothing in the field of psychiatry to be compared to Amazon or Airbnb at present, it is feasible that this will change much sooner than general opinion. In the following sections, a summary of some of the innovations that have been made as well as some of the barriers that have been faced in these three areas, including evaluation, treatment, and integration of care are presented.

4 Digital Interventions Designed to Address Access and Delay Issues are the Treatments

Beginning with telepsychiatry and early attempts to shift evidence-based therapy online, there is a large body of research that supports the use of digital technologies for the treatment of mental health conditions, primarily motivated by the need to overcome obstacles in treatment access and delivery times. Recently, several research have been conducted to investigate the efficacy of digital mental health interventions. Efficacy can be defined as a measurement of how well an intervention leads to the desired results in an ideal or controlled setting. However, there have only been a limited number of studies that have directly examined the effectiveness of these fast-developing technologies. Effectiveness can be defined as the degree to which an intervention operates well under real-world situations. Despite this, however, the available research points to the value of digital interventions in comparison to face-to-face interventions as a means of increasing access to therapies that are supported by evidence.

5 The Available Proof that it Works

Among 3,414 participants in 18 randomized controlled trials (RCTs), a recent meta-analysis of 22 smartphone-based apps for depression found a significant decrease in depressive symptoms from baseline (Hedges' g [a measure of the standardized mean difference between study groups] $= 0.38$; 95% confidence interval [CI]: 0.24–0.52; p0.001), including all 18 studies, and a larger effect when smartphone-based interventions were compared with inactive controls $g = 0.56$. Although the authors were limited in their ability to conduct subgroup analyses due to the small number of trials, a meta-analysis of nine RCTs of smartphone apps that targeted anxiety found that the overall effect size for the smartphone interventions was significant ($g = 0.325$, 95% CI=0.17– 0.48, p0.01). The apps were designed to treat anxiety (e.g., interventions with and without face-to-face supplementation; 22), and the included studies included a wide range of sample sizes (ranging from $N = 15$ to 248 each arm), mean ages (ranging from 18 to 43 years), and outcome measures (including the seven-item Generalized Anxiety Disorder Scale and the Depression Anxiety Stress Scales). The authors of the meta-analyses on depression and anxiety found no evidence of publication bias among the articles that were included in either of the analyses.

Insomnia, post-traumatic stress disorder (PTSD), psychosis, and substance use disorders are all conditions that have been shown to benefit from the use of digital therapies; however, research in each of these areas is still infant, and this promising field continues to face challenges due to the relatively small number of published RCTs across the field of psychiatry (and an even smaller number that include children and adolescents), the significant heterogeneity among studies (such as inclusion criteria, use of in-person supplementation of digital interventions, control conditions, and outcome measures), and relatively short study durations (usually one to three months). If the goal is access, then the change from efficacy to effectiveness will be the litmus test, and this shift will need the widespread adoption of digital treatments as well as continued engagement.

6 Emerging Tides in the World of Digital Interventions

There are three positive tendencies in the field of interventions that should be noted. First, there is the application of digital therapies to individuals suffering from severe mental illness. This formerly difficult-to-reach demographic demonstrates significant rates of adoption of mobile applications that provide peer support, medication adherence, and cognitive retraining and the apps are promising. The second opportunity is the possibility of integrating digital methods with more conventional ones. The United States Food and Drug Administration (FDA) approved the first mobile app for substance use disorders among adults as "a prescription digital therapeutic" (basically, digital cognitive–behavioral therapy [CBT]) to accompany standard outpatient treatment after a pivotal multisite RCT, and because of this certification, healthcare professionals are now authorized to recommend the reSET (Pear Pharmaceutics) mobile application to patients as part of an all-encompassing care plan that also incorporates traditional, in-person therapy for substance abuse.

The utilization of "chatbots," which are supported by more advanced forms of AI, is the third and most cutting-edge trend. A recent RCT compared the effects of a fully automated conversational agent that reinforced CBT techniques in a text-message format with an information-only control group and found that individuals in the intervention group experienced a significantly greater reduction in depressive symptoms than those in the information-only control group. Interventions such as chatbots with sophisticated AI are yet to undergo rigorous testing at scale, although they appear to be a potential answer to the problems of access and latency. It is possible that the majority of people who have a mental illness but are not receiving treatment due to a lack of access or negative attitudes toward psychiatry do not share our assumption that our patients would prefer face-to-face interaction to interaction with a bot. While we may assume that our patients would prefer face-to-face interaction, this assumption may not hold for the majority of people who have a mental illness [9].

The creation of chatbots is just one indication of how recent advances in technology may modify intervention strategies. There is evidence that video games that help train attention or executive function are effective, and the FDA is looking at whether or not they qualify as a "medical device" that can be potentially used in the treatment of attention deficit hyperactivity disorder (ADHD). Over the course of the last decade [10], advancements in virtual reality (VR) technology have resulted in the creation of highly immersive digital experiences, mostly for use in gaming. Alongside these advancements in virtual reality gaming, there has been a proliferation of virtual reality-based treatments for a variety of psychiatric illnesses. For example, several businesses have developed VR applications that imitate fear-inducing scenarios, capitalizing on the empirical support for exposure therapy in the treatment of PTSD and specific phobias. VR technology can supplement in vitro therapy, particularly in situations when in vivo exposure is either not practical or unacceptable, rather than taking the place of traditional in-person treatment (which would improve access). In addition, many virtual reality environments can be customized to precisely resemble the particular circumstances and stimuli that bring on the patient's most severe symptoms, which is a significant advantage.

7 Problems Associated with Digital Interventions

The difference between efficacy and effectiveness is not a meaningless distinction; however, most attempts to put digital treatments discovered in research into reality have been unsuccessful, and patients and providers do not embrace or adhere to online treatments outside of the guidelines established for the study. Mohr et al. [11] remind us that, going forward, we need to think about digital interventions as technology-enabled services rather than stand-alone products, integrating them into the fabric of a patient's life and the workflow of a provider's practice. This is something that we need to do to ensure that they are effective, and it is anticipated that the next generation of digital interventions will appear less like internet-based manualized treatment and more like video games for ADHD or immersive VR. This will be done to boost acceptance and adherence.

Although we have placed a strong emphasis on the evidence supporting efficacy in this article, in the world of software development, success is defined not by efficacy or effectiveness but rather by engagement and scalability. Because software is constantly being changed and improved iteratively to increase adoption and engagement, it is important to recognize that digital interventions may not fit the pharmaceutical development model with RCTs and FDA-approved phases of development. Recognizing this is important because software is constantly changing. When put into reality, this indicates that the software that was evaluated in an RCT and published within the past year (or within the past week) is almost probably no longer relevant and is unlikely to be the same software that patients are using today. If digital therapies are going to be successful in this area of psychiatry, adoption and engagement are going to be just as vital as their efficacy to tackle the challenges of access and delay.

8 New Methods and Resources for Mental Health

In addition to developments in assessment, therapy, and the integration of care, there are a few new technologies that are being developed that have the potential to completely transform mental health. The smartphone, which is now practically ubiquitous, is, without a doubt, the most essential piece of technology in terms of its potential to disrupt diagnosis and treatment. Although the use of smartphones, particularly among younger generations, maybe more commonly described as a contributor to the problem rather than a contributor to the solution, the intensive and widespread use of these powerful computers presents psychiatry with an opportunity to influence public health that has never been seen before. In the following paragraph, we will discuss a few additional strategies in particular domains that have the potential to be just as disruptive.

9 Online Therapy Disadvantages

Online therapy can be effective for some, but it has risks and disadvantages over regular therapy.

- **Not covered by insurance**
  E-therapy insurance coverage varies by state and insurance. Some insurance coverage doesn't cover online treatment, and some professionals don't accept insurance. Psychotherapy can be expensive.
- **Some states prohibit out-of-state providers.**
  Many states ban out-of-state psychologists. In such circumstances, your provider must be licensed in both states. Deborah Baker, an APA legal expert, explained that certain states allow psychologists to provide out-of-state mental health services for a limited time. 9 10 to 30 days per year [12].
- **Unreliable technology, confidentiality, and privacy**
  Online psychotherapy complicates the issue of privacy in psychotherapy. Online therapy is as confidential as traditional treatment. Online information transmission increases the risk of breaches and hacks. Technology issues can make it hard to get needed therapy.
- **Unresolved crises**
  Since online therapists are far from their clients, they can't respond swiftly in a crisis.
- **Not for severe mental illness**
  E-therapy can be effective in some situations, but not for persons who need direct treatment or in-person intervention. If you have a significant addiction or severe mental health problems, internet counseling may not be recommended unless you also receive in-person care. Online counseling may not be useful for complex problems due to its limited scope.
- **Body language**
  Text-based therapy doesn't show facial expressions, voice cues, or body language. These signals can tell the therapist a lot about your feelings, thoughts, moods, and behaviors. Voice-over-internet and video chats can provide a clearer picture, but they lack the warmth and complexity of real-world encounters. Some people may feel more comfortable with digital therapy, especially younger people who are more experienced with it, but others—therapists and patients alike—may benefit more from direct human interaction.
- **Ethical/legal issues**
  Online therapy removes regional restrictions, making legal and ethical enforcement problematic. Many states have various licensure and treatment regulations for therapists. Before starting therapy, check your therapist's credentials and experience.

10 Limitations and Plans for the Future

Even though recent years have witnessed the exponential rise of digital mental health, we are just at the beginning of some of the most innovative and possibly disruptive advances. This was discussed earlier. Both digital interventions, such as certain apps for depression and anxiety, which currently have supporting scientific evidence but have not been widely adopted in care, and digital phenotyping, which is just beginning to demonstrate its value in care, are in the early stages of their respective adoption processes.

The existing state of affairs in the realm of digital mental health has several other significant constraints. Given the intricate nature of the legislative framework that underpins the digital world, one of the most serious issues is the security of information about mental health that is contained within these technologies. To be more specific, it appears that, as of the time that this article was written, the Security Rule and Privacy Rule of the Health Insurance Portability and Accountability Act are only applicable to data collected on digital platforms for mental health if those platforms also collect personally identifiable health information [13]. Similarly, there is a possibility that developers will use information collected from users to produce data for marketing purposes. Before entrusting an app with sensitive, personal information, patients and professionals should carefully analyze the terms of service provided by the app. Specifically, they should examine what data will be collected, who will have access to that data, and how privacy will be secured before moving forward with the project. This is an especially significant topic in the context of recent high-profile breaches of personal information from platforms such as Facebook, which have led to calls for greater data-security measures. This has led to increased requests for improved data-security measures. The use of content-free phone data for phenotyping or anonymized text for peer support is two examples of possible solutions to problems with privacy that are essential for maintaining public trust.

Second, even though digital technologies have the potential to eliminate inequalities in mental health treatment, the gaps between those who have access to digital care and those who do not may expand as these technologies continue to advance. With increasing market competition among software developers and nearly universal ownership of smartphones in developed countries, the issue of cost is becoming less of a concern; however, individuals with lower digital fluency may be intimidated and feel alienated by these digital resources, and they may find it difficult to engage with them. Userexperience leaders in the larger realm of digital technology are researching ways to make websites, smartphone interfaces, and mobile apps accessible for those with a variety of disabilities ranging from physical (such as visual impairment) to cognitive impairments (e.g., dementia). This consideration is especially important in digital interventions for mental health conditions, given the high rates of cognitive impairment (for example, impaired working memory and executive functioning in schizophrenia) and interfering behaviors (for example, motor tics in Tourette syndrome) that are associated with psychiatric disorders and that could potentially hinder the successful use of these technologies. The phenomenon known as "digital exclusion" may be on the decline as the Internet and cell phones become more ingrained in people's daily lives, but the obstacles that still exist need to be actively addressed so that they can accommodate users with a wide range of backgrounds and skills.

11 Limitations and Plans for the Future

It can be difficult for a single doctor to make sense of the bewildering selection of mobile applications, artificial intelligence resources, and VR-based treatments that are currently on the market because this selection is constantly evolving. In this regard, we have included a list of considerations for clinicians to take into account when particularly assessing a mental health app to incorporate it into their practice. The authors identify three primary categories: app capabilities and functions (e.g., psychoeducational materials versus symptom tracking, availability of conversational agents, or chatbots), workflow issues (e.g., accommodation of patients' daily routines, appeal of the app design), and cultural or access issues. Each of these categories is broken down into subcategories (e.g., accounting for technological literacy and access issues). Standardized scales, such as the 23-item Mobile App Rating Scale that is available to the public, can be used by physicians to assist in providing structure to this review. A "five-step app evaluation approach" has been developed by the American Psychiatric Association to assist physicians in determining the usefulness and efficacy of a mobile application (app).

These rating tools are useful when thinking about a single app because either the patient asks about a particular app or the clinician has come across an app through his or her search. However, they are less useful when thinking about a problem (such as depression) and then searching for the "best" app to address the clinical concern. In these situations, which may be more common than one may think, doctors can examine regularly updated rating guides, such as those kept up to date by the Anxiety and Depression Association of America and the PsyberGuide, which is a component of the One Mind Institute, a nonprofit organization.

However, in the end, it is up to the clinician to decide whether or not to recommend an app, or any other type of digital health technology, to a patient. On the other hand, the decision to use online treatments is typically made by the patient, with or without the knowledge and consent of a clinician. As was discussed in this article, there is growing evidence to support the use of tools for better measurement and the usefulness of numerous mobile apps for treatment, in addition to promising digital technologies to coordinate care. These tools and technologies include: Having said that, we are still in the beginning stages of a highly dynamic field. A famous innovator in the field of technology Bill Gates once issued the following word of caution: "We always overestimate the change that will occur in the next two years and underestimate the change that will occur in the next 10." Our patients are more accustomed to living in a world where services are oriented to the needs of the consumer and are provided in real-time. That does not adequately define the field of mental health practice in the modern era. Technology might not revolutionize the way we diagnose and treat mental illness in the next two years, but it could do so in the next ten years, allowing us to circumvent problems associated with access, delay, negative attitudes, fragmentation, and a lack of measurement.

References

1. Fairburn, C.G., Patel, V.: The impact of digital technology on psychological treatments and their dissemination. Behav. Res. Ther. **88**, 19–25 (2017)
2. Heeren, A.: Commentary: the impact of digital technology on psychological treatments and their dissemination. Front. Psychol. **9**, 1571 (2018)
3. De Witte, N.A., Joris, S., Van Assche, E., Van Daele, T.: Technological and digital interventions for mental health and wellbeing: an overview of systematic reviews. Front. Digit. Health **3** (2021)
4. Brailas, A.: Psychotherapy in the era of artificial intelligence: therapist Panoptes. Homo Virtualis **2**(1), 68 (2019)

5. Edition, F.: Diagnostic and statistical manual of mental disorders. Am. Psychiatr. Assoc. **21**(21), 591–643 (5th edn, 2013)
6. Haggerty, D.J.: The Relationships Among Organizational Climate, Leader Situation, and the Machiavellianism of Elementary School Principals. New York University, New York (1979)
7. Rogers, C.R.: The necessary and sufficient of therapeutic personality change. J. Consult. Psychol. **21**, 95–103 (1957)
8. Poznanski, B., Silva, K., Conroy, K., Georgiadis, C., Comer, J.S.: Expanding the reach of evidence-based psychotherapy through remote technologies. In: Handbook of Evidence-Based Therapies for Children and Adolescents, pp. 369–380. Springer, Cham (2020)
9. Bunge, E.L., Dickter, B., Jones, M.K., Alie, G., Spear, A., Perales, R.: Behavioral intervention technologies and psychotherapy with youth: a review of the literature. Curr. Psychiatr. Rev. **12**(1), 14–28 (2016)
10. Hirschtritt, M.E., Insel, T.R.: Digital technologies in psychiatry: present and future. Focus **16**(3), 251–258 (2018)
11. Mohr, D.C., Weingardt, K.R., Reddy, M., Schueller, S.M.: Three problems with current digital mental health research... and three things we can do about them. Psychiatr. Serv. **68**(5), 427–429 (2017)
12. Fox, R.E., DeLeon, P.H., Newman, R., Sammons, M.T., Dunivin, D.L., Baker, D.C.: Prescriptive authority and psychology: a status report. Am. Psychol. **64**(4), 257 (2009)
13. Mühleisen, M.: The long and short of the digital revolution. Finance Dev. **55**(002) (2018)

Advances in Technology Enhanced Learning and Teaching

Intersectionality Between Open Educational Resources and Sustainable Development Goals: Future Perspectives

Piergiorgio Guarini[✉] [iD], Martina Rossi [iD], Francesco Pio Savino [iD], and Francesca Finestrone [iD]

Learning Science institute, University of Foggia, Via Arpi 176, Foggia, Italy
`piergiorgio.guarini@gmail.com`

Abstract. The Open Educational Resources (OER) are the new frontier of the accessibility to knowledge. This new philosophy allows every person, in every part of the world to access to every Open Resource, with a view to the lifelong learning. This contribution tries to connect the Open philosophy with the Objective 4 of the Sustainable Development Goals (SDGs) of 2030 Agenda, which aims at improving basic education all over the world and decrease the illiteracy rate worldwide. Infrastructural interventions are of course needed: school buildings, digital and technological tools are essential to have access to OER; nevertheless, this can be the viaticum to fulfill the Objective 4 of SDGs, following the still ongoing questioning of the Humboldtian conception of knowledge and university organization. The Open Access is already changing (and simplifying) the way of learning: this work presents an overview of the possibilities offered by the Open philosophy in order to improve knowledge and social possibilities all over the world.

Keywords: Open Educational Resources · Sustainable Development Goals · Distance Learning

1 Philosophy, University and "Open" Resources

The adjective "Open" is now commonly used to indicate freedom of access and participation, referring both to physical spaces and events and to the use of contents and tools. It is a philosophy present in many aspects of society, as well as in education (open education) and in education (open universities) [1].

As far as education is concerned, the open movement began to develop in the 1960s and 1970s, when the mission of the Humboldtian university (a place of study managed and administered by the elite of society, to maintain this status) was questioned and universities become more accessible places, enrollments increase and culture becomes a mass product, usable by an increasingly heterogeneous audience of students [2].

The idea behind the open movement is that culture and knowledge are and must be accessible as a path of liberation for the masses [3] through an autonomous path of delineation of an academic and customizable learning path [4] and that allows access to university courses even for people who have not completed their education in a canonical manner [5]. It is not the initiative of a small marginal group of scholars dissatisfied with the communication system, but the affirmation of the position of communication as the foundation of scientific activity [6].

The first open university, the UK Open University (UKOU), was founded in London in 1969 and became the model of inspiration for all the open universities that would be founded in the following years.

Today, there are about 60 open or Distance universities Teaching Universities (DTU) in the world; most of them are in Asia [7]. They are also engaged in research activities of the highest profile, such as appearing in the international rankings dedicated to the quality of research alongside historical and noble universities. Among the top 500 universities in the world [9], we find The Open University (England), the Universitat Oberta de Catalunya (Barcelona, Spain), and the Universidade Aberta (Lisbon, Portugal). Italy, unfortunately, does not include open universities in this ranking.

Open universities, therefore, tend to break the paradigm of the classical university didactic organization, proposing a flexible, plastic education, adaptable to the different needs of individual students: courses and digital tools that can be used online, with the minimum necessary requirement of having an internet connection [9].

A further declination of the open philosophy is represented by Open Educational Resources (OER), literally "open educational/didactic resources": these are all "Teaching, learning and research materials on any medium that can be composed of copyrighted materials. Released under an open license, non-copyrighted materials, materials for which copyright protection has expired, or a combination of these conditions" [10]. They are the expression of a movement that aims to radically change the historically perpetrated paradigm of the production, use and dissemination of knowledge in a traditional way [11], which is reserved for a few people and carried out in a formal and frontal way.

The OERs are mainly digital, published with a free use license [1]; this means that the contribution can be downloaded and used free of charge, and is usable, modifiable and distributable without any kind of cost for the user [12]. All these characteristics have been summarized by the definition given by UNESCO in 2012 [9, p. 31].

To check if a resource is an OER, we must refer to the 5R Framework: a resource is open if it can be stored, modified, combined, reused and redistributed [13]. Over the years, the framework has been criticized for being too rigid, so much so that most of the existing open resources do not fully satisfy the Wiley Framework [14].

The emergence of the open mentality is reflected in teaching, questioning the organization of school systems and teaching methodologies that we know, such as the chronological linearity of school-academic paths (diploma, degree, doctorate/master) [9] and academic coherence ("binding" to a scientific disciplinary sector for one's experience and career).

The original thinking behind OER, in summary, is to create universally accessible educational resources that can improve the quality of teaching, learning and the related processes [15]. The OER "represent the utopia of democratic liberation enacted by the Internet, in relation to Pierre Lévy's idea according to which collective intelligence is more efficient than individual intelligence" [16]; they tend towards the internationalization of knowledge and the recognition of skills, intercepting a demand coming from any part of the world. Open culture has enormous power – a great ability to penetrate globally [17].

The most famous example, used and enjoyed by OER is represented by Massive Open Online Courses (MOOCs) – online courses open to a very wide audience, accessible on online platforms with free and free attendance. This was started in 2008, when George Siemens, Dave Cormier and Stephen Downes made what is considered the first MOOC at Manitoba University in Canada, "Connectivism and Connective Knowledge (CCK08)", which had an audience of 2,200 spectators worldwide.

The model of this MOOC has become the reference model, which has inspired the creation of large online user platforms such as Coursera, edX, Udacity, FutureLearn and others, which, in a few years have managed to reach millions of users at the same time. Today, MOOCs reach an audience of over 110 million students through over 15,000 courses offered (Fig. 1). A platform has also been developed in Italy that offers MOOCs. This is EduOpen, an experience born in 2014, which today has 21 participating universities and 6 other associated institutions, reaching over 50,000 users. Unlike larger platforms, EduOpen adopts a truly open approach, "releasing all its contents as OER and favoring the creation of training courses made up of MOOCs from the various partner universities" [18].

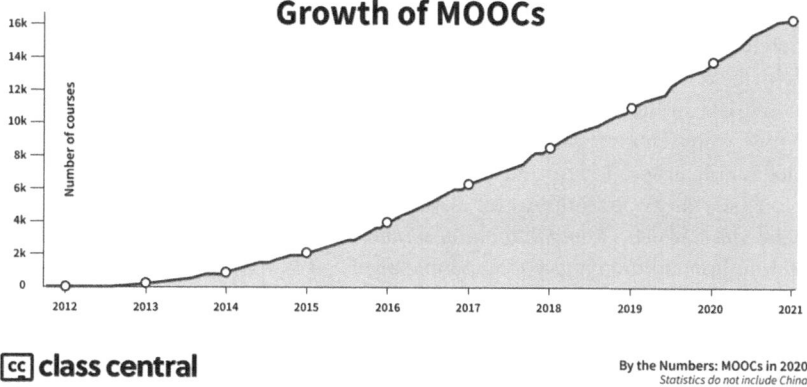

Fig. 1. Number of MOOCs Registered by Class Central up to 2021.

Other OERs are,

- repositories, such as the OpenCourse Ware of the Massachussets Institute of Technology (MIT), a free educational archive that allows free consultation of high-level content, regardless of one's level of education;
- open textbooks, or open textbooks, created thanks to the participation of the writing work of the teachers themselves and, sometimes, also of the students;
- open research, i.e., online publications accessible for free because they are published on open journals, open educational journals, open data, tools and data generally used

to analyze various sectors of public administration and used by public bodies to plan social innovation.

2 The Evolution of Interventions by the International Community for Accessible Education: The 2030 Agenda and the Sustainable Development Goals (SDGs), Objective 4

The international community has been trying for several decades to plan a series of initiatives and interventions to solve problems related to economic development and to promote the environment and human life. The United Nations Organization (UN) is at the forefront in this regard.

The UN's commitment starts with Agenda 21 for the promotion of sustainable development, approved in 1992, to evolve, during the Millennium Summit in 2000, into the Millennium Declaration containing a list of 8 Millennium Development Goals (MDGs), including making primary education universal (Goal 2) [19].

The objectives were not met, so much so that reports *Reimagine the future. Innovation for every child* [20] and *Fixing the broken promise of education for all. Finding from Global Initiative on Out-of-School Children* [21], found that around one in 11 children have not attended primary school and 121 million children and adolescents have never started or have ever started school. Abandoned, despite the international community's commitment to education for all.

The next step of the UN took place during the Summit on Sustainable Development, in which the 193 member states ratified the 2030 Agenda for Sustainable Development [22], with the related 17 Millennium Development Goals (SDGs). At the time of signing, there were 103 million young people in the world in a situation of lack of literacy, of which 60% were female. For this reason, Objective number 4, "Quality Education", was provided for the promotion of a quality, inclusive and equal education, and the guarantee of lifelong learning opportunities for all people.

In *A Future Stolen: Young and out of school* [23], a first interim survey, it was found that 303 million children and young people aged 5–17 do not attend school – a third of the world population of school age (25% of whom live in countries affected by conflicts or disasters, 50% if we consider only the reference age of primary school).

Following demographic trends, the 10–19-year-old population will increase to 1.3 billion in 2030, increasing by 8%. This population that will live, in most cases, in lowmiddle-income countries, making further interventions necessary to expand the possibilities of using education, and ensuring that the education proposed is of quality, as per SDG 4.

According to Irina Bokova, Director-General of UNESCO, and Anthony Lake, Director-General of UNICEF, it is not enough to increase teachers, facilities and teaching materials to increase and improve access to education: a global commitment is needed to increase the number of boys and girls attending primary school and continuing education with secondary school, because the reasons that lead boys and girls to leave school or do not allow them to attend at all (displaced families, girls forced to stay at home, children with disabilities, child workers) are intrinsically linked to the economic situation of families and the countries themselves.

Increasing the possibilities of access to education means, upstream, aiming at solving structural problems linked to the economic situation of developing countries (DCs) and underdeveloped countries, with interventions that would weigh heavily on the coffers of individual countries, and they would include a political commitment that is often disregarded in these countries.

Although there is still a lot to do, there has been progress in guaranteeing access to quality primary education for as many boys and girls in the world as possible: preschooling one year before entry into primary school went from 62% in 2010 to 67% in 2018, and the primary school completion rate went from 70% in 2000 to 84% in 2018. In *The Sustainable Development Goals Report 2019* [24], we find an exemplary table (Fig. 2) of the progress made in accessing education and consistency in attending school.

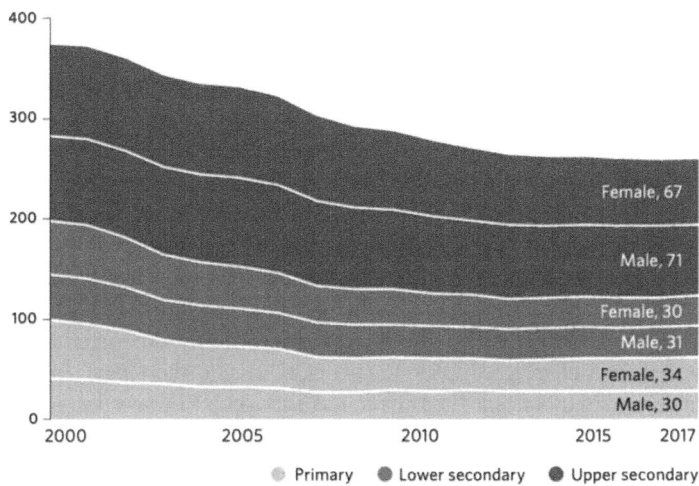

Fig. 2. Number of children in out-of-school age in the world by level of education and gender. Note: figures in millions for the period 2000–2017 – UN, The Sustainable Development Goals Report 2019.

That the data were improving is evident from the decidedly downward trend of the data; that there is still a lot to do, is testified by the fact that there are still 258 million children and young people of compulsory school age who do not attend school, which would be 17% of the world population, which includes 6–17 years old.

Obviously, there are differences between the various geographical areas of the world, between the countries belonging to them, and between the same people who live in the same country. For example, South Asia is home to nearly half of the world's illiterate population, and Sub-Saharan Africa is home to another quarter; in the latter, less than half of the schools had computers available, had access to the internet and basic services such as electricity; there are also differences between different social backgrounds: only 1% of countries have achieved parity for education between rich and poor children and adolescents, and only in 25% of cases with regard to primary education. Moreover, differences in the possibility of access between boys and girls persist, especially in primary school. Gender differences are far from being resolved or overcome.

3 OERs Before the Covid-19 Pandemic

At the institutional level, in 2017, the Second UNESCO World Congress on OER launched the OER Action Plan, which recognizes an important role for OER as a tool to aim for the fulfillment of Objective 4 of the SDGs. From this Action Plan the work continued, until reaching the UNESCO Recommendation on OER of November 2019 [18], which already noted that education was rapidly diversifying in the world and also noted the lack of a framework that allowed the provision of OER for international cooperation and for strengthening capacity building [25].

The 2019 Recommendation has reinforced and corroborated the use of OERs in various countries of the world, because they increase student performance, allow easy and free access to teaching materials by eliminating learning barriers, promoting the sharing of teaching materials [26].

Often the OER narrative focuses on Europe and North America, homelands of the Open mentality and OER, which has been extensively discussed in the previous paragraphs. In the rest of the world too, OERs are clearly used and, before the pandemic, they were enjoying great success, albeit with some limitations and objections.

In China, since 2003, numerous initiatives have been launched by the government itself – institutions and organizations to facilitate the adoption of OER. Most of the studies on OER are recent (2015–2018) and show Chinese ministerial initiatives to facilitate access and sharing of OER [27]. In Sri Lanka, the Open University of Sri Lanka (OUSL) and in Indonesia, the Universitas Terbuka (UT) have designed, developed and implemented support services for distance education and in Open form, to become modern Open universities, using new technologies in teaching and learning processes and in the management of their services [28]. In Australia, despite the absence of federal government support on OER and Open Educational Practice (OEP), universities have invested time and resources in experimenting and continually refining MOOCs and are taking specialist positions to support OEPs and MOOCs [29].

In Morocco, the national strategy "Morocco Digital 2020" has been developed in recent years, which succeeds "Maroc Numeric 2013". The initiative is based on three pillars, the third of which aims to develop courses and skills in computing ICT. This path was strengthened in 2016 with the launch of the Moroccan declaration on OER, addressed to all school actors of all levels and all people involved in education and training [30]. In South Africa, many universities share teaching material online, making it free as OER, an initiative that is coupled with numerous political and institutional initiatives in this sense, even if the idea is widely shared that the development and use of OER does not automatically mean greater access to education; as long as there are barriers preventing access to education, OER alone will not solve these problems [31]. In Latin America, the practice of use and reuse of OER is not covered by public or institutional policies: the main actors are teachers, who are organized in groups that support the adoption of OER and consider it an integral part of development and transformation of the educational offer [32].

The reading of many contributions of the scientific literature on OER makes it clear how these resources were entering the daily life of teachers and students of all types and grades of school. The debate was lively and even in countries farthest from the place where the Open mentality was conceived and developed, institutional policies or inter-university working groups were being developed to encourage the adoption, development and use of OER [33].

4   The Effects of the Covid-19 Pandemic on Education

As is widely known, the Covid-19 pandemic has upset and profoundly changed, perhaps forever, habits and practices of our daily life that have been consolidated for decades, if not, in some cases, for centuries. The methods of fruition and access to education have not been exempt from these upheavals.

The common feature of these changes, as well as the only possible tool to continue carrying out our social activities, was the increased use of Information and Communication Technologies (ICT), that is, the set of methods and techniques that are used, in various fields, in the transmission, reception and processing of data, concepts, information and knowledge [34]. This general definition can be specified and interpreted or adapted based on the specific field being referred to.

During lockdown periods, to prevent contagion, the normal daily activities of communication, work, social interaction and even food shopping moved entirely and exclusively to digital platforms, video conference software and delivery apps, (home delivery), of any type and for any need.

Until the first months of 2020, the provision and use of online educational courses was in some cases a possibility, chosen above all by higher education institutes, such as universities, and in others a targeted, precise methodological choice, such as for example telematic universities, to provide courses and educational activities exclusively online.

From the first lockdowns, however, organizing educational activities in online mode was no longer a choice, but a necessity dictated by the impossibility of leaving the house and meeting indoors, as a preventive measure against contagion [35]. An illustrative figure concerns the increase, in March 2020, of enrollments in Coursera courses up to 650% compared to 2019, which is an unprecedented increase [18].

No country has managed to make this transition completely smoothly and painlessly. Although there have been some virtuous examples of moving online teaching activities without particular problems, especially from the university world, most academic and educational institutions of any order and degree found themselves totally unprepared to face this forced change.

Understandably, the countries with a higher rate of diffusion of knowledge and technological devices encountered fewer difficulties in adapting and managed to resolve those encountered in a reasonable time. The fundamental element for the successful delivery of online teaching was certainly the previous digital competence of the socalled digital native students [36]; in an overturning of the classic teaching paradigm, it were the teachers who had to adapt and learn to use tools and practices which the students were (and are) already practical and experienced.

The Humboldtian modality of planning and teaching delivery, with which this contribution opens, has undergone substantial changes in the space of a few weeks, if not a few days: of course, the methodology has remained mainly the frontal and formal lesson and the teaching tools were unchanged, but the learning environment was digital and not physical; the teacher's ability to control and call attention is less or, in any case, is considerably reduced, and instead, it increases the physical freedom of the student, who can make himself "comfortable" and not be forced to sit in the same position for hours.

The fundamental turning point was the change in concept regarding the digital device: from a distraction tool, usually forbidden in classrooms, to an indispensable tool for cultural transmission and teacher-student interaction; on the contrary, the possibility of using multiple devices at the same time during the lesson (PC or laptop and smartphone) increases and expands the possibilities of research and, therefore, of learning for students.

This forced change in the methods of delivery of educational content has led to major problems of use by students: the phenomenon of the digital divide has fully shown its effects during the lockdown period.

Students unable to have a digital device and/or an available sufficient internet connection, both in terms of stability (we consider low-quality supply or people who live in areas where the possibility of connecting to the internet is scarce or completely absent) and that of consumption possibilities (limited tariff plans, lack of a fixed unlimited connection and limited use of data for internet connection), were heavily penalized. The lack of the possibility of being constantly part of this change, that is to be able to be constantly connected to follow the lessons, did not allow all these students to follow the lessons consistently and constantly, as they could have done if the lessons had taken place in a classroom of a physical school and in the presence [37, 38].

All these problems have been exacerbated by the lack of access to the internet connection and the lack of digital devices in developing countries and less developed countries.

Data from the UN agency that studies communication technologies (ITU), collected in the December 2021 edition of the *Measuring Digital Development, Facts and Figures* [39] report shows that despite an increase in 13% regarding internet penetration in developing countries, in December 2021, 37% of the world population has never used the internet. It is measured to be approximately 2.9 billion people offline, of which 96% live in developing countries or countries less developed. In the latter, the increase in penetration reaches 20%, but in real terms, three out of four people still do not have the possibility to access the internet, and the proportion increases to four out of five if we take into consideration only the female gender.

According to these data, it is confirmed that the biggest obstacle to access to education, albeit in a completely digital form and in these two years of pandemic, has been the economic factor.

According to UN estimates from *The Sustainable Development Goals Report 2021* [40], during the pandemic, there was an increase of 101 million children and young people, in primary and lower secondary school, who did not achieve the minimal reading skills; the rate of completion of the primary school path, globally, went from 82% in 2000 to "only" 85% in 2019, with a ridiculous increase compared to 2018.

In developing countries, schools with access to drinking water are 56%, while the percentage stops at 33% if schools with access to the electricity grid are considered.

Although it was known even before the pandemic that regardless of the interventions implemented, Objective 4 of the SDGs would not have been met by 2030, today we know that we risk taking huge steps backwards on expanding access to education. Quality: Covid-19 canceled 20 years of advances in education. The *What have we learned* [41] shows a worrying picture: only 20% of low-income countries managed to count distance learning days as official school days and only 40% of governments asked schools to continue teaching despite the closure of schools (against 90% of developed countries).

UNICEF data speak of 1.2 billion school-age children affected by school closures due to interventions to combat the infection, given that it must be contextualized with the lack of internet access for more than half of the population in 71 countries around the world; the Remote Learning Readiness Index [42] report attests that at least 200 million students live in 31 low and middle-income countries who are still unprepared to organize and support remote education in the event of a new school closure.

Covid-19 was the worst crisis for children that UNICEF has ever recorded in 75 years of activity [43]: children living in poverty increased by 100 million, or 10% in more than in 2019, and up to 1.6 billion students missed school due to national closures during the pandemic.

5 OER Characteristics and Their Implementation Around the Globe

The open mentality and OERs are born in the framework of Western universities by academics who wanted to break the tradition of top-down cultural transmission, with the teacher being the absolute protagonist of the teaching and learning processes because he is the only depositary and possible dispenser of knowledge.

Open Education therefore aims at overcoming this organizational methodology and at the democratization of learning and the creation of teaching materials [44] as, from an ideological point of view, the open movement and the Open Education in particular are linked to social justice and start from the fundamental premise that education must be a leading actor in correcting social disparities [45].

The open movement, however, can go further and be a solution not only of the social disparities within that developed part of the world, but also of the same disparities within developing countries and low-income countries and between these countries and the so-called developed ones.

The benefits of adopting an open mindset regarding production and access to educational resources are manifold:

- access, with the elimination or overcoming of technological and economic obstacles to the use of resources;
- inclusion, with the possibility of adapting resources to one's specific needs, of content or context;
- experimentation, through the use of non-traditional pedagogical methodologies, especially linked to processes of co-creation and co-planning of resources;
- improvement of the quality of the resources, allowing the analysis and the critical comment also to the final users of the resources;

- efficiency, allowing teachers to deal with highly educated realities and archives for the organization of lessons;
- improving the reputation of teachers, being able to reach an unimaginable number of students or trainees with traditional structures;
- increase in revenue, both through the material sale of "premium" access, and through the return in terms of visibility by the institutes that offer free courses, and the collection of data on participants in MOOCs, with which to set up the future offer.

These characteristics would have been important and fundamental to enhance the possibilities of access to education in those countries where this rate is still low as well as to increase the quality of teaching itself, already in the period preceding the outbreak of the pandemic, even more so they can be today, especially in light of the educational inequalities highlighted by the global pandemic from Covid-19 [46].

It is not just a question of numbers: the quality of the educational offer itself is insufficient in many cases, to the point that 617 million children and adolescents in the world do not acquire the minimum skills in the field of reading and mathematics, while 20% of school-age children worldwide still do not have access to education [47].

In the words of Robert Jenkins, UNICEF Head of Education, "Access to the technologies and materials needed to continue learning while schools are closed is vastly uneven. Likewise, children with limited learning support at home have almost no means to support their education. Providing a set of learning tools and accelerating internet access for every school and every child is essential".

In recent years, especially those of the pandemic, OERs have been increasingly protagonists in the debate on access and quality of education, and some initiatives have already been proposed: the UNESCO Recommendation on OER of 2019 confirms the objectives of the Open and sparked a rich discussion, with non-governmental actors such as the Commonwealth of Learning, Creative Commons, the International Council for Open and Distance Education (ICDE), the Open Education Global consortium, the Slovenian National Commission for UNESCO and SPARC, an NGO that deals with Open Knowledge [18]. UNESCO itself has tried to involve governments of countries and private companies in a global sharing of OER to support these objectives (Call to Support Learning and Knowledge through OER, 2020). The OER Foundation, through the OER, has promoted the OER4Covid initiative, i.e., free courses for teachers on the use of open resources and the International Council for Open and Distance Education (ICDE) has launched Learning together.

We cannot fail to mention the commitment and initiatives of UNICEF: "Reimagine Education" aims to promote equal access to digital and quality education for approximately 3.5 billion children and young people in the world. The initiative involves partners from both the public and private sectors, with a time target of 2030, and is supported by "giga", a global project in collaboration with ITU to connect every school in the world to the internet, including its surrounding community. In October 2021, there were 1 million schools mapped in 41 countries, with the connection to the network of 3,000 institutes, for the benefit of over 700,000 students and their respective communities. "Learning Passport", a learning platform created in collaboration with Microsoft and accessible from anywhere in the world, reached over one and a half million students during the forced closure of schools.

OERs have a significant impact and possibility of penetration and some organizations are trying to make the most of these characteristics, trying to overcome or, at least, reduce the barriers that prevent OER from being used and exploited one hundred percent. These barriers were five, according to the Beyond OER report [48], and at least four are still present: among these, the most studied one is certainly the problem of the (lack of) perception of OER qualities [49]; the other three are the limited institutional support, the lack of skills on the part of the teachers (or the time needed to acquire them) and the opportunities for sharing resources and skills which, at various levels, are not grasped.

Are still viewed with distrust, since the most famous resource globally, namely Wikipedia, is an example of how anyone can access the modification of a content, sometimes inserting false information for various reasons and for the most disparate reasons. This does not mean that open access is a failure; it is quite the contrary: with the possibility of making changes and, above all, of reporting "suspicious" updates to the staff, the Wikipedia community shows us how quality monitoring information is very broad and constant.

This wide range of controllers is the exemplification of the bottom-up attitude at the base of OER and of the open mentality, which is in stark contrast to the top-down philosophy at the base of the didactic resources produced and, above all, on the methods of control, all within the traditional publishing circuit. The fewer the number people controlling a content, the easier it is for an error to go unnoticed and, statistically, the easier it is for the content or its revision to be influenced by personal views and not be neutral.

A further tool for measuring quality is the introduction of a social approach on the platforms that contain OER, allowing to measure the quality of resources and their authors through the popularity achieved among students and teachers [50].

6 OER to Meet the SDGs of the Third Millennium: Future Perspectives

OER, if organized in an organic way in academic institutions of all types and levels, and if inserted in a broader perspective of collaboration between countries and between the countries themselves and the organizations that deal with guaranteeing ever greater access to education and an ever-increasing quality of the latter, could be the turning point to bring us ever closer to Objective 4 of the SDGs, that is to allow accessibility to quality education for all boys and girls in the world, eliminating the illiteracy. The Open movement, which some international governmental organizations and non-governmental stakeholders have moved in the last few years, proposing concrete actions to create an increasingly open culture, open right from the planning stages of resources and teaching tools, is accessible in a totally free and a horizontal and transversal way by anyone in any part of the world, regardless of their age and level of education.

The effects of the impact of OER, as seen in the course of this contribution, are highly positive.

The transition towards the use of OER in teaching and learning processes and the integration of hybrid and online teaching has already begun, peremptorily required by external factors to the organization of the production and supply systems of cultural content and tools.

OERs can be the right tool to allow institutions and individual institutes to offer at least the same quality of the educational paths that take place through traditional teaching but to a wider audience, if not to improve the educational offer.

It is not a change that can happen in a short time, because it requires major structural and economic interventions: the first, but no less trivial (indeed), is to be able to equip all schools and students with the necessary digital tools and minimum internet connection that allows the use of OER. The pandemic has already shown us that progress in this direction has proved necessary.

OERs allow the possibility of making up for the shortcomings that may derive from school learning confined to a single physical place and from the presence of teachers who do not have the possibility or even the will to take time for their own continuous self-training. Not seizing this opportunity, not integrating the open movement into future strategies on maintaining and increasing access to quality education, could mean both being caught unprepared for the next event, which could force us to re-propose a forced closure of schools, and try to fill the educational gap over a much longer time horizon.

All this, added to the immobility of investments and internal interventions in individual countries, could block the great results achieved in the level of access to education, if not even make us go back, as it once happened due to the great lack of preparation for teaching globally, during the Covid-19 pandemic.

Universities, places of production and use of culture par excellence, can be fundamental strategic actors for the development and increase of use of OER by both institutions and final users, in order to make access to education of quality a concrete and above all fair possibility, anywhere in the world.

Being "Open" goes in the opposite direction to a competitive university way, which is very proud and "protective" of the fruits of their research and their work. Convincing more and more teachers and universities to embrace the "Open" approach, with the consequent freeing up of access to the resources and research products of individual universities and teachers is not easy; it requires tireless and punctual work, which shows the enormous advantages at the local and global level, of the freedom of access to educational and teaching resources. In an ideal (and probably utopian) perspective, if all the universities of the world were converted into Open Universities, all the resources that would be made available would make free access to an education of the highest quality and, in cascade, everyone would benefit from it. This includes the actors and all the phases of the processes of creation, submission and use of educational resources: the training of the actors of the didactic planning and educational interventions, the quality of the lessons and the use by the students, the possibility of bringing educational contents of the highest level in the most isolated places in the world, thanks to a "simple" internet line.

The open movement is no longer a niche movement but is central and protagonist in the global debate on education. The new challenge for the movement is to be able to maintain its spirit, its goals and its direction without being influenced by the market value achieved by openness, as is happening to MOOC companies financed by venture capitalists [51].

References

1. Guerrini, M.: La filosofia open: paradigma del servizio contemporaneo. Biblioteche oggi **35**, 12–21 (2017)
2. Brandser, G.C.: Humboldt Revisited: The Institutional Drama of Academic Identity. Berghahn Books, New York (2022)
3. Freire, P.: L'educazione come pratica della libertà (L. Bimbi, Trans.). Milano: Arnoldo Mondadori (Original work published 1973)
4. Silari, F.: Massive Open Online Course: "Un audace esperimento di apprendimento distribuito" nelle università. Firenze University Press, Firenze (2019)
5. Zawacki-Richter, O., et al.: Elements of open education: an invitation to future research. Int. Rev. Res. Open Distrib. Learn. **21**(3), 319–334 (2020)
6. Guédon, J.C.: Open access: toward the internet of the mind. Budapest Open Access Initiative (2017)
7. Tait, A.: Open Universities: the next phase. Asian Assoc. Open Univ. J. **31**(1/2018), 13–23 (2018)
8. Times Higher Education (THE): World University Rankings 2022 (2022). https://www.timeshighereducation.com/world-university-rankings/2022
9. Nascimbeni, F.: Open Education: Oer, mooc e pratiche didattiche aperte verso l'inclusione digitale educativa. Milano: Franco Angeli Open Education (2020)
10. UNESCO: Recommendation on Open Educational Resources (OER). Paris: UNESCO (2019). https://www.unesco.org/en/legal-affairs/recommendation-open-educational-resources-oer
11. Bell, S.: Course MATERIALS ADOPTION: A FACULTY SURVEY and Outlook for the OER Landscape. Temple University Libraries, Philadelphia (2018)
12. Wiley, D.: On the sustainability of open educational resource initiatives in higher education. Centre for Educational Research and Innovation (CERI) (2007). https://www.oecd.org/education/ceri/38645447.pdf
13. Wiley, D., Bliss, T.J., McEwen, M.: Open educational resources: a review of the literature. In: Spector, J.M., Merrill, M.D., Elen, J., Bishop, M.J. (A cura di) Handbook of Research on Educational Communications and Technology, pp. 781–789. Springer, New York (2014)
14. Bliss, T.J., Smith, M.: A brief history of open educational resources. In: Jhangiani, R.S., Biswas-Diener, R., (A cura di) Open: The Philosophy and Practices that are Revolutionizing Education and Science. Ubiquity Press, London (2017)
15. Mishra, S.: Open educational resources: removing barriers from within. Distance Educ. **38**(3), 369–380 (2017)
16. Toto, G.A., Limone, P.: Hybrid digital learning environments for college student education. In: Second Symposium on Psychology-Based Technologies Psychology Based Technologies PSYCHOBIT 2020, pp. 1–8. CEUR (2020). https://www.nytimes.com/2013/01/29/opinion/online-courses-possibilities-and-pitfalls.html
17. Weller, M., Jordan, K., DeVries, I., Rolfe, V.: Mapping the open education landscape: citation network analysis of historical open and distance education research. Open Praxis **10**(2) (2018)
18. Nascimbeni, F.: Breve storia dell'Open Education, per una riflessione sull'open in Italia. BRICKS. Rivista Online per Promuovere l'innovazione Nella Scuola, **2**, 176–194 (2022)
19. United Nations: Millenium Development Goals (MDGs). New York: UN (2000). https://documents-dds-ny.un.org/doc/UNDOC/GEN/N00/559/51/PDF/N0055951.pdf?OpenElement
20. UNICEF.: Reimagine the future. Innovation for every child. New York: UNICEF (2016). https://www.unicef.org/serbia/en/reports/reimagine-future-innovation-every-child
21. Hawke, A.: Fixing the Broken Promise of Education for All: Findings from the Global Initiative on Out-of-School Children. UNICEF, New York (2015)

22. United Nations: Transforming our world: the 2030 Agenda for Sustainable Development. New York: UN (2015). https://sdgs.un.org/2030agenda
23. UNICEF: A Future Stolen: Young and out of school. New York: UNICEF (2018). https://www.unicef.org/eap/reports/future-stolen-young-and-out-school
24. United Nations: The Sustainable Development Goals Report 2019. New York: UN (2019). https://unstats.un.org/sdgs/report/2019/
25. Ossiannilsson, E.: OER and OEP for access, equity, equality, quality, inclusiveness, and empowering lifelong learning. Int. J. Open Educ. Resourc. **1**(2), 25058 (2019)
26. Wong, B.T., Li, K.C.: Using open educational resources for teaching in higher education: a review of case studies. In: 2019 International Symposium on Educational Technology (ISET), pp. 186–190. IEEE (2019)
27. Tlili, A., Huang, R., Chang, T.W., Nascimbeni, F., Burgos, D.: Open educational resources and practices in China: a systematic literature review. Sustainability **11**(18), 4867 (2019)
28. Zuhairi, A., Karthikeyan, N., Priyadarshana, S.T.: Supporting students to succeed in open and distance learning in the Open University of Sri Lanka and Universitas Terbuka, Indonesia. Asian Assoc. Open Univ. J. **15**(1), 13–35 (2019)
29. Stagg, A., Nguyen, L., Bossu, C., Partridge, H., Funk, J., Judith, K.: Open educational practices in Australia: a first-phase national audit of higher education. Int. Rev. Res. Open Distrib. Learn. **19**(3) (2018)
30. Zaatri, I., Kharki, K.E., Bendaoud, R., Berrada, K.: The use of open educational resources at Cadi Ayyad University: state of art review. In: 2019 7th International Conference on ICT and Accessibility (ICTA), pp. 1–4. IEEE (2019)
31. Chikuni, P.R., Cox, G., Czerniewicz, L.: Exploring the institutional OER policy landscape in South Africa: dominant discourses and assumptions. Int. J. Educ. Dev. Using Inf. Commun. Technol. **15**(4), 165–179 (2019)
32. Rodés, V., Gewerc-Barujel, A., Llamas-Nistal, M.: University teachers and open educational resources: case studies from Latin America. Int. Rev. Res. Open Distrib. Learn. **20**(1) (2019)
33. Shear, L., Means, B., Lundh, P.: Research on open: OER research hub review and futures for research on OER. Menlo Park: SRI International (2015)
34. Limone, P., Toto, G.A.: The psychological constructs and dimensions applied to sports performance: a change of theoretical paradigms. J. Phys. Educ. Sport **18**, 2034 (2018)
35. Trentin, G.: Didattica con e nella rete. Dall'emergenza all'uso ordinario. Milano: Franco Angeli (2020)
36. Ferri, P.: Nativi digitali. Milano: Mondadori (2011)
37. Albanese, V.E.: Geografie della pandemia e capitalismo della sorveglianza: riflessioni italiane. Documenti geografici **2**, 53–80 (2021)
38. Lai, J., Widmar, N.O.: Revisiting the digital divide in the COVID-19 era. Appl. Econ. Perspect. Policy **43**(1), 458–464 (2021). Lai, J., & Widmar, N. O.: Revisiting the digital divide in the COVID-19 era. Applied economic perspectives and policy, 43(1), 458–464 (2021)
39. International Telecommunication Union (ITU): Measuring Digital Development, Facts and Figures. Geneva: ITU (2021). https://www.itu.int/en/ITU-D/Statistics/Pages/facts/default.aspx
40. United Nations: The Sustainable Development Goals Report 2021. New York: UN (2021). https://unstats.un.org/sdgs/report/2021/
41. UNESCO, UNICEF & World Bank (WB): What have we learnt? Overview of findings from a survey of ministries of education on nation responses to COVID-19. New York: UNESCO, UNICEF & WB (2020). http://uis.unesco.org/sites/default/files/documents/national-education-responses-tocovid-19-web-final_en_0.pdf
42. UNICEF: Remote Learning Readiness Index. New York: UNICEF (2021). https://data.unicef.org/resources/remote-learning-readiness-index-dashboard/

43. UNICEF: Preventing a lost decade. Urgent action to reverse the devastating impact of COVID-19 on children and young people. New York: UNICEF (2021). https://www.unicef.org/reports/unicef-75-preventing-a-lost-decade
44. Blessinger, P., Bliss T.J.: Open Education: International Perspectives in Higher Education. Cambridge: Open Book Publishers (2016)
45. Almeida, N.: Open educational resources and rhetorical paradox in the Neoliberal Univers(ity). J. Critic. Libr. Inf. Stud. **1**(1) (2017)
46. Murphy, M.P.A.: COVID-19 and emergency eLearning: consequences of the securitization of higher education for post-pandemic pedagogy. Contemp. Secur. Policy **41**(3) (2020)
47. United Nations: International Day of Education. New York: UN (2022). https://www.un.org/en/observances/education-day
48. Andrade, A.,: Beyond OER–shifting focus to open educational practices: OPAL Report 2011 (2011)
49. Stracke, C.M.: The quality of MOOCs: how to improve the design of open education and online courses for learners?. In: International Conference on Learning and Collaboration Technologies, pp. 285–293. Londra: Springer (2017)
50. De La Higuera C.: Foreword. In: Burgos, D. (a cura di) Radical Solutions and Open Science. Singapore: Springer (2020)
51. Aliprandi, S., Giglia, E., Weller, M.: La battaglia per l'open: come l'open ha vinto, ma non sembra una vittoria. La battaglia per l'open, pp. 1–306. Milano: Ledizioni (2021)

Italian Teachers and TPACK-G: An Exploratory Study of Its Relationship with Attitudes Towards DGBL and Digital Self-efficacy

Roberta Renati[1]([✉])[iD], Natale Salvatore Bonfiglio[1] [iD], Maria Lidia Mascia[1] [iD], Dolores Rollo[2] [iD], and Maria Pietronilla Penna[1] [iD]

[1] University of Cagliari, 09123 Cagliari, Italy
roberta.renati@unica.it
[2] University of Parma, 43121 Parma, Italy

Abstract. Numerous studies have highlighted the opportunities offered by digital game-based teaching on cohorts of students at all levels of education. Positive effects on motivation, learning and relationships have been highlighted.

The teacher needs specific knowledge, skills, and attitudes to implement this pedagogical approach effectively, which, because of the specific nature of digital game-based learning (DGBL), has a close relationship to digital competence. In particular, the question of what skills the teacher needs to develop to introduce this instructional innovation into teaching and learning processes remains an overlooked area of study. This study aimed at exploring TPACK-G in a sample of Italian teachers, deepening the relationship between GK, GPK and GPCK, and critical variables such as Digital self-efficacy and attitudes towards digital game-based learning. Results highlight the crucial role of teacher Experience with games (EWG) and Game knowledge (GK) in predicting Game pedagogical content knowledge.

Keywords: TPACK-G · Teacher Digital Self-Efficacy · Teacher Attitudes Towards Digital Games

1 Introduction

Teaching is a challenging practice that requires teachers to master both specialised knowledge and specific competencies, both helpful to manage the complexity of the specific school context in which they work and the dynamic nature of the classroom in which they teach. Teachers are called upon to constantly readjust elements of their teaching practices to meet the multifaceted needs of their students, supporting them in their learning process and autonomy development. Therefore, effective teaching depends on knowing different domains and having specific competencies, which today cannot fail to include new technologies.

In the contemporary scenario of digitalisation of education, and in light of the European Union Digital Education Action Plan (2021–2027), teachers' literacy on innovative technologies and digital games seems to be a crucial key priority (Kapp, 2007; 2012).

The development of teacher competencies can have positive effects by reducing the gap between the learning styles that characterise IGen students and teaching practices, promoting students' positive involvement in their learning path and the construction of their knowledge (Clark, Tanner-Smith, Killinsworth, 2016).

Although play is generally considered a frivolous activity in contrast to learning, which is viewed as a "serious activity", many scholars in the field of game-based learning (GBL) have emphasised the usefulness of play in learning processes, both for young children (Connolly et al., 2012) and adults (Romero et al., 2015). Particularly, in recent years, a considerable number of scientific studies have been conducted and have highlighted the opportunities offered by the introduction of game-based teaching approaches in educational activities (Johnson et al. 2014; Nousiainen et al., 2018; Prensky, 2008; Razak et al., 2021; Quian & Clark, 2016). By their experiential nature, games are tools with enormous potential, able to support motivational processes and promote peer collaboration, with positive effects on learning, social development, reasoning and decision-making skills (Granic et al., 2014). Despite this positive evidence, integrating digital games into teaching practices, especially within compulsory education, is still an overlooked and scarcely implemented teaching practice. Resistance to the adoption of these methodologies seems to be due to multiple factors, including lack of adequate resources in terms of technology (Assaf et al., 2021; Brooks et al., 2019), lack of time (Assaf et al., 2021; Brooks et al. 2019), as well as insufficient technological skills (Blume, 2020; Chen et al., 2020) and low teachers' self-efficacy concerning the implementation of digital game-based teaching (Becker, 2007; Dele-Ajayi et al., 2017). It should also not be forgotten that digital games are still often viewed as a radically new form of information technology (Hamari & Nousiainen, 2015), so it may be difficult for teachers to fully understand their educational potential. This may have negative implications for their adoption, partly in light of the numerous misconceptions about digital games, which are often perceived as a mere entertainment tool (Bourgonjon, 2013), especially by those who do not have personal experience with digital games (De Grove, Bourgonjon, & Van Looy, 2012).

Four main approaches to digital game-based learning have been identified in the literature (Nousiainen et al., 2015; Nousiainen et al., 2018): educational games, entertainment games, learning through game creation, and gamification. Each of these approaches has specific characteristics and its implementation with students requires specific knowledge and competencies of teachers.

Most studies have been conducted on small samples of teachers and tend to provide limited descriptions of the pedagogical choices and teachers' specific skills in implementing digital game-based teaching activities. In general, there seems to be a lack of knowledge among teachers about digital game-based pedagogy, both with respect to the pedagogical models that delineate the teachers' role in digital game-based learning activities and about practical issues related to the implementation of digital game-based learning in the classroom, which requires the application of specialised pedagogical and digital knowledge and skills.

Thus, the implementation of game-based pedagogy requires the teacher to have appropriate knowledge, skills and attitudes (Binkley et al., 2012; Nousiainen et al.,

2018), which, by the specific nature of digital game-based learning, have a close relationship with teachers' digital competencies. Digital skills and positive attitudes towards innovation and technologies can be seen as crucial factors in addressing the challenge of an uncertain and complex world and key elements in developing meaningful learning ecosystems. Specifically, the integration of digital technologies into teaching and learning practices makes possible the promotion of innovative, virtuous and accessible learning environments where learning processes can be improved and enhanced, giving value to inclusion and personalization.

1.1 From TPACK Framework to TPACK-Game

According to Koehler et al. (2013), the possibility of virtuous teaching through the use of technology depends on three basic components that interact with each other: content, pedagogy and technology. These elements are the core of the Technology, Pedagogy and Content Knowledge (TPACK) framework (Mishra & Koehler, 2008; Mishra & Koehler, 2006). Thus, TPACK represents an aggregate of knowledge and competencies teachers must possess and master to teach 21st-century students effectively.

Although the TPACK provides a fundamental theoretical framework for integrating technology into teaching and learning processes, it lacks specificity (Voogt et al., 2013). Chai et al. (2011) pointed out that the theoretical framework needs to be contextualised for specific content, technology, or pedagogy. Starting from this observation, Hsu et al. (2013, 2015, 2020a, 2020b) proposed a framework for teaching with digital games called Technological Pedagogical Content Knowledge-Games (TPACK-G).

The TPACK-G framework consists of four components: game knowledge (GK), game pedagogical knowledge (GPK), game content knowledge (GCK), and game pedagogical content knowledge (GPCK). The GK component describes teachers' knowledge about the general use of digital games (e.g., knowing how to play digital games and having the technical skills to play games effectively). This kind of knowledge requires teachers to keep up to date with new games and innovative technologies related to games. The GPK component refers to understanding how digital games can be implemented pedagogically through appropriate teaching methods; this implies that the teacher is aware of the pedagogical constraints and possibilities of different digital games and a range of pedagogical strategies. It should be remembered that many digital games (entertainment games) are not designed with a primary educational intent. However, they can still be used flexibly, innovatively integrating them into teaching practice. Teachers need to develop the ability to look beyond the most common uses of digital games, reconfiguring them to meet personalised pedagogical goals. The GCK refers to the knowledge of how games can be used to represent the content of a specific subject, and the comprehension of how digital games and content can influence each other. The GPCK refers to knowledge that goes beyond the three components described above (GK, GPK, GCK), and it represents the teacher's awareness of how games and the pedagogical and content aspects of the subject matter can be appropriately integrated, including the specific teaching context in which learning occurs. This complex knowledge underlies effective teaching through digital games.

1.2 Teachers' Attitudes in Using Digital Games in Education

Attitudes can be defined as complex mental states involving a person's beliefs and feelings. Attitudes are organised through experience and influence a person's responses to situations with which they relate. Regarding the implementation of digital game-based pedagogy, it is crucial to examine teachers' attitudes towards using digital games because they influence their use in the classroom (Kreijns et al., 2014; Raghunath et al., 2018).

The scientific literature identified individual teacher-specific factors that affect the implementation of digital games in the classroom. These include demographics such as age, gender, and years of teaching experience (Assaf et al., 2021), perceived self-efficacy (Chen et al., 2020; Dele-Ajayi et al., 2017; Hsu et al. 2020a, 2020b; Scherer et al., 2018), and knowledge of digital games (Kaimara et al., 2021; Munkvold & Sigurdardottir, 2018). One particularly relevant factor seems to be teacher's experience with games (Hsu et al., 2013; Martín del Pozo et al., 2017; Sánchez-Mena et al., 2017); teachers lacking such exposure exhibit negative attitudes towards digital game-based learning and appear to be more reluctant towards this instructional innovation. In addition, teachers with specific training in special education, who are likely to be more flexible in adapting teaching strategies, seem to have more positive attitudes towards using digital games in teaching. A study conducted on a sample of kindergarten teachers to investigate TPACK-G (Hsu et al., 2013) found that teachers' attitudes towards digital game-based learning played an essential role in fostering their confidence in GK and GPK, the two critical components contributing to GPCK. Similar results were shown in another study by Hsu et al. (2017), which showed that the GK and GPK of elementary and middle school teachers are both positive predictors of GPCK.

Starting from Hsu et al. (2013, 2015, 2020a, 2020b) studies, the purpose of the present study was to extend the limited research on TPACK-G by exploring the relationship between teachers' confidence in GK, GPK and GPCK, their attitudes towards digital games, and their digital self-efficacy.

The research questions of this study were:

1) What is the relationship between Italian teachers' games pedagogical knowledge, attitude towards digital games, and digital self-efficacy?
2) What role do attitudes towards digital games and digital self-efficacy play in relation to teachers' technological pedagogical content knowledge about digital games?

2 Methodology

2.1 Participants

The group of participants consisted of 170 Italian in-service teachers with an average age of 44.1 years (SD = 9.03); 27 were male, and 143 were female, which is consistent with the distribution of teachers in Italy. Recruitment took place on a voluntary basis among teachers involved in in-service training courses, who received the link to fill out the anonymous questionnaire via e-mail or WhatsApp. Most respondents were from northern Italy (N = 80) and the islands (N = 77). Few were from central (N = 4) and southern (N = 9) Italy. Most of the participants were university graduates (Bachelor's degree N = 10; Master's degree N = 130), a minority had obtained a Ph.D. (N =

4), and the remaining group of participants obtained a high school education diploma (N = 26). Concerning the grade of school in which the teachers worked, 17 teachers reported teaching at preschool, 52 in elementary schools, 36 in middle schools, and 64 in secondary schools; 1 teacher did not answer the question. In relation to professional experience, the teachers were classified into three career stages: novice, up to four years' seniority (N = 64); experienced, between five- and nineteen years seniority (N = 73); and expert, with more than 20 years seniority (N = 32), one teacher did not answer the question.

2.2 Instruments

Technological Pedagogical Content Knowledge-Games TPACK-G
The TPACK-G was developed by Hsu et al. (2013) to ascertain teachers' confidence in using digital games in teaching and learning. The questionnaire consists of 22 items divided into four factors, described as follows:

Game Knowledge (GK) refers to teachers' confidence in using digital games (e.g. "I can learn digital games easily").

Game Pedagogical Knowledge (GPK) refers to teachers' confidence in using digital games to enhance students' learning (e.g. "I know how to use the characteristics of digital games to support teaching").

Game Content Knowledge (GCK) refers to teachers' confidence in selecting games appropriately to represent specific content (e.g. "I can tell whether the digital games represent the targeted subject matter knowledge").

Game Pedagogical Content Knowledge (GPCK) refers to teachers' confidence in using digital games combined with appropriate pedagogical strategies to teach specific content (e.g. "I can use appropriate digital games to display the subject I teach").

In the present study, an abbreviated version of the instrument was administered, consisting of 14 items referring only to the GK, GPK and GPCK scales. The GCK scale (a combination of play and content knowledge that excludes pedagogy) was eliminated because the study sample included preschool teachers. As pointed out by Hsu et al. (2013) and Liang et al. (2013), when preschool teachers use games to represent content for younger children, they automatically incorporate this kind of knowledge into teaching activities; this may make it difficult for them to have a clear understanding of what GCK is.

Acceptance of Digital Game-Based Learning (ADGBL)
The ADGBL was developed by Hsu et al. (2013) to assess some aspects related to teachers' acceptance of using digital games. The questionnaire consists of 22 items divided into four factors, described as follows:

Learning Opportunities (LO): the scale is composed of 7 items. It refers to the extent to which teachers believe that using games in the classroom can provide students with learning opportunities, such as "Digital games offer opportunities to experiment with knowledge".

Experience with games (EWG): the scale is composed of 7 items and refers to the teachers' experience with digital games, such as "I play different types of digital games".

Preference for Games (PFG): the scale is composed of 3 items and refers to the extent to which teachers prefer using games in the classroom, such as "I am enthusiastic about using games in the classroom".

Attitudes towards Game-Based Learning (ATT): the scale is composed of 6 items. It refers to the extent to which teachers have a positive attitude towards the use of digital games in teaching and learning, such as, "Digital games can enhance teaching skills". Concerning our cultural context, it was deemed opportune to add an item to this scale: 'Digital games can promote inclusion".

All the items are presented on a 7-point Likert scale: 1 = Strongly disagree; 2 = Disagree; 3 = Slightly disagree; 4 = Neither agree nor disagree; 5 = Slightly agree; 6 = Agree; 7 = Strongly Agree.

Teachers' Digital Self-efficacy Scale

The digital self-efficacy scale was constructed for the purposes of this paper and is based on the DigCompEdu framework (Redecker, 2017) and the SELFIEforTEACHERS tool developed by the European Commission. The scale consists of 7 items that were translated and adapted from the SELFIEforTEACHERS self-reflection questionnaire. The items refer to the extent to which teachers can use digital technologies in their daily professional practice to communicate, collaborate, teach and develop their professional skills. Example items are: "Design and implement learning experiences using digital technologies" and "Use search and selection criteria to identify digital resources useful for my teaching practice."

All the items are presented on a 7-point Likert scale: 1 = Not at all capable; 2 = Scarcely capable; 3 = Slightly capable; 4 = Neither capable nor incapable; 5 = Slightly capable; 6 = Largely capable; 7 = Completely capable.

In the present study, the Cronbach alpha coefficient of the scale was .96.

For all the above instruments, the translation and the back-translation were reviewed and verified by two experts, one of whom was a native English speaker with excellent competence and fluency in Italian.

2.3 Data Analysis

The EFA for the Digital Self-Efficacy Scale questionnaire was conducted using Principal Component Analysis as extraction method, and Promax as a rotation method. Scree-plot was used to extract factors. In addition, to explore differences within subjects ANOVA analysis was conducted. Finally, multiple linear regression and path analysis were performed to further examine the relations among the TPACK-G factors, teachers' digital self-efficacy and attitudes toward digital games.

Results

The participants' responses were grouped into only one orthogonal factor defined as Digital Self-Efficacy (Table 1). The cumulative variance explained by the factor was 79%.

Table 1. Items contents and factor's loading for the Digital Self-Efficacy Scale

Digital Self-Efficacy Scale items	Factor's loadings
Use digital technologies to communicate with colleagues, families and students	.87
Use digital technologies to collaborate with colleagues and/or other educational stakeholders	.92
Use digital technologies (e.g. devices, platforms and software) and infrastructures (e.g.Internet access) available in my school to improve my teaching practice	.94
Using digital technologies for my professional learning	.93
Engage in professional learning activities for the development of digital competence	.87
Use search and selection criteria to identify digital resources useful for my teaching	.90
Use search and selection criteria to identify digital resources useful for my students' learning	.92

With regard to the TPACK-G and ADGBL questionnaires, we used the 3-factor structure proposed by Hsu et al. (2013). The mean, standard deviation, and reliability values for all scales are given in Table 2.

Table 2. Means, Standard Deviation (SD) and Cronbach's Alpha for all the instrument scales.

Instruments	Scales	Cronbach's Alpha	Means	SD
Technological Pedagogical Content Knowledge-Games	GK	0.83	4.62	1.2
	GPK	0.94	4.47	1.4
	GPCK	0.92	4.2	1.4
Acceptance of Digital Game-Based Learning	LO	0.93	5.5	1
	EWG	0.92	3.29	1.5
	PFC	0.9	5.14	1.4
	ATT	0.96	5.59	1.2
Digital Self-Efficacy Scale	DSES	0.96	4.78	1.35

Note: GK = Game Knowledge, GPK = Game Pedagogical Knowledge, GPCK = Game Pedagogical Content Knowledge, LO = Learning Opportunities, EWG = Experience with games, PFG = Preference for Games, ATT = Attitudes towards Game-Based Learning, DSES = Digital Self-Efficacy

The within-subject ANOVA between the TPACK-G scales scores showed that the GK scores ($M = 4.62$) were higher than GPK scores ($M = 4.47$) and GPCK scores ($M = 4.16$ per item) ($F(2,336) = 20.5, p < .001$). This finding reveals that Italian teachers tend to have more confidence in their GK than the other components of TPACK-G. Moreover, the within-subject ANOVA between ADGBL scales scores showed that ATT scores ($M = 5.59$) were higher than LO scores ($M = 5.50$), PFG scores ($M = 5.14$) and EWG scores ($M = 3.29$) ($F(3,468) = 268, p < .001$). This finding shows that participating teachers had the highest scores in "Attitude towards DGBL" (ATT) and the lowest scores in confidence in their "Experience with Play" (EWG).

Table 3 reports the results of the Pearson correlation coefficients between the scales instruments. All factors were positively correlated with each other. The higher correlations ($>.50$) between EWG and GK, GPK and GPGK and between DSES and GK are noteworthy.

Table 3. Correlation matrix

Instrument Scales	1	2	3	4	5	6	7	8
1. GK	—							
2. GPK	.708**	—						
3. GPGK	.699**	.850**	—					
4. LO	.406**	.399**	.367**	—				
5. EWG	.630**	.684**	.714**	.374**	—			
6. PFG	.447**	.449**	.448**	.751*	.509**	—		
7. ATT	.425**	.417**	.409**	.818**	.452**	.861**	—	
8. DSES	.554**	.418**	.377**	.324**	.350**	.241*	.22*	—

Note. * $p < .01$, ** $p < .001$

Regarding Path Analysis, ADGBL and DSES scales were considered predictors, and the TPACK-G scales were outcome variables. In particular, GK and GPK have respectively entered as predictors of GPCK. A collinearity analysis showed that all the VIF (Variance Inflation Factor) and Tolerance indexes have acceptable values (VIF: EWG = 1.35, ATT = 1.25, DESE = 1.15; Tolerance: EWG = .74, ATT = .70, DSES = .87), suggesting no multicollinearity in the models (O'Brien, 2007).

The path model indicates several significant relations between the scales, as reported in Fig. 1.

First, the results highlight how personal "Experience with games" (EWG), "Attitude towards DGBL" (ATT), and "Digital Self-efficacy" (DSES) are closely interrelated constructs. In particular, a strong relationship between "digital self-efficacy" (DSES) and "experience with games" (EWG) and between "attitude towards DGBL" (ATT) and personal "experience with games" (EWG) emerges. Second, "Experience with games" (EWG), "Attitude towards DGBL" (ATT) and "Digital Self-Efficacy" (DSES) could significantly explain the outcome of GK (respectively, $\beta = .45\ p < .001$; $\beta = .137, p = .025$; $\beta = .36, p < .001$). Teachers who report more experience with games (EWG), a more positive attitude towards game-based digital learning (ATT), and greater digital self-efficacy (DSES) have stronger confidence in their knowledge of games (GK). Third, "Experience with games" (EWG) and GK played a positive role in GPK (respectively, β

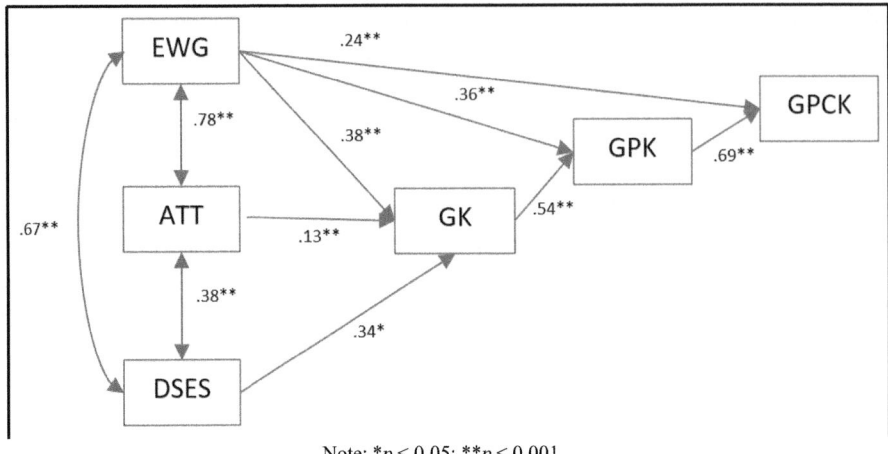

Fig. 1. The structural model of TPACK-G, ADGBL and DSES.

$= .37, p < .001; \beta = .47, p < .001$). This finding reveals that teachers who had more confidence in their knowledge of games and higher confidence in their knowledge of games seemed to have more confidence in GPK. Fourth, both "Experience with games" (EWG) and GPK directly predicted GPCK ($\beta = .25, p < .001; \beta = .70, p < .001$), indicating that teachers' GPK and their personal experience with games contribute significantly to the development of their GPCK.

3 Discussion

This study aimed to explore confidence in TPACK-G in a sample of Italian teachers by analyzing the relationship between teachers' confidence in GK, GPK and GPCK, their attitudes towards digital games and their digital self-efficacy. The results showed that in our sample, the mean scores of the TPACK-G components were below 5, indicating that teachers have low confidence, particularly concerning their GPCK, which appears to be the component with the lowest mean score. What emerged is in line with previous studies conducted in other countries (Hsu et al., 2020) and with the findings in Williamson's (2009) work that highlighted a weakness in teachers with respect to their knowledge of how to use games in teaching and learning practices.

With reference to the acceptance of digital game-based learning, it emerges that teachers have a "very poor" experience of gaming (EWG, which is around a mean score of 3) but a tendency to have a positive attitude towards the use of digital games at school, with mean scores on the LO, PFG and ATT scales hovering around a value of 5. The mean value for digital self-efficacy is around 4, a score indicating that the teachers surveyed seem to be struggling to define how capable they feel of using digital technologies to communicate, collaborate, teach, and for their own professional development.

A path analysis was conducted to examine the relationship between participants' TPACK-G, ADGBL and DSES. The results showed that experience with games, attitude towards digital game-based learning, and digital self-efficacy play a crucial role in fostering teachers' confidence in their GK. Experience with games (EWG) also plays an essential role in promoting GPK and GPCK. The results suggest that increased game experience can contribute to improved GK, GPK and GPCK. In contrast to previous studies (Hsu et al., 2013; Lee and Tsai, 2010), GPK is directly predicted by experience with games (EWG) and GK.

The GK component, indicating the teacher's familiarity with digital games, combined with the concrete experience with digital games, within the model represents the basic elements to build the GPK, and the GPCK represents the knowledge needed to implement the DGBL in the classroom. The GPK alone may not be sufficient to predict actual pedagogical use by teachers. The model is only partially congruent with the previous study by Hsu et al. (2013) conducted with a sample of preschool teachers in Taiwan. What emerges is that teachers need to be familiar with the game environment to adapt digital games to the pedagogical needs of the specific classroom (GPCK).

The evidence from this study enables researchers and practitioners to gain new insights into developing teachers' competencies in digital game-based pedagogy.

Teachers' professional identity, digital games literacy, attitudes towards digital games, and perceived self-efficacy must be considered when developing training programmes on digital game-based pedagogy. Teacher training is required to help the development of digital competence and self-efficacy, as well as to prevent risks of technostress and technostrain (Salanova et al., 2013; Syvanen et al., 2016; Sulla et al., 2022). To virtuously integrate this methodological and technological innovation into the curriculum, the active involvement of the entire school system is necessary, which would enable the development of methodological guidelines on digital game-based pedagogy. In particular, it is essential to develop tools that can support the teacher in designing and implementing game-based teaching activities.

Teacher training in this area is still in its early stages. It requires a comprehensive approach involving the synergy of all stakeholders to support the full development of teachers' skills: the school context, ministries in charge of developing educational policies and ministerial programmes, and digital game developers and researchers in the field of education and new technologies.

This study has some limitations; first, the need to expand the sample to have a representative population of teachers concerning the different school levels In addition, in future studies it would be appropriate to integrate TPACK-G with the PCK component, which was not examined in this study. It might also be interesting to complement the questionnaires by exploring specific aspects of the teacher, such as openness to experience, grit (Sulla et al., 2018), coping, and resilience (Bonfiglio et al., 2020) in relation to attitude towards technologies and TPACK-G.

It would be appropriate to integrate qualitative instruments capable of capturing teachers' instructional design to have a more precise and realistic picture of teachers' competencies and overcome the bias related to the limitations inherent in self-report questionnaires.

References

Assaf, M., Spil, T., Bruinsma, G.: Supporting teachers adopting game-based learning in formal education: a systematic literature review. In: European Conference on Games Based Learning, pp. 33-XXI. Academic Conferences International Limited (2021)

Bonfiglio, N.S., Renati, R., Costa, S., Rollo, D., Sulla, F., Penna, M.P.: An exploratory study on the relationship between video game addiction and the constructs of coping and resilience. In: 2020 IEEE International Symposium on Medical Measurements and Applications (MeMeA), pp. 1–5. IEEE (2020)

Chai, C.S., Koh, J.H.L., Tsai, C.C., Tan, L.L.W.: Modeling primary school pre-service teachers' Technological Pedagogical Content Knowledge (TPACK) for meaningful learning with information and communication technology (ICT). Comput. Educ. **57**(1), 1184–1193 (2011)

Chen, S., Zhang, S., Qi, G.Y., Yang, J.: Games literacy for teacher education: towards the implementation of game-based learning. Educ. Technol. Soc. **23**(2), 77–92 (2020). https://www.jstor.org/stable/26921135

Clark, D.B., Tanner-Smith, E.E., Killingsworth, S.S.: Digital games, design, and learning: a systematic review and meta-analysis. Rev. Educ. Res. **86**(1), 79–122 (2016)

Connolly, T.M., Boyle, E.A., MacArthur, E., Hainey, T., Boyle, J.M.: A systematic literature review of empirical evidence on computer games and serious games. Comput. Educ. **59**(2), 661–686 (2012)

Dele-Ajayi, O., Strachan, R., Sanderson, J., Pickard, A.A: Modified TAM for predicting acceptance of digital educational games by teachers. In: Proceedings of 2017 IEEE Global Engineering Education Conference (EDUCON 2017), pp. 961–968. IEEE (2017)

EU Commission webpage. https://education.ec.europa.eu/focus-topics/digital-education/action-plan

Hsu, C.Y., Liang, J.C., Su, Y.C.: The role of the TPACK in game-based teaching: Does instructional sequence matter? Asia Pac. Educ. Res. **24**(3), 463–470 (2015)

Hsu, C.Y., Liang, J.C., Chai, C.S., Tsai, C.C.: Exploring preschool teachers' technological pedagogical content knowledge of educational games. J. Educ. Comput. Res. **49**(4), 461–479 (2013)

Hsu, C.-Y., Liang, J.C., Tsai, M.-J.: Probing the structural relationships between teachers' beliefs about game-based teaching and their perceptions of technological pedagogical and content knowledge of games. Technol. Pedagogy Educ. **29**(3), 297–309 (2020)

Hsu, C.-Y., Liang, J.-C., Chuang, T.-Y., Chai, C.S., Tsai, C.-C.: Probing in-service elementary school teachers' perceptions of Tpack for games, attitudes towards games, and actual teaching usage: a study of their structural models and teaching experiences. Educ. Stud. **47**(6), 734–750 (2020)

Hsu, C.-Y., Tsai, M.-J., Chang, Y.-H., Liang, J.-C.: Surveying In-service teachers' beliefs about game-based learning and perceptions of technological pedagogical and content knowledge of games. Educ. Technol. Soc. **20**(1), 134–143 (2017). INT FORUM EDUCATIONAL TECHNOLOGY & SOC

Jayatilleke, A., Shah, M.: Examining the technological pedagogical content characteristics of games for medical education. Med. Sci. Educ. **30**(1), 529–536 (2020)

Kaimara, P., Fokides, E., Oikonomou, A., Deliyannis, I.: Potential barriers to the implementation of digital game-based learning in the classroom: pre-service teachers' views. Technol. Knowl. Learn. **26**(4), 825–844 (2021)

Kapp, K.M.: Tools and techniques for transferring know-how from boomers to gamers. Glob. Bus. Organ. Excell. **26**(5), 22–37 (2007)

Kapp, K.M.: The Gamification of Learning and Instruction: Game-Based Methods and Strategies for Training and Education. Wiley, Hoboken (2012)

Koehler, M.J., Mishra, P., Cain, W.: What is technological pedagogical content knowledge (TPACK)? J. Educ. **193**(3), 13–19 (2013)

Kreijns, K., Van Acker, F., Vermeulen, M., Van Buuren, H.: Community of inquiry: social presence revisited. E-learning Digit. Media **11**(1), 5–18 (2014)

Lee, M.H., Tsai, C.C.: Exploring teachers' perceived self-efficacy and technological pedagogical content knowledge with respect to educational use of the World Wide Web. Instr. Sci. **38**(1), 1–21 (2010)

Liang, J.C., Chai, C.S., Koh, J.H.L., Yang, C.J., Tsai, C.C.: Surveying in-service preschool teachers' technological pedagogical content knowledge. Australas. J. Educ. Technol. **29**(4) (2013)

Martín del Pozo, M., Basilotta Gómez-Pablos, V., García-Valcárcel Muñoz-Repiso, A.A.: Quantitative approach to pre-service primary school teachers' attitudes towards collaborative learning with video games: previous experience with video games can make the difference. Int. J. Educ. Technol. High. Educ. **14**(1), 1–18 (2017)

Mishra, P., Koehler, M.J.: Technological pedagogical content knowledge: a framework for teacher knowledge. Teach. Coll. Rec. **108**(6), 1017–1054 (2006)

Mishra, P., Koehler, M.J.: Introducing technological pedagogical content knowledge. In: Annual Meeting of the American Educational Research Association, vol. 1, p. 16 (2008)

Munkvold, R.I., Sigurdardottir, H.D.I.: Norwegian game-based learning practices: age, gender, game-playing and DGBL. In: Proceedings of the 12th European Conference on Game-Based Learning, pp. 460–468 (2018)

O'brien, R. M.: A caution regarding rules of thumb for variance inflation factors. Qual. Quant. **41**(5), 673–690 (2007)

Qian, M., Clark, K.R.: Game-based Learning and 21st century skills: a review of recent research. Comput. Hum. Behav. **63**, 50–58 (2016)

Raghunath, R., Anker, C., Nortcliffe, A.: Are academics ready for smart learning? Br. J. Edu. Technol. **49**(1), 182–197 (2018)

Razak, A.A., Connolly, T., Hainey, T.: Teachers' views on the approach of digital games-based learning within the curriculum for excellence. Int. J. Game-Based Learn. (IJGBL) **2**(1), 33–51 (2012)

Redecker, C., Punie, Y.: European Framework for the Digital Competence of Educators: DigCompEdu, EUR 28775 EN, Publications Office of the European Union, Luxembourg (2017). https://doi.org/10.2760/178382 (print). https://doi.org/10.2760/159770 (online), JRC107466

Romero, M., Usart, M., Ott, M.: Can serious games contribute to developing and sustaining 21st century skills? Games Cult. **10**(2), 148–177 (2015)

Salanova, M., Llorens, S., Cifre, E.: The dark side of technologies: technostress among users of information and communication technologies. Int. J. Psychol. **48**(3), 422–436 (2016)

Sánchez-Mena, A., Martí-Parreño, J.: teachers' acceptance of educational video games: a comprehensive literature review. J. e-Learn. Knowl. Soc. **13**(2) (2017). https://www.learntechlib.org/p/188115/

Scherer, R., Tondeur, J., Siddiq, F., Baran, E.: The importance of attitudes toward technology for pre-service teachers' technological, pedagogical, and content knowledge: comparing structural equation modeling approaches. Comput. Hum. Behav. **80**, 67–80 (2018)

Sulla, F., Renati, R., Bonfiglio, S., Rollo, D.: Italian students and the Grit-S: a self-report questionnaire for measuring perseverance and passion for long-term goals. In: 2018 IEEE International Symposium on Medical Measurements and Applications (MeMeA), pp. 1–5. IEEE, June 2018

Sulla, F., Ragni, B., D'Angelo, M., Rollo, D.: Teachers' emotions, technostress, and burnout in distance learning during the COVID-19 pandemic. In: Proceedings of the Third Workshop on Technology Enhanced Learning Environments for Blended Education, Foggia, Italy, 10–11 June 2022 (2020)

Syvänen, A., Mäkiniemi, J.-P., Syrjä, S., Heikkilä-Tammi, K., Viteli, J.: When does the educational use of ICT become a source of technostress for Finnish teachers? Seminar.Net **12**(2) 2016

Voogt, J., Fisser, P., Pareja Roblin, N., Tondeur, J., van Braak, J.: Technological pedagogical content knowledge–a review of the literature. J. Comput. Assist. Learn. **29**(2), 109–121 (2013)

Williamson, B.: Computer Games, Schools, and Young People: A Report for Educators on Using Games for Learning. Futurelab, Bristol (2009)

Traditional, Flipped Learning, or Blended Learning Classroom: Which Method Improves Students' Engagement in Gamified Digital Storytelling Environment?

Vahid Norouzi Larsari(✉)

Faculty of Education, Charles University, Prague, Czech Republic
`vahid.larsari@gmail.com`

Abstract. Digital technology is a fundamental part of the learning environment. The objective of the research is to investigate the collaborative creation of digital storytelling using gamification and its effect on EFL Grammar learning in flipped, blended, and traditional classes. The design of the study is based on quasi-experimental group theory. This research included 75 EFL students who were learning English at English language institutions. The students were chosen at random from three intermediate-level intact English classrooms and were allocated to one of three conditions: mixed structure (N = 26), flipped instruction (N = 24), or conventional teaching (N = 25). This study lasted around eight weeks and was split into three key phases: (1) teaching the structure (past tense), (2) assisting students in creating stories in the past tense and cultivating presenting abilities, and (3) an assessment phase for overall evaluation of learning and instruction. The researcher performed the treatment for flipped, blended context, and traditional classes. In flipped and blended classes, the teacher sent a video of teaching past tense in an online platform then student used storyboard app to make their stories in a gamified environment, in flipped classroom students presented their lecture in their online class. But in blended classroom student came to class to present their lecture in a real environment (not virtual). In traditional class, they didn't have online class, they didn't have any digital apps to use, they learned past tense and present their stories in class by playing the role of the character in their stories in front of their classmates. Following the treatments, all students took the grammar test. Pretest and post-test results were analyzed to note similarities and differences in grammar retention. The results showed that the gamified instruction with collaborative creation of digital storytelling on English grammar learning in a blended learning setting improved the participants' involvement, compelling them to be active, and significantly increased their competency of grammar, showing that the blended learning was successful in achieving the instructional goals of the class.

Keywords: Digital Storytelling · Gamification · flipped Learning · Blended learning · EFL Learners

1 Introduction

Nowadays, digital technology is a fundamental part of the learning environment. To achieve exceptional education for everyone by 2030, sophisticated innovation must be integrated into the educational system. The key to technology is using new innovation to transform the conventional learning system into a contemporary and digitalized learning framework. With the support of human rights and dignity, digital technology offers the chance to bridge the gap between traditional learning and modern approaches. Technology in education can be defined as a tool that is used to enhance all phases of instruction and simplify the jobs of those involved in education. It is based on the design, implementation, assessment, and rebuilding of instruction in line with the findings of evaluations and draws its fundamentals from the instruction hypothesis and research, pointing to permitting the highest level of learning in individuals [1]. On the other hand, in a digital learning environment, students have access to computerized resources including a computer, mobile devices, the web, peer-user gadgets, various facilities, video exercises, mock test centers, and different analysis software. Learning aids can help students and instructors at almost every level of the learning process. It increases learning motivation. The computerized learning environment may have the potential to improve ability, inventiveness, cooperation, independence, and personalisation.

Due to this transformation, inadequate teaching and learning methods have emerged, and questions have been raised regarding how well cutting-edge teaching strategies alike blended learning and flipped classrooms should be used. A learning strategy known as blended learning incorporates traditional face-to-face and online learning experiences. Teachers and students can both benefit from virtual learning environments (VLEs). Students are differentiated from one another in the classroom and are encouraged to collaborate and communicate with one another. Students develop collaborative skills and issue-understanding strategies while working on projects with their peers. VLEs, however, also necessitate financial speculation, technical assistance, and additional instructor preparation [2]. The flipped or inverted classroom may be a novel and popular instructional strategy in which activities typically carried out in the classroom (such as the introduction of substances) end up as domestic activities, and activities often considered homework end up as classroom activities [3]. In a flipped classroom, the teacher makes a difference by engaging the students rather than just imparting information. The students take responsibility for their learning and choose their own pace [4]. The teacher may engage students via other learning activities, including conversation, addressing concerns raised by the students, hands-on exercises, and guidance since classroom time isn't used to transfer knowledge to students through addresses. Since its popularization in the early 2015's, gamification, the approach of employing gameful planning in diverse settings for the goal of inducing experiences recognizable from games to endorse unique actions [5], has remained a well-known theme within both industry and academia. Gamification has received a lot of attention recently, especially in educational settings [6]. Gamifying education and learning has a lengthy and intuitively obvious history since entertainment plans and learning theories rely heavily on the same psychological theoretical underpinnings [7]. The application of gamification in pedagogy has developed as a consequence of technology improvements that allow more computerized learning settings, as well as the application of hypothetical technical results generated in connection to video games to establish engrossing and lock-in learning environments. For the most part, "design components from games," such as identifications and rankings, are "implemented in non-game settings" in gamification [8] with the goal of encouraging individuals. Duolingo®, a foreign language learning programme, and Codecademy®, an online platform for learning how to code, are two popular examples. Because millions of people play games for hours every day, the assumption is that such diversions are innately motivating [9]. On the one hand, there is intrinsic inspiration, which is characterized by emotions of pleasure and involvement while doing an activity [10]. The other kinds of inspiration are extrinsic in nature, which indicates that the directives originated-at least initially-outside of the activity [10]. When people feel confined by such outer constraints, they prefer to conceal this kind of drive, making it a part of their internal selves. According to Kosa [11], storytelling is beneficial to student learning because it appeals to a broader range of learners with diverse perceptual preferences because it covers kinesthetic, tactile, aural, and visual modalities. Using stories as extensive reading in English classrooms encourages students to read more, even outside of class, and allows them to make educated guesses about what they are reading [12]. Teaching short fiction improves the development of creative thinking, innovativeness, and mindfulness in EFL students. Students learn about "the creation and capacity of sentences, the range of possible structures, and the numerous techniques of linking concepts" via reading and writing [13]. Consequently, learners have a wonderful chance to observe new words and grammatical structures in context as well as examine syntactic or lexical topics they already know. In other words, when EFL instructors are going to improve EFL learners' language abilities, such as grammatical understanding, by using short stories, they have the benefit of doing so in context [14]. Many studies have shown that incorporating real materials in general and short narratives in particular, in English language education, improves students' performance [15, 16]. Therefore, the following research question was investigated in this present study:

(1) Is there a statistically significant distinction in the grammatical accomplishments of EFL students who participate in the three modalities of teaching using gamified digital story-telling?

2 The aims of the Study

The aims of this present paper is to see if there is any significant difference in the grammar achievement of those EFL students who undergo the gamified digital storytelling in the three modes of instruction including flipped instructional mode, blended learning mode, and traditional learning mode.

3 Methods

3.1 Study Design and Setting

This study used a quasi-experimental approach to look at the impacts of three different educational structures on EFL students' learning to determine whether using gamified digital storytelling techniques in the flipped and blended learning situations could affect EFL learners' grammatical performance. The classes were the flipped classroom approach, a blended classroom approach, and traditional structured.

3.2 Respondents

This research included 75 EFL students aged 20 to 25 who were learning English at an English language institution. The students were from three intermediate levels, each randomly selected and assigned to one of the following conditions: blended instruction (N = 26), flipped instruction (N = 24), and traditional instruction (N = 25). The participants had weekly three 50-min class periods.

3.3 Materials and Instrumentations

3.3.1 Oxford Placement Test (OPT)

The researchers employed an Oxford Placement Test to assess students' general language skills at the start of the study and ensure their homogeneity.

3.3.2 Stories

As a storyteller, the educator used short tales in the class to explain certain English language challenges and analyse the examination theory. In this scenario, the stories were created by the storyteller. He also straightened out the plot and made the main characters adjustable so that they could change or manage the accounts based on the needs and reactions of the pupils. The language was appropriate for the pupils' linguistic level. It included rapid jargon such as pronouns, colours, descriptive terms, bodily parts, and numbers. It also included a kind of past tense. The expert used the necessary resources to depict the major events.

3.3.3 Storyboard Software and Microsoft Team Online Platform

It is a kind of online platform that its software for establishing digital stories is used in blended and flip groups as a digital app for kids to make their stories in a gamified environment. A free online platform (Microsoft team) was presented to share the data, and all instructors and students used this programme to form an online class for chatting, presenting, and sharing their content. The environment of this storyboard software is formed virtually, and video as well as audio can be provided, like video calls in the Whatsapp program, but with the higher ability that was used in blended and flipped classrooms.

3.3.4 Book

The syntactic structures (past tense) were taught using grammar reviews from the Headway Beginner Students' Book. The syntactic structures (pasttense) were taught using grammar reviews from the Headway Beginner Students' Book. Liz and John Soars planned this book; Oxford University Press (OUP) will publish it. The instructor employed Sections 1 (Hello!), 2 (Your world), 3 (Personal information), and 4 (Family and friends), all of which include past tense kinds.

3.3.5 Grammar Test

3.3.5.1 Pretest of Grammar

It is a 30-item grammar test which was designed and piloted by the researcher using the grammatical rules presented in the sentences and expressions of the selected short stories for the experimental study. The pretest of grammar was used at the beginning of the study to test the participants' degree of familiarity with the target structures. This test consists of multiple-choice (10 items); fill-in-the-blank items (10 items), and writing words to complete a text (10).

3.3.5.2 Post-test of Grammar

It is a parallel form of the 30-item pretest in which the sequencing and organization of items have been changed to remove the effect of learning and memorization of items. It was used to test the participants' short-term memory regarding the instructed syntactical rules at the end of the treatment sessions.

3.3.5.3 Reliability and Validity of Grammar Tests

The pre-test and post-test were parallel-form tests. The reliability for the two tests was calculated using the KR-21 method. The correlation coefficients for pre-test and post-test turned out to be 0.79 and 0.72. The validity of the grammar tests was also computed through calculating the amount of correlation coefficient between these tests and the subtest of a TOEFL test in a pilot study. This indicated that the correlation coefficient for the grammar pretest and post-test was 0.65 and 0.59.

3.4 Data Collection Procedures

Before the process started, all the participants took an Oxford Placement Test (OPT) to measure their skills. The findings (Mean = 557.68; SD = 41.37) revealed that the majority of the 75 participants (80%) were at the intermediate level. Three intact and homogeneous classes (with an average size of 25) in three language institutes were randomly selected. The students were assigned to one of the following conditions: blended instruction (N = 26), flipped instruction (N = 24), or traditional instruction (N = 25). One person was the teacher and instructor of these three classes and the whole process. These language learners share the same first language and are expected not to differ greatly in terms of their English language proficiency. Then, all the participants of three groups took a pretest of grammar; the pretest of grammar was used at the beginning of the study to test the participants' degree of familiarity with the target structures. This study lasted roughly eight weeks and was split into three key phases:

(1) teaching the structure (past tense), (2) assisting students in defining tasks (making tales in the past tense), and (3) a testing phase for overall assessment of teaching and learning. To commence, the preparation phase began in the first week of, with each group receiving instructions. Next step was about three English teaching lessons that took time about six-week period, and the lesson themes. For evaluations, each session required two 50-min class times each week for two weeks.

3.4.1 Flipped Learning Classroom

At the primary step, a free online platform (Microsoft team) was presented to hold on online classes and share the data. This programme duration was eight weeks and divided into three main phases: (1) teaching the framework (past tense); (2) assisting students in defining tasks (making stories in the past tense) and cultivating presentation skills; and (3) a testing phase for overall evaluation of learning and instruction. To begin with, this intervention group received an orientation in the use of the Microsoft team during the first week, then the teacher sent a video of teaching past tense and teach students how to make story with storyboard application in online platform.in the second phase, they were encouraged to make use of these learning strategies and make stories in the past tense with storyboard software. The students were told what they were supposed to get out of the main project, which was digital storytelling and required them to do a number of tasks. To accomplish the complicated task of digital storytelling, students were directed step by step to (1) find topics for making stories in past tense (2) learn to utilize story board software, (3) make stories with storyboard and discuss what they found and after that present their lecture in online class, (4) work in groups to create a digital tale in the past tense. Every lesson consumed two 50-min class times every week.

3.4.2 Blended Learning Classroom

The integrated classroom was allocated to the second experimental group. At the primary step, a free online platform (Microsoft team) was presented to share the data. This study lasted eight weeks and was split into three key stages: (1) teaching the instruction (past tense) (2) making stories in past tense (3) an evaluation phase. To commence, during the first week of this intervention group, the instructor transmitted a video to the internet platform, taught how to make sentences in past tense grammar and how to make story with storyboard application. Then they were encouraged to make use of this app to make stories in past tense and present it in attendance class. The students were instructed of their anticipated result in the primary assignment, digital storytelling, which needed them to participate in a series of activities in order to fulfill the complex work of digital storytelling. They performed their seminar within the classroom in front of their speaker and peers. Meanwhile, each evaluates and reviewed others exhibitions agreeing to the scale and given in their evaluation of both exhibitions to their teacher. They could collaborate in pairs to create a digital narrative to present in class using story board software. They were given three lessons every week, each lasting two 50-min class sessions.

3.4.3 Traditional Learning Classroom

The third experimental group was assigned to the traditional classroom. This study took eight weeks and was split into three key stages, (1) teaching the instruction (past tense) (2) making stories in past tense (3) an evaluation phase. To initiate this, the preparation step occurred during the intervention group's first week, the teacher explained the past tense structure on the whiteboard and used the Headway Beginner Students' Book grammar, and there were three lessons. Every lesson required two 50-min class times each week. The pupils were told what they may anticipate from the key job, storytelling. In the second phase students were encouraged to make stories in past tense and shared their presentation in the class; the students made stories in past tense then presented their stories in class by playing the role of the character in their stories in front of their classmates, the students moved about the room, listening to the narrative and acting out the roles. Finally, they sat down in a circle. The participants give their thoughts and comments on each other's tales. Students participate by correctly identifying tale components and choosing characters. The second arrangement (while-storytelling) incorporated the story's presentation as well as inquiries.

4 Data Analysis

In this study, the data was gathered from English-language institutes. Cronbach's alpha is an estimated reliability of the tests, including the OPT test and Grammar test. The data was collected through placement tests, pretests, and posttests of grammar test scores in order to answer the research question. The results of both tests were analyzed separately so as to find the mean and standard deviation of the pretest and posttest Grammar tests. Meanwhile, in order to investigate the comparison of group differences in EFL grammar learning with a collaborative digital storytelling approach, the researcher used a one-way analysis of variance (ANOVA) test.

5 Results

5.1 Research Question

The research question for the study is, "Is there any significant distinction in the grammatical success of those EFL learners who endure gamified digital storytelling in the flipped instructional style and the blended teaching mode? Table 1 shows the comparison of group differences in pretest and post-test in grammar learning with a collaborative gamified digital storytelling approach.

Table 1. Comparison of Group differences in EFL Grammar learning with Collaborative Digital Storytelling Approach

Teaching Model	N	Grammar Achievement (Pretest)		Grammar Achievement (Post-test)	
		Mean	SD	Mean	SD
Flipped Instruction	24	72.88	7.15	78.88	6.71
Blended Instruction	26	74.71	6.15	83.31	5.24
Traditional Instruction	25	73.76	6.25	75.52	4.87
ANOVA		F = 0.47, p = .625		F = 12.24, p = .000	

An one-way analysis of variance (ANOVA) was conducted in Table 1 to look for any discrepancies in the findings. The data revealed significant variations in the mean scores of the post test and pretest (F = 0.47, p = .625 and F = 12.24, p.05, respectively). According to Table 1, participants in the blended classroom performed significantly better than those in the flipped-structured classroom and traditional classroom (blended > flipped, blended > traditional mode, p.05), but the performance of participants in the flipped-structured classroom and conventional classroom did not differ significantly (traditional < flipped). These findings about student performance indicate that, in general, the organized blended classroom assisted student learning in courses better than the conventional classroom. Participants in the organized mixed classroom improved the most in the past tense and obtained the highest mean score of 83.31 overall among the three groups.

6 Discussion

As an initial effort to use applicable strategies in the classroom, the study detailed here describes How language instructors can create attractive classes for learners Does gamified digital storytelling educate and active learning methodology have an effect on students' grammar learning? The findings revealed that employing gamified digital storytelling helps improve learning sentence structures and grammatical usage standards in the English language. The post-test findings indicate that the mean of the experimental groups (blended mean = 83.31; flipped mean = 78.88) was higher than the conventional mean (mean = 75.52). The favorable findings of this study are consequently limited to the unique research setting and technology instruments employed in the learning environment. The results from this work cannot be generalized owing to the limited sample size since the important purpose of this study was to evaluate a gamified digital storytelling technique for English grammar EFL learners. This research contributes to the literature by comparing the gamified-digital storytelling classroom method to traditional techniques. In contrast to previous research in large-scale, lecture-based programmes [17], this study revealed the feasibility of employing gamified digital storytelling to help small groups of English language learners grasp grammar. Concerning the particular benefits of this academic technique on student learning, the present research discovered considerable gains in students' involvement, achievement, and fulfillment. To begin, the findings of this study showed most of the study on active learner engagement and participation in STEM fields [18]. In that flip and blended education allow EFL learners to evaluate their own pace, such as looking for words, investigating new ideas, learning, and discovering new resources. Second, the outcomes of [17] give compelling evidence that most learners are happier with learning grammar via narrative in a flipped or blended classroom than in a traditional classroom, and the same was discovered in this study. Third, this present research affirms the result reported in [19] which the mixed classroom is related with higher achievement, whereas traditional classrooms are little successful.

7 Conclusion

This research affirmed that students learn more viably in a mixed learning (blended) environment with well-structured than in an environment with as if it were online (flipped) or face-to-face (traditional) learning; the change in student victory and satisfaction when compared with face-to-face courses; The combination of modern advances, digital and gamified lessons with traditional instructing strategies has the potential to improve students' grammar learning. Using social media, blended can break down the walls of traditional classrooms and school campuses. In the study, the students who took part in a gamified blended classroom were more successful at grammar learning. As shown, after an online class they used a gamified digital app (storyboard) to make their stories, and then they had to take part in an attendance class to present their lecture in front of their teacher and classmates. The results revealed that the gamified instruction with collaborative creation of storytelling on EFL grammar learning in a blended context not only enhanced the participants' motivation, making them more active, but also significantly improved their grammar knowledge, indicating that the blended learning was more successful in achieving the instructional goals of the class than two other groups.

References

1. Akcay, M.: Internal and transitional ballistic solution for spherical and perforated propellants and verification with experimental results. Isı Bilimi ve Tekniği Dergisi (J. Thermal Sci. Technol.) **37**(1), 35–44 (2017)
2. Paddick, S.M., et al.: Development and community-based validation of the IDEA study Instrumental Activities of Daily Living (IDEA-IADL) questionnaire. Global Health Action **7**(1), 25988 (2014)
3. Sohrabi, B., Iraj, H.: Implementing flipped classroom using digital media: a comparison of two demographically different groups perceptions. Comput. Hum. Behav. **60**, 514–524 (2016)
4. Lai, C.L., Chang, C.Y., Hwang, G.J.: Trends and research issues of mobile learning studies in nursing education: a review of academic publications from 1971 to 2016. Comput. Educ. **116**, 28–48 (2018)
5. Huotari, K., Hamari, J.: A definition for gamification: anchoring gamification in the service marketing literature. Electron. Mark. **27**(1), 21–31 (2017)
6. Koivisto, J., Morschheuser, B., Hamari, J., Maedche, A.: Gamified crowdsourcing: conceptualization, literature review, and future agenda. Int. J. Hum. Comput. Stud. **106**, 26–43 (2017)
7. Landers, R.N.: Developing a theory of gamified learning: linking serious games and gamification of learning. Simul. Gaming **45**(6), 752–768 (2014)
8. Seaborn, K., Fels, D.I.: Gamification in theory and action: a survey. Int. J. Hum. Comput. Stud. **74**, 14–31 (2015)
9. Su, C.H., Cheng, C.H.: A mobile gamification learning system for improving the learning motivation and achievements. J. Comput. Assist. Learn. **31**(3), 268–286 (2015)
10. Ryan, Richard M., Deci, Edward L.: A self-determination theory perspective on social, institutional, cultural, and economic supports for autonomy and their importance for well-being. In: Chirkov, V.I., Ryan, R.M., Sheldon, K.M. (eds.) Human Autonomy in Cross-Cultural Context: Perspectives on the Psychology of Agency, Freedom, and Well-Being, pp. 45–64. Springer, Dordrecht (2011). https://doi.org/10.1007/978-90-481-9667-8_3
11. Kosa, T., Güven, B.: The effect of dynamic geometry software on student mathematics teachers' spatial visualization skills. Turk. Online J. Educ. Technol. TOJET **7**(4), 100–107 (2008)
12. Khatib, M., Rezaei, S., Derakhshan, A.: Literature in EFL/ESL classroom. Engl. Lang. Teach. **4**(1), 201–208 (2011)
13. Collie, J., Slater, S.: Literature in the Language Classroom: A Resource Book of Ideas and Activities. Ernst Klett Sprachen, Stuttgart (1987)

14. Parvareshbar, F., Ghoorchaei, B.: The effect of using short stories on vocabulary learning of Iranian EFL learners. In: Theory and Practice in Language Studies, vol. 1377, no. 2, pp. 1476–1483. Academy Publication (2016)
15. Erkaya, O.R.: Benefits of Using Short Stories in the EFL Context. Online Submission (2005)
16. Khodabandeh, F.: The impact of storytelling techniques through virtual instruction on English students' speaking ability. Teach. Engl. Technol. **18**(1), 24–36 (2018)
17. Palomino, P., Toda, A., Oliveira, W., Rodrigues, L., Cristea, A., Isotani, S.: Exploring content game elements to support gamification design in educational systems: narrative and storytelling. In: Brazilian Symposium on Computers in Education (Simpósio Brasileiro de Informática na Educação-SBIE), vol. 30, no. 1, p. 773 (2019)
18. Afrilyasanti, R., Cahyono, B.Y., Astuti, U.P.: Effect of flipped classroom model on Indonesian EFL students' writing ability across and individual differences in learning. Int. J. Engl. Lang. Linguist. Res. **4**(5), 65–81 (2016)
19. Kennedy, K., Ferdig, R.E.: Handbook of Research of K12 Online and Blended Learning. ETC Press, Pittsburgh (2018)

Training Teachers to "Play Seriously": Testing a Game Design Activity for Assessment During a Teacher Training Course

Marco di Furia(✉) , Guendalina Peconio , and Benedetta Ragni

Learning Science Hub, University of Foggia, Via Arpi 176, 71121 Foggia, Italy
marco.difuria@unifg.it

Abstract. The introductory part of this article offers a glimpse of the state of teacher education in Italy, with specific reference to the digital skills required, at the national and European level, of future teachers. Serious Games (SGs), i.e., videogames developed for educational purposes, and more generally the gamification of educational processes represent one of the latest frontiers of educational design. Rethinking the traditional model of teaching is necessary: global governance is rebuilding paradigms, tools and methodologies, relying on the benefits of new technologies. The purpose of the present study is to report a teacher training experience consisting of an exercise on Game Design, introducing students to the basic elements of game-based learning with integration of contemporary technological elements. The methodology for developing educational games adopted is that created by The Chang School of Continuing Education at Ryerson University in Toronto. The authors present the products produced at the end of the educational activities, proposing an innovative model for returning and evaluating assignments.

Keywords: Serious Games · Game Design · Teacher Training

1 Introduction

1.1 New Teacher Configurations

The Covid-19 pandemic has deeply shaken well-established patterns and traditions in world societies, starting with those inherent in the systems of work and education. Millions of workers, teachers and students around the world have necessarily had to transfer their activities to digital environments, converting their relationships into a virtual format that, for many, had been completely unexplored until then. Over the past year, many researchers have investigated the perceptions of teachers and students with respect to the new, sudden modalities of interaction aimed at teaching and learning [1–3], coming to the common conclusion that the traumatic change experienced as a result of the Coronavirus has highlighted the need to implement teachers' digital skills, revising

---

All authors contributed equally to the paper.

teacher training pathways [4] and implementing technologies and systems for evaluating and monitoring teaching activity [5]. So, broadly speaking, the contemporary education sector is clamoring for the need to innovate teacher training programs at all levels, with a specific focus on educational technologies that can, on the one hand, enrich and enhance educational offerings; and, on the other hand, prepare learning communities for other situations of emergency that may occur in the future.

In the recent Horizon 2021 report, compiled by EDUCAUSE, some recent trends inherent in the world of education and training are pointed out in light of the upheavals of the last two years [6]. EDUCAUSE is "a higher education technology association and the largest community of IT leaders and professionals committed to advancing higher education. Technology, IT roles and responsibilities, and higher education are dynamically changing. Formed in 1998, EDUCAUSE supports those who lead, manage, and use information technology to anticipate and adapt to these changes, advancing strategic IT decision-making at every level within higher education. EDUCAUSE is a global nonprofit organization whose members include US and international higher education institutions, corporations, not-for-profit organizations, and K–12 institutions" and it counts more than 100,000 stakeholders from all over the world, trying to collect as much information and perspectives as possible.

The report's authors identified 6 key technologies and practices around which education should center its progress, namely:

1. Artificial intelligence
2. Blended and Hybrid Course Models
3. Learning Analytics
4. Microcredentialing
5. Open Educational Resources
6. Quality Online Learning

Among these topics, gamification and game-based learning take a little space; despite this, the potentialities of game-based learning, as mentioned in very recent studies [7, 8], represent a line of research that has interested several scholars in the educational field over the years. Plus, each of the topics valorized by the Horizon 2021 Report fits perfectly with the processes of game-based learning: in particular, as a specific case reported by EDUCAUSE itself within the section dedicated to microcredentials [6], game-based online training and gamification-based learning mechanisms could be seen as a fertile soil for future educational research. AI, Virtual Reality, Online Education and Learning Analytics actually are eligible for implementation with game logic, so this area is expected to grow more and more in recent years. For this reason, educating teachers and future teachers on these particular aspects of contemporary educational practice seems to be a prerogative of new teacher training programs. *Game Design* in teacher education is the focus we intend to analyze within this article.

By this term we mean the actual design of a videogame product, useful both for setting up the processes of gamification - according to Deterding's famous definition, in fact, gamification is "the use of game design elements in non-game contexts" [9] - and for understanding the intrinsic rationale of a videogame for education, i.e., a Serious Game. Initiating or refreshing teachers with respect to this particular subject thus becomes a source of benefit, on the one hand, for the teachers themselves, who acquire knowledge of alternative methods and tools to foster student academic achievements; on the other hand, for students of all levels, who, by means of innovative expedients that can be adopted at school, such as Serious Games, can enjoy more engaging, personalized and satisfying learning experiences [10].

1.2 Training Teachers in Educational Technology: Current Status in Italy

In Italy, the new law No. 79 of June 29th, 2022, which regulates initial teacher training, emphasizes several times that among the objectives of initial training there should be the acquisition of digital literacy.

Digital Literacy is one of the key competencies that the European Union has established since 2006. Based on the European Qualifications Framework (EQF), DigComp is the first framework for transversal digital competencies, developed by the European Commission's Joint Research Center (JRC), and now in its second version, DigiComp 2.2. It is a common European framework that provides a reference point for member state initiatives to develop, improve and support the development of citizens' digital competencies. Specifically, the model identifies and describes digital competencies in terms of knowledge, skills and attitudes.

Digital technologies, which are increasingly present in classrooms starting as early as kindergarten [11], hold enormous potential for enriching the educational experience, since they are resources with vast applicability and capable of promoting learning processes [12]; plus, the context of social and health emergencies given by the spread of Covid-19 around the world has further highlighted their value and fundamental role in education. However, data on teacher preparation with respect to e-learning practices are not encouraging: the SIRD 2020 report on DAD, i.e. distance learning, found that only 12% total of Italian teachers (corresponding to: 7.5% preschool teachers, 9.3% primary teachers, 13.9% secondary teachers, 17.4% secondary teachers) had participated in training on e-learning practices [13]. These data support a need for revision of teacher training pathways. Indeed, the drastic testing ground of Covid-19 has challenged many teachers [14, 15], underscoring the importance of training education professionals in the use of platforms, media, and innovative tools that can improve students' learning experiences [11].

The scientific literature highlights the benefits of teacher training aimed at promoting digital skills in education [16]. Indeed, several studies have shown how teachers who report having good digital skills are able to integrate digital technologies into their educational curriculum activities on a daily basis, thus promoting their students' digital learning and active engagement during classroom instruction [17, 18]. In order for technology to mediate learning and teaching processes by enhancing them, it is necessary for the teacher to serve as a role model and facilitate the development of digital skills in students through pedagogical and educational choices geared toward the use of technologies in innovative ways [19]. Students alone are unable to develop the knowledge and skills needed to use technologies creatively. A teacher trained in this regard is able to foster a high-quality educational environment, contributing not only to the development of students' digital skills in the short term, but also in the long term, enabling them to face daily challenges not only in everyday life but also and especially in the work environment, from a lifelong perspective [20].

In addition to this, recent literature has highlighted technology as a potential tool that can foster and support the teacher-student relationship. According to a recent literature review [21], technology increases the frequency, duration, and quality of communication between teachers and students, promoting greater academic success. It can also serve as a reliable and useful collaboration tool. Indeed, thanks to technology, teachers and students can work together on curricular content while confronting each other within active and interactive relationships, including one-on-one, thus fostering the creation of student-centered learning environments [21].

Typically, the trainings that are offered to teachers fail to train "the teachers of the future" in terms of essential digital skills [22, 23] because they present an incongruence between content and theoretical knowledge conveyed and the practical application of the latter in the real context, within which the demands that teachers receive and their expectations turn out to be different [24, 25]. Developing teachers' digital competencies requires the application of differentiated and complex strategies. Teachers' digital competencies cannot be developed and enhanced only by transferring theoretical knowledge but also and especially through realistic experiences that show teachers how to integrate digital technologies themselves into learning-teaching processes [24, 25]. In accordance with the theoretical framework TPACK (Technology, Pedagogy And Content Knowledge) [26], the preparation of future teachers must therefore take into account the dynamic relationship between three components: technological, disciplinary, and pedagogical. These skills, in turn, require mastering and integrating three components: content, pedagogical, and technological skills. The effective use of technologies is only possible if the teacher manages to integrate these three dimensions, and it is necessary, therefore, to go beyond the teaching of individual skills, encouraging the development of meaningful connections between these different domains [11, 27].

Given this, effective digital skills training is expected to include, in addition to purely theoretical content, active teaching activities, such as laboratory exercises, collaborative activities with colleagues, supportive moments that actively guide teachers in using specific digital tools to create their lesson content, innovative assessment methods that involve technologies and include feedback and reflective moments aimed at enhancing metacognition [16].

2 "Play Seriously": Introducing Teachers to the Videogame Medium with Game Design Exercises

2.1 Context

In Italy, teacher training involves a multidisciplinary course of practice and theory, called TFA (Tirocinio Formativo Attivo[1]). Special educational needs (SEN) teachers follow an ad hoc, one-year course, which is accessed by an admission test. At the end of the specialization course, which includes theoretical training entrusted to centers of higher education and a period of peer tutoring at school, they are expected to take a final exam; after that, specialized students are deemed eligible to pursue the profession independently.

---

[1] Formative Active Training.

The University of Foggia runs specific courses to train SEN teachers, composing a varied training offering that consists of elements of psychology, pedagogy and neuroscience, with a specific focus on SEN (BES, Bisogni Educativi Speciali, in italian).

The development of digital skills and knowledge of educational technologies represent two leading training objectives in courses for the specialization of SEN teachers: as part of the ICT course, a number of topics and practical exercises concerning Information and Communication Technologies applied to education are proposed to the trainees; among these, Serious Games are particularly emphasized, given the recent attention that international educational research has given to them [28–30].

In a preliminary phase prior to ICT classes, we experimented with a Game Design exercise with our TFA students. The exercise was proposed not only as a moment of active and executive learning, but also as a formative assessment tool at the end of the "Developmental Psychology: Models of Learning" module. By formative assessment we mean the definition established by the Council of Chief State School Officers' (CCSSO), which refers to FA as a "process used by all students and teachers during learning and teaching to elicit and use evidence of student learning to improve student understanding of intended disciplinary learning outcomes and to support students to become more self-directed learners" [31].

2.2 Methodology

After a brief theoretical introduction on Game Design imprinted with notions from an up-to-date textbook on the subject [10] and under the knowledge acquired at the end of the "Education and Developmental Psychology" module, the trainees were invited to design a Serious Game, envisaging content, storytelling, game mechanics and learning outcomes of the product. Being a specialization course focused on SEN, the working groups imagined a videogame with special benefit of pupils with disabilities in terms of mechanics, storytelling content and accessibility; 70 trainees belonging to the course for future secondary school teachers participated in the creative exercise; the participants, divided into seven working teams, produced a total of seven Game Design products, corroborating their skills in teamwork, time management and task analysis.

Specifically, for conducting the training exercise, the methodology "The Art of Serious Game Design" [32] (by Digital Education Strategies, The Chang School of Continuing Education, Ryerson University) was used. This methodology represents an adaptation of the Design, Play, and Experience (DPE) Framework, developed by Brian Winn [33], which represents a formal process to guide game design.

The Art of Serious Game Design conceptual framework is represented by a circle divided into four equal quadrants (Fig. 1), each representing a game element: Learning, Storytelling, Gameplay and User Experience. The components within each of these game elements are connected with double-ended arrows, representing iteration and the interconnectedness between the framework's layers.

In particular, Learning refers to the content to be learned by players through the game; Storytelling refers to the background story of the game and includes characters' description, the setting, and the goal of the game; Gameplay refers to the way in which the player interacts with the game, or with other players and includes the type of activity found in the game; User Experience refers to the player's emotions and attitudes while playing the game and how the player interacts with the game.

In addition to this, according to the model, the innermost Design layer represents all the elements that the designer introduces to the game that will allow the player to play the game; the middle layer, Play, represents the "mediated experience" between the player and design input through play; the outermost Experience layer represents the play experiences that players can have depending on their backgrounds.

The Art of Serious Game Design methodology helps teams to engage in guided brainstorming using ideation cards that contain questions. Specifically, in our study participants worked with cards for Brainstorming Part 1. The titles and colors on the front of the cards match those of the four core elements of the circle (learning, storytelling, gameplay and user experience).

The facilitator instructs the group to select one team member to take on the role of reading the card questions and another team member to write the answers. The main aim of this session is for team members to answer as many of the questions as possible.

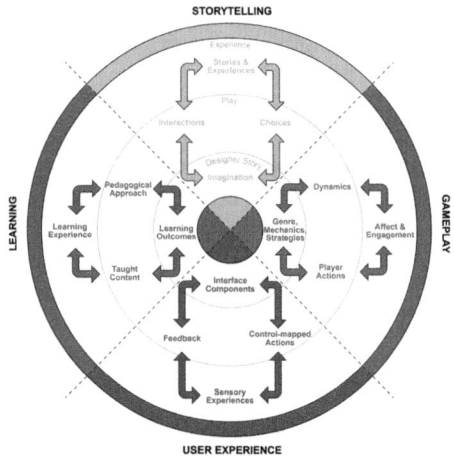

Fig. 1. Conceptual framework for Game Design, created by Digital Education Strategies.

2.3 Results and Discussion

All participants equally participated in the exercise, as trainers reported. During the exercise session, two trainers were present to guide the participants in the process of brainstorming and game design, promoting contamination of ideas, mingling of personal skills, strategies of time management and practical tips to organize the creative flow [34]. Nevertheless, trainers' guidance was reduced to the barest necessary, so that the participants were left free to decide the contents of their work, the division of tasks, and the outcomes to reach. Overall, 7 projects were realized by the groups. Each project was presented in class and converted in a presentation, using PowerPoint or Genially; just one project was transcripted in a Word document. All the projects were collected through our e-learning platform, which is developed in LMS Moodle [35]. In Table 1 we provide the complete list of Serious Games designed by trainees, reporting their main characteristics, according to the guidelines provided by The Chang School of Continuing Education of Toronto:

Certainly, it is important to emphasize that the Game Design exercise effectively achieved two purposes:

1. Instructing the trainees operationally on the basic mechanisms and features of a Serious Game: all trainees successfully executed the design, responding to all the steps and questions within the prescribed time, enhancing their skills of time management, task analysis and team working;
2. To elicit in the trainees an applied reflection on the notions learned in the Psychology and Pedagogy modules followed up to that moment: references to specific disabilities; innovative teaching methodologies such as PBL, tinkering, task analysis, cooperative learning; soft and hard skills fundamental to learning communities appear in the SG design of each group (Fig. 2).

Specifically, 3 projects involve SGs to support, respectively, students with intellectual disabilities (*It's raining wast*e), students with ADHD (*Escape Castle*), and students with developmental disabilities (*A city for all*). The other products, on the other hand, make use of cooperative learning or multiplayer dynamics in general, with potential positive effects on motivation, positive interdependence, stigma reduction, and enhancement of social skills [36].

All the proposed projects contain a more or less accurate description of the game mechanics, with details regarding the input and output devices involved, the user experience and the emotions evoked; in particular, some products (i.e., the SG *A city for all* draws on the bring-your-own-device approach). In terms of accessibility, it can be said that the game mechanics are deliberately simplified in order to make the product inclusive for all types of learners (e.g., the click-and-play dynamics of *The Odyssey: 7 challenges for Nobody* and *Grow up* do not require special executive skills). For a possible and effective development of the products presented, and their implementation for students with SEN, it would be useful to work precipitously on tools and processes that make SGs as accessible as possible (with the addition of subtitles, tangible elements or sound feedback for sensory disabilities, etc.); in this sense, there are some useful tools for this purpose in the literature, such as the accessibility scale recently elaborated by Jaramillo-Alcázar et al. [37]. For a possible continuation of the research, therefore, a reconnaissance of studies regarding tools and strategies for Game Design would undoubtedly represent the first step (Fig. 3).

Table 1. Analytical table of Game Design projects.

Title	Storytelling	Gameplay	User experience	Learning outcomes
It's raining waste	The main character is Mr. Green, a superhero who lives in Bin-city. He must defeat Skyser, a god-like monster from the sky that decided to avenge air pollution by raining garbage on the planet. The player is tasked with leading Mr. Green in cleaning up the city.	It is a simulation game in which the player performs actions of collecting and discerning garbage according to the rules of garbage recycling. The emotions involved are mainly disgust and contentment. The time available for each task is 10–15 s, according to 3 difficulty levels: easy, medium, hard.	Players receive 3 types of visual feedback: *Ops!*, *Oh no!*, and *Good job!*, which work as reinforcements. Game mechanics are not specified, although interaction with touchscreen is mentioned.	The SG is specifically designed for students with intellectual disability. The use of the game fits into a learning unit within the civic education program. The main outcome concerns notions about recycling collection. Expected skills are: Emotional alphabetization, empathy, active citizenship. Pedagogical approach: learning by doing.
Escape Castle	The user is a traveler setting out to explore new lands, but suddenly kidnapped and taken to some unknown location. The aim is to get out and keep your captors from seeing you. The game consists of getting through the levels by solving puzzles, choosing the right objects, finding coins to earn skills and reach the exit.	It is an exploration game in which players find themselves in a maze consisting of six levels of increasing difficulty. The character can jump over obstacles, run, interact with key-objects, interact with characters to solve puzzles, collect coins to earn bonuses (reinforcements). The setting is spooky; there are enemies and allies.	The player can pause the game and save progress at checkpoints in case of fatigue, so that he/she can continue the adventure later on. The avatar is customizable. A controller is required; tactile feedback in the form of vibrations are given, together with sounds that indicate success or failure.	The SG is designed for implementing executive functions and attention in students with Attention Deficit/Hyperactivity Disorder (ADHD). Expected skills are problem solving and self regulation/self control. Pedagogical approach: tinkering, Problem based learning, token economy.
Escape Room: Quiz Detective	Students have been locked inside the school by a mischievous genius; the goal is to escape the building, gaining not only freedom but also the satisfaction of having defeated a tricky character.	It is an online exploration game in which players must solve puzzles spread over seven progressive-access levels, within a time limit. Characters can move freely all around the place to find objects used to solve the math-based puzzles.	Mouse and keyboard are required. Players are able to share their results, within a challenge based situation; they can save their progress and pause the game. There is no information about feedback and avatars.	Students are divided into teams. The game fits in at the end of a teaching unit, serving as a reinforcement for the final assessment. The academic outcome is game-based strengthening of mathematical knowledge Pedagogical approach: cooperative learning, problem based learning.

(continued)

Table 1. (*continued*)

Title	Storytelling	Gameplay	User experience	Learning outcomes
Master cooking	Players participate in a simulated cooking competition with a number of difficulties to cope with (expired food, broken utensils, etc.). The game is inspired by the Italian version of Masterchef: characters' helper is an actual Italian chef who participates in the TV programme.	It is a simulation game in which the player performs a recipe through written instructions and video-modeling; the recipe will be evaluated by some judges; the action is articulated in 3 steps (apprentice, chef assistant, cooking master); activities (choice of ingredients, plating, etc.) must be performed within a time limit.	Mouse and keyboard are required. The progress will be shown within special interfaces. The game can be paused in case players need to receive support from the teacher. A prompt will be given by clicking on the helper's figure (chef Cannavacciuolo). Players are provided with visual feedback in case of success (e.g., the helper claps his hands as social mediated reinforcement).	The SG is designed for catering school, and it serves as an exercise to consolidate acquired knowledge (food science, dining services, gastronomy) and train stress management, self-efficacy, emotional self regulation Pedagogical approach: learning by doing.
A city for all	Once upon a time, there was a class of 20 kids from a small town in southern Italy. One of the classmates has a motor disability that forces him to use a wheelchair and he faces daily difficulties in navigating town routes. The teachers issue a challenge to the class: to recognize and eliminate the town's architectural barriers.	The game includes 4 pathways: Home-School, School-Library, Library-Gym, Gym-Home Each scenario includes 10 barriers for each. The final stage is the Town Hall, where players can communicate the difficulties encountered and request solutions Characters can move freely around the town.	Recognize architectural barriers in the path and point them with appropriate markers; visual feedback is provided (red/green light to indicate presence/absence of the obstacle), together with sound feedback (cheerful/annoying sound). A smartphone is required to play the game, since it is developed as an app.	Ideal players are a student with motor disabilities and his/her classmates. Players are expected to learn how to identify architectural barriers and report them through institutional communication. The game is designed to raise class awareness of disability, civics and active citizenship. The game is embedded within a cross curricular learning unit.

(*continued*)

Table 1. (*continued*)

Title	Storytelling	Gameplay	User experience	Learning outcomes
Grow up	A student moves around the school, encounters different situations and has to make decisions Each choice is followed by a positive or negative effect; at the end of the game, one can start again to change the course of the storyline.	It is a 'click-and-play' simulation game in which players must manage difficult situations with moral implications (e.g., reacting to a bully who write Homophobic insults on the wall) Undefined levels of difficulty are mentioned.	Visual feedback is provided (right/wrong answer); game controls are very simple, since it is a conceptual reasoning genre of game, in which choices are the actual actions performed. A *keep growing* message appears whenever the user makes the wrong decision.	Expected skills are: emotional alphabetization, empathy Pedagogical approach: learning by doing.
The Odyssey:7 challenges for Nobody	The player plays Ulysses. To reach the motherland after the Trojan War, the Greek hero will have to overcome 7 feats. In each of these challenges the player will have to answer correctly three questions to move to the next level next. Having passed all the challenges, Odysseus will be reunited with his wife Penelope. The setting is Ancient Greece Homer will pose the questions; enemies are inspired by the poem (e.g., Circe, the sirens)	This 'click and play' game has an epic matrix. It will elicit tension, suspense, surprise. The game consists of 7 levels (each level corresponds to some of the feats that Ulysses accomplished during his journey). The player will have to answer questions with multiple choice questions related to the poem. For each correct answer, the player will get 1 star, upon reaching 3 stars, he will advance to the next level. The time available to answer is 20 s.	A mouse is required Players will be able to share the results with others. A table will appear with the ranking of scores in real time. Players are able to put the game in pause mode, save the results and consult them. The player who reaches the last level with the highest score will receive a voucher for the purchase of a real game.	This SG is designed to enhance the knowledge of the poem or to acquire new knowledge of Greek literature through a GBL approach.

Fig. 2. First slide from *It's raining waste* eco-game presentation.

Fig. 3. *City for all* game designed logo.

3 Conclusions

Bringing concrete reflections on new technologies is one of the inescapable directions that higher education institutions pursue today in addressing the delicate process of teacher education, in accordance with frameworks and reference guidelines established in recent years by international governance [38]. Within these reflections, the reasoning on the use of innovative tools such as Serious Games in the field of education occupies a privileged position, since the students who populate schools and educational environments, 'digital natives' by definition, massively consume videogame content, every day, acquiring its languages, symbologies and cognitive implants. Not surprisingly, the percentages of gamers continue to grow year after year [39, 40].

As a result, a good teacher cannot remain ignorant of notions regarding the videogame industry because, on the one hand, it can provide products that can foster students' motivation to learn; on the other hand, appropriate literacy with respect to the video game dimension allows the teacher to have the tools to carry out his or her task as a *media educator*, who guides students toward a balanced, conscious and profitable use of the videogame medium, contrasting, for example, dangerous forms of addiction that become even more acute in situations of isolation, as happened during the Coronavirus pandemic [40].

In the present article, we proposed a practical example of literacy for teachers in training with respect to the medium of videogames, consisting of an exercise on Game Design that also served as a formative assessment tool. Adopting this type of project-based training activity allowed us, first of all, to test the methodology with the trainees, recording the results and obtaining, on the whole, a positive response from all the participants, who excelled in completing the task by making use of the knowledge they had received so far during the training course.

This operational exercise model, subjected to its very first testing in TFA course, can, in the future, not only be used as an innovative evaluative practice of project-based learning for different subject areas and subjects of study, but also lend itself to quantitative measurement, taking into account, for example, students' levels of motivation and self-efficacy or their learning outcomes in the area of digital knowledge. In addition, the same model could also be used outside formal educational settings, for example in the stimulation of creative processes within companies that are involved in the development of software and technology solutions for personal services.

References

1. Dash, F.: Pandemic induced e-learning and the impact on the stakeholders: mediating role of satisfaction and moderating role of choice. Athens J. Educ. **9**, 1–22 (2022)
2. Shariq, M., Lutfy, K., Alahdal, A., Abdullah Aldhali, F.I.: Teachers and learners' perceptions of e-learning implementation in special times: evaluating relevance and internationalization prospects at Saudi universities. Sustainability **14**(10), 6063 (2022)
3. Shambour, M.K.Y., Abu-Hashem, M.A.: Analysing lecturers' perceptions on traditional vs. distance learning: a conceptual study of emergency transferring to distance learning during COVID-19 pandemic. Educ. Inf. Technol. **27**(3), 3225–3245 (2022)
4. Luy, D.T.T.: Remote teaching amid the Covid-19 pandemic in Vietnam: primary school EFL teachers' practices and perceptions. AsiaCALL Online J. **13**(1), 1–21 (2022)
5. Saha, S.M., Pranty, S.A., Rana, M.J., Islam, M.J., Hossain, M.E.: Teaching during a pandemic: do university teachers prefer online teaching? Heliyon **8**(1), e08663 (2022)
6. Pelletier, K., et al.: EDUCAUSE Horizon Report, Teaching and Learning edn. Boulder, CO (2021)
7. Limone, P., Toto, G.A.: Manuale TIC. Per una didattica inclusiva. McGraw-Hill, Milano (2022)
8. Toto, G.A., Scarinci, A., di Furia, M., Rossi, M.: Serious Games e strategie didattiche contemporanee: una revisione sistematica e meta analisi. Nuova Secondaria Ricerca **2**, 267–284 (2022)
9. Deterding, S., Dixon, D., Khaled, R., Nacke, L.: From game design elements to gamefulness: defining gamification. In: Proceedings of the 15th International Academic MindTrek Conference, Envisioning Future Media Environments, pp. 9–15. Association for Computing Machinery, Tampere (2011)
10. Egenfeldt-Nielsen, S., Heide Smith, J., Pajares Tosca, S.: Understanding Video Games. The Essential Introduction, 4th edn. Routledge, New York and London (2020)

11. Toto, G.A.: Didattica digitale e drop-out: osservazioni da un corso di formazione iniziale degli insegnanti durante la pandemia da Covid-19. J. Incl. Methodol. Technol. Learn. Teach. **1**(1) (2021)
12. Pascoletti, S.: Le tecnologie didattiche nella progettazione del curricolo inclusivo. In: Cottini, L. (ed.) Universal design for learning e curricolo inclusive, pp. 38–50. Giunti, Firenze (2019)
13. Girelli, C.: La scuola e la didattica a distanza nell'emergenza Covid-19: Primi esiti della ricerca nazionale condotta dalla SIRD (Società Italiana di Ricerca Didattica) in collaborazione con le associazioni degli insegnanti (AIMC, CIDI, FNISM, MCE, SALTAMURI, UCIIM). RicercAzione **12**(1), 203–208 (2020)
14. Hurwitz, S., Garman-McClaine, B., Carlock, K.: Special education for students with autism during the COVID-19 pandemic: "Each day brings new challenges." Autism **26**(4), 889–899 (2022)
15. Stambekova, A., Zhakipbekova, S., Tussubekova, K., Mazhinov, B., Shmidt, M., Rymhanova, A: Education for the disabled in accordance with the quality of inclusive education in the distance education process. World J. Educ. Technol. Current Issues **14**(1), 316–328 (2022)
16. Reisoğlu, İ.: How does digital competence training affect teachers' professional development and activities? Technol. Knowl. Learn. **27**(3), 721–748 (2022)
17. Dinçer, S.: Are preservice teachers really literate enough to integrate technology in their classroom practice? Determining the technology literacy level of preservice teachers. Educ. Inf. Technol. **23**(6), 2699–2718 (2022)
18. Silva, J.S., Usart, M.U., Lázaro-Cantabrana, J.L.L.C., Silva, J., Usart, M., Lázaro-Cantabrana, J.L.: Teacher's digital competence among final year Pedagogy students in Chile and Uruguay, Comunicar. Media Educ. Res. J. **27**(2), 31–40 (2019)
19. Krumsvik, R.J., Jones, L.Ø., Øfstegaard, M., Eikeland, O.J.: Upper secondary school teachers' digital competence: analysed by demographic, personal and professional characteristics. Nordic J. Digit. Lit. **11**(3), 143–164 (2016)
20. Redecker, C.: European framework for the digital competence of educators: DigCompEdu, JRC Working Papers JRC107466, Joint Research Centre (Seville site) (2017)
21. Harper, B.: Technology and teacher–student interactions: a review of empirical research. J. Res. Technol. Educ. **50**(3), 214–225 (2018)
22. Fernández-Batanero, J.M., Montenegro-Rueda, M., Fernández-Cerero, J., García-Martínez, I.: Digital competences for teacher professional development. Syst. Rev. Eur. J. Teacher Educ. **45**, 513–531 (2020)
23. Gudmundsdottir, G.B., Hatlevik, O.E.: Newly qualified teachers' professional digital competence: implications for teacher education. Eur. J. Teach. Educ. **41**(2), 214–231 (2018)
24. Tondeur, J., van Braak, J., Siddiq, F., Scherer, R.: Time for a new approach to prepare future teachers for educational technology use: its meaning and measurement. Comput. Educ. **94**, 134–150 (2016)
25. Tondeur, J., Pareja Roblin, N., van Braak, J., Voogt, J., Prestridge, S.: Preparing beginning teachers for technology integration in education: ready for take-off? Technol. Pedagog. Educ. **26**(2), 157–177 (2017)
26. Mishra, P., Koehler, M.J.: Technological pedagogical content knowledge: a framework for teacher knowledge. Teach. Coll. Rec. **108**(6), 1017–1054 (2006)
27. Bonaiuti, G., Calvani, A., Menichetti, L., Vivanet, G.: Le tecnologie educative. Criteri per una scelta basata su evidenze, pp. 1–280. Carocci, Roma (2017)
28. Papoutsi, C., Drigas, A.S., Skianis, C.: Serious games for emotional intelligence's skills development for inner balance and quality of life: a literature review. Retos: nuevas tendencias en educación física, deporte y recreación **46**, 199–208 (2022)
29. Ullah, M., et al.: Serious games in science education. Syst. Lit. Rev. Virt. Real. Intell. Hardw. **4**(3), 189–209 (2022)

30. Alencar, N.E.S., Pinto, M.A.O., Leite, N.T., Silva, C.M.V.D.: Serious games para educação sexual de adolescentes e jovens: revisão integrativa de literatura. Cien. Saude Colet. **27**, 3129–3138 (2022)
31. Close Council of Chief State School Officers: Attributes of effective formative assessment, Council of Chief State Schools Officers, Washington, DC (2017)
32. https://de.ryerson.ca/games/research/_/Game_Design_Textbook.pdf
33. Winn, B.: The design, play and experience framework. In: Ferdig, R., (ed.) Handbook of Research on Effective Electronic Gaming in Education, pp. 388–401. IGI Global, Hershey (2009)
34. Sari, H.P., Sofansyah, N.A., Saputra, R.H.: Enhancing pre-service teacher's creativity through "Youtube" project based learning. EDUCATIO J. Educ. **7**(2), 79–91 (2022)
35. Borrelli, L., Perrella, S.: Progettazione didattica nell'e-learning: l'esperienza Unifg durante l'emergenza Covid-19. In: Limone, P., Toto, G.A., Sansone, N. (eds.) Didattica Universitaria a distanza: tra emergenze e futuro, pp. 37–46. Progedit, Bari (2020)
36. Lopez, A.G.: Cooperazione e gioco. In: De Serio, B., Toto, G.A. (eds.) Media ed emozioni: una sfida per l'apprendimento, pp. 45–56. FrancoAngeli, Milano (2020)
37. Jaramillo-Alcázar, A., Cortez-Silva, P., Galarza-Castillo, M., Luján-Mora, S.: A method to develop accessible online serious games for people with disabilities: a case study. Sustainability **12**(22), 9584 (2020)
38. Reisoğlu, İ., Çebi, A.: How can the digital competences of pre-service teachers be developed? Examining a case study through the lens of DigComp and DigCompEdu. Comput. Educ. **156**, 103940 (2020)
39. Nielsen. https://www.nielsen.com/it/insights/2018/us-games-360-report-2018/. Accessed 30 Oct 2022
40. Gómez-Galán, J., Lázaro-Pérez, C., Martínez-López, J.Á.: Exploratory study on video game addiction of college students in a pandemic scenario. J. New Approach. Educ. Res. **10**(2), 330–346 (2021)

Bilingualism and Second Language Learning

Bilingualism and Second Language Learning through the Use of Social Robots: A Scoping Review

Carla Cirasa and Daniela Conti(✉)

Department of Humanities, University of Catania, 95124 Catania, Italy
daniela.conti@unict.it

Abstract. In this digital era, the use of technology has affected all sectors. In particular, recent studies have focused on how social robots can improve second language learning. In this study, we present a scoping review of the last ten years (from January 2012 to September 2022), where consider the articles that have argued the impact of using a social robot on second language learning. The SCOPUS electronic database was used, and data were collected in September 2022 from the database. A total of 227 articles were identified in the databases as relevant. Finally, after screening by inclusion and exclusion criteria, 46 articles were eligible for this scoping review. From the selected articles we observe that in the last ten years the "Robot-Assisted Language Learning (RALL)" topic increased exponentially in the last three years, while from 2012 to 2015 no studies have been identified. Most of the studies have used the NAO social robot, and the 80.95% consisted of quantitative studies, preferring in 94.65% of cases the direct interaction with the social robot. In 50% of the selected articles, the mother tongue of the sample of participants was not specified, while for the second language 56.52% provided for the learning of English with the support of a social robot. In conclusion, the increasing interest in this topic suggests that research on human-robot interaction could provide meaningful contributions to this field.

Keywords: Robot-Assisted Language Learning · Social Robots · Scoping Review

1 Introduction

The Robot-Assisted Language Learning (RALL) is a new field of research, with most of the work conducted in the previous decade. Numerous researchers show how interaction with physical robots improved student learning achievements significantly compared with virtual interaction [1]. Most studies on learning foreign languages have indicated how the use of social robots can help reduce anxiety, especially during dialogue exercises [2, 3].

According to Bartneck & Forlizzi [4], a social robot can be defined as "autonomous or semi-autonomous robot that interacts and communicates with humans following the rules behavioral expected by the people with whom the robot intended to interact".

Social robots are considerate as mechanical tools with social interaction skills that generate responses in the users with whom they relate. These robots are able to communicate both verbally and non-verbally. The interaction is facilitated by their humanoid aspect (see [5] for a systematic review on the definition of social robots).

Different robot designs are currently studied in the research community, ranging from mechanically looking (e.g. Pioneer1 robots) to zoomorphic robots (e.g. the AIBO), to humanoids such as NAO, Pepper or Furhat. Moreover, robot design kits are available (e.g. LEGO Mindstorms) [6].

An embedded system, such as a humanoid social robot, is more challenging for the dialogue and the language, compared with devices without these characteristics [7, 8]. As suggested by Konjin et al. [9], this perceived humanity creates the potential for social robots to take on the role of teachers, tutor or peer for learning tasks.

According to studies by Belpaeme [10], social robots have shown to be effective tutors, capable of improving concentration and academic performance thanks to their profitable use for the language development in children, primarily in aged children preschool. Specifically, the level of involvement and motivation was positively related to expressive behavior in robotic narration, the whose effectiveness is comparable to that of a human being with the same behavior than a human being with characteristics of static and inexpressiveness [11].

During the learning tasks, the robot tutor can therefore be perceived as less intimidating than a peer or a teacher [12]. Therefore in a recent study on second language learning conducted by van den Berghe [13], it proved to be the children who perceived the robot as more human at the end of the tutoring activity knew a superior number of words compared to the control group. Konjin et al. [14] showed how interacting with humanoids, people may feel an emotional bond between them and the robot.

Recent literature shows that moments of uncertainty are frequent for students during practice of a second language [15]. For this reason, proper management of events could help avoid the development of frustration and ensure benefits for the learner experience. This potential benefit was discovered in both children and adults.

There are numerous studies in the literature that demonstrate the benefits of learning in primary school children. Specifically, for adults, there are fewer studies and these mainly concern migrant adults and language schools. For example, the study conducted by De Carolis et al. [16] programmed the NAO robot to teach culturally related gestures to young unaccompanied foreigners to facilitate their integration into the territory.

An interesting study conducted by Vogt et al. [17] evaluated the use of a social robot in second language learning sections in young adults with severe learning problems. In their qualitative study, Fuglerud & Sollheim [18] evaluated the use of the NAO robot [19] to support second language learning in a group of primary school children with autism spectrum disorder. Moreover, thanks to gestures, the social robots can be useful for both children and adults with learning difficulties.

Social robots can play the role of assistants to the human teacher, as an autonomous tutors, as a peer, as a partner to perform a task with or as a game adversary [11].

Positive effects from robot-assisted language learning have also been reported, such as an increase in vocabulary acquisition, speaking ability, pronunciation, confidence in learning, and storytelling skills [10, 20].

To maximize the effect of social robots in learning contexts, some studies have focused on the different styles of robot interaction and on the response produced by the participants who interact with a social robot. For example, Engwall et al. [21] have developed four different styles of interaction with the Furhat social robot. The social robot conducted an oral conversation with two simultaneous language learners, based on the interaction styles of the human language bar moderators [21].

Moreover, numerous studies on the influence of the use and type of feedback provided by the robot during a second language learning section were conducted. To study how a robot's use of feedback can affect children's engagement and support second language learning. De Haas et al. [22] conducted an experiment with three different conditions: preferred feedback, unwelcome feedback and no feedback. The results showed that the preferred feedback, compared to the other two conditions, resulted in greater engagement with the robot and the activity. The same authors [23], in 2022, conducted a further experiment to understand if there were differences in the child's interaction with the robot that produced iconic gestures, without iconic gestures or with a tablet. The results reported that children were more involved in interactions where robots used iconic gestures [23].

De Wit et al. [24] found that, contrary to what most of the existing research suggests, the robot's use of gestures did not result in increased learning outcomes, compared to a robot that did not use gestures. However, in the two conditions in which the robot used gestures, the involvement was greater.

Another aspect examined was the individual differences between children during the learning tasks. Van den Berghe et al. [13] studied the moderating role of three individual characteristics of the child considered relevant for language learning: knowledge of first language vocabulary (L1), phonological memory and selective attention. The authors found numerous moderating effects. A final aspect on which current scientific research has focused is the understanding of the influences exerted by a social robot within a group.

Recent studies measured the influence of a social robot in a social interaction between two participants during a second language learning section [9]. Gillet et al. [25] assessed whether the social robot can balance the level of participation in a language skill-based game played by a native speaker and a second language learner. The study showed that the robot's adaptive gaze behavior could shape the interaction between the participants leading to more uniform participation during the game.

This set of observations led us to carry out a scoping review of the literature over the past 10 years which takes into account a rigorous approach in the choice of inclusion criteria to select articles. We report below the procedure used for the selection of the articles and the results and conclusions that emerge.

2 Method

In this article, is important to highlight that while a systematic review "attempts to gather empirical evidence" for a targeted research question [26] the scoping review allows the literature on a specific topic to be described and based on the intention to synthesize the research on the ground [27]. However, a scoping review is not a less rigorous adaptation of a systematic review, because they are two approaches with different objectives [26].

With this premise, we have explored in detail all the studies on "Robot-assisted language learning" (RALL) topic.

The SCOPUS electronic databases were searched, using prespecified search terms, for peer-reviewed articles and unpublished literature. Specifically, we conducted a search with the following search terms: ab (learning * robot *) AND accept * (n = 67); ab (second language * robot *) AND accepts * (n = 26); ab (social robot *) AND accepts * (n = 134). This search included 227 articles.

Specifically, we focused on language learning with social robots according to three aims: a) explore existing empirical research on second language learning and social robots; b) identify the used measures; c) select reference literature from January 2012 to September 2022.

The PRISMA Flow diagram [28] presents the inclusion and exclusion procedures performed from SCOPUS electronic databases. The diagram shows the selection of 46 articles in total for 227 articles initially identified (see Fig. 1). This synthesis aims to give a descriptive overview, a picture, of where we are in the study of second language learning and robotics.

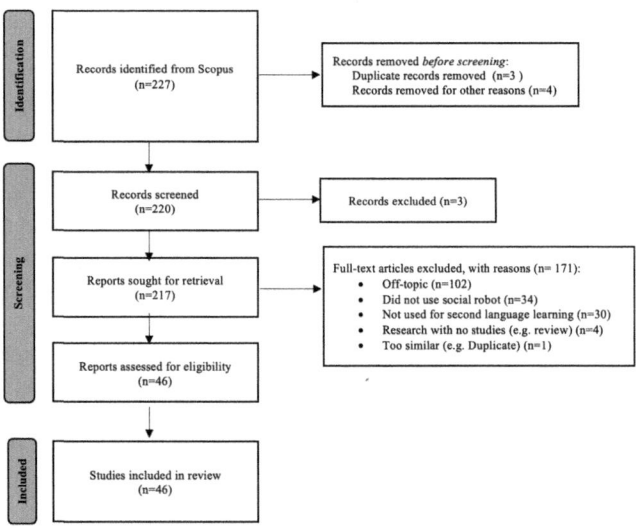

Fig. 1. The PRISMA Flow Diagram of the scoping review.

Finally, the authors exported the 227 articles found in the databases into an Excel table with their metadata (e.g., author, title, DOI, etc.), and a total of 46 articles resulted from this selection and their data were added to a single clean Excel file. (see Table 1). Table 1 reports for each selected article the type of study (quantitative or qualitative), the type of robot used, whether the interaction between the robot and the subject was direct or mediated and how many subjects or robots interacted, the age of the sample, the nationality of the sample, the size of the sample, the language spoken, the language learned, the steps of the experiment.

Table 1. Articles selected from Scopus database.

N.	Title	Type of Study	Social Robot	Interaction	Type of Sample	Sample Nationality	Sample Size	Mother Tongue	Language (Robots as Tutors in Language Learning)	Analysis methods used
1	Robots in situated learning classrooms with immediate feedback mechanisms to improve students' learning performance [1]	QT	ZENBO, from ASUS	Direct (1 robot) (group)	Students of junior high school (Age 15)	Taiwan	101	N.S.	English	Pre and post-test to examine students' learning achievement; questionnaire to measure the students' learning motivation and engagement
2	An innovative approach of incorporating a humanoid robot into teaching EFL learnes with intellectual disabilities [29]	Case study	NAO	Direct (1 robot) (Group)	Participants of the Down Syndrome Center of Iran (DSCI). (Average:30)	Iran	10	N.S.	English	Pre-test; post-test; delayed post-test
3	Employing Humanoid Robots for Teaching English Language in Iranian Junior High-Schools [2]	QT	NAO	Direct (1 robot) (Group)	Junior high school students. (Average age of 12)	Iran	46	N.S.	Iranian English	Pre-test; post-test

(continued)

Table 1. (*continued*)

N.	Title	Type of Study	Social Robot	Interaction	Type of Sample	Sample Nationality	Sample Size	Mother Tongue	Language (Robots as Tutors in Language Learning)	Analysis methods used
4	Adoption of social robots as pedagogical aids for efficient learning of second language vocabulary to children [30]	QT, QL	EMYS (EMotive headY System)	Direct (1 robot) (1 subject)	Students of third primary grade	Algeria	54	N.S.	English	Reading pre-test; reading post-test; writing test; Pronunciation progress; learning time
5	Influence of the NAO robot as a teaching assistant on university students' vocabulary learning and attitudes [31]	QT, QL	NAO	Direct (1 robot) (Group)	University students (Around age 20)	North Cyprus	65	N.S.	English	Pre-test; post-test;
6	Guidelines for Designing Social Robots as Second Language Tutors [10]	QT	NAO	Direct (+ Tablet) (1 robot) (1 subject)	Preschool children (around age of 5 years)	Holland	46	Dutch	English	Pre-test; post-test
7	Teaching L1 and L2 communication skills with a robotic head [32]	QT	Robotic head Furhat (furhatrobotics.com)	Direct (1 robot) (1 subject)	Patients of various levels of communication deficits	N.S	10	Slovak	Slovak	Questionnaire; Post-test
8	Detection of Listener Uncertainty in Robot-Led Second Language Conversation Practice [15]	QT	Robotic head Furhat (furhatrobotics.com)	Direct (1 robot) (1 subject)	Students from a Swedish Immigrants school (ages 21–51)	N.S	27	N.S.	Swedish	Different response states

(*continued*)

Table 1. (*continued*)

N.	Title	Type of Study	Social Robot	Interaction	Type of Sample	Sample Nationality	Sample Size	Mother Tongue	Language (Robots as Tutors in Language Learning)	Analysis methods used
9	Uncertainty in Robot Assisted Second Language Conversation Practice [33]	QT	Robotic head Furhat (furhatrobotics.com)	Direct (1 robot) (1 subject)	Students from a Swedish Immigrants school (ages 21–51)	N.S	27	N.S.	Swedish	Different response states
10	Social robot supporting the inclusion of unaccompanied migrant children: teaching the meaning of culture-related gestures [16]	QT	NAO with Microsoft Kinect	Direct (1 robot) (1 subject)	Migrants (ages 19–24)	N.S	6	N.S.	Italian	Measuring of culture-related gestures
					Italian children (ages 6–10)	Italy	4	Italian	Italian	Measuring of culture-related gesture
11	The Effects of Feedback on Children's Engagement and Learning Outcomes in Robot-Assisted Second Language Learning [22]	QT	NAO	Direct (+ tablet) (1 robot) (1 subject)	Children (ages 5–6)	N.S	72	N.S.	English	Pre-test; post-test
12	When Pre-schoolers Interact with an Educational Robot, Does Robot Feedback Influence Engagement?[34]	QT	NAO	Direct (1 robot) (1 subject)	Children (age 3–4)	Netherlands	58	Dutch	English	Pre-test; post-test

(*continued*)

Table 1. (continued)

N.	Title	Type of Study	Social Robot	Interaction	Type of Sample	Sample Nationality	Sample Size	Mother Tongue	Language (Robots as Tutors in Language Learning)	Analysis methods used
13	Engagement in longitudinal child-robot language learning interactions: Disentangling robot and task engagement [23]	QT	NAO	Direct (+ tablet) (1 robot) (1 subject)	Primary school (age 5)	Netherlands	194	Dutch	English	Pre-test; post-test
14	Varied Human-Like Gestures for Social Robots: Investigating the Effects on Children's Engagement and Language Learning [24]	QT	NAO	Direct (+ tablet) (1 robot) (1 subject)	Primary school (ages 4–6)	Netherlands	94	Dutch	English	Pre-test; post-test
15	The Effect of a Robot's Gestures and Adaptive Tutoring on Children's Acquisition of Second Language Vocabularies [35]	QT	NAO	Direct (+ tablet) (1 robot) (1 subject)	Primary school (ages 4–6)	Netherlands	61	Dutch	English	Pre-test; post-test
16	Designing and Evaluating Iconic Gestures for Child-Robot Second Language Learning [36]	QT	NAO	Direct (+ tablet) (1 robot) (1 subject)	Primary school (ages 5)	Netherlands	194	Dutch	English	Pre-test; post-test

(continued)

Table 1. (*continued*)

N.	Title	Type of Study	Social Robot	Interaction	Type of Sample	Sample Nationality	Sample Size	Mother Tongue	Language (Robots as Tutors in Language Learning)	Analysis methods used
17	L2 Vocabulary Teaching by Social Robots: The Role of Gestures and On-Screen Cues as Scaffold [37]	QT	NAO	Direct (+ PC) (1 robot) (1 subject)	Preschools (ages 5)	Turkey	72	Turkish	English	Pre-test; post-test
18	Identification of Low-engaged Learners in Robot-led Second Language Conversations with Adults [21]	QT	Robotic head Furhat (furhatrobotics.com)	Direct (1 robot) (2 subject)	Students from a Swedish Immigrants school (ages 20–54)	Sweden	33	N.S.	Swedish	Expression of engagement; audio recordings; manual annotation of facial expressions
19	Interaction and collaboration in robot-assisted language learning for adults [38]	QL, QT	Robotic head Furhat (furhatrobotics.com)	Direct (1 robot) (2 subject)	Students from a Swedish Immigrants school (ages 20–54)	Sweden	33	N.S.	Swedish	Questionnaire; analysis of learner interaction; collaboration and learner ratings for the different robot behaviors
20	Robot Interaction Styles for Conversation Practice in Second Language Learning [39]	QT	Robotic head Furhat (furhatrobotics.com)	Direct (1 robot) (2 subject)	Students Swedish from hosting language cafés	Sweden	32	N.S.	Swedish	Audio-video recordings; survey

(*continued*)

Table 1. (continued)

N.	Title	Type of Study	Social Robot	Interaction	Type of Sample	Sample Nationality	Sample Size	Mother Tongue	Language (Robots as Tutors in Language Learning)	Analysis methods used
21	Learner and teacher perspectives on robot-led L2 conversation practice [40]	QT	Robotic head Furhat (furhatrobotics.com)	Direct (1 robot) (2 subject)	Students Swedish from immigrants course (Ages 24–60)	Sweden	24	N.S.	Swedish	Post-session interviews; teachers' ratings of the robot's behavior; analyses of the video-recorded conversations
22	The use of social robots for supporting language training of children [18]	QL	NAO, from Aldebaran Robotics	Direct (+ tablet) (1 robot) (1 subject)	Children migrant in kindergartens	N.S	10–16	N.S.	Norwegian	Observations of the children; interviews with teachers
				Direct (+ tablet) (1 robot) (1 subject)	Children whit autism spectrum disorder (ASD) in primary school	N.S	2	N.S.	Norwegian	Observations of the children; interviews with teachers; focus group meeting with the parents
23	Robot Gaze Can Mediate Participation Imbalance in Groups with Different Skill Levels [25]	QT	Robotic head Furhat (furhatrobotics.com)	Direct (1 robot) (2 subject)	Volunteers (ages 18–67)	N.S	36 pair	N.S. (1 native speaker, 1 language learner)	Swedish	Pre- and post-experiment questionnaire
24	Utilization of socially assistive robot's activity for teaching pontic dialect [41]	QT	NAO, from Aldebaran Robotics	Direct (1 robot) (1 subject)	Students of university (Age 20–60)	Macedonia	30	N.S.	Pontic dialect	Observation; interview

(continued)

Table 1. (*continued*)

N.	Title	Type of Study	Social Robot	Interaction	Type of Sample	Sample Nationality	Sample Size	Mother Tongue	Language (Robots as Tutors in Language Learning)	Analysis methods used
25	Affective Personalization of a Social Robot Tutor for Children's Second Language Skills [42]	QT	Tega by Personal Robots Group at the MIT Media Lab.	Direct (+ tablet) (1 robot) (1 subject)	preschool classrooms (ages 3–5)	Boston (U.S.A.)	34	English	Spanish	Digital pre- and post-assessment test
26	Robot with Embodied Interactive Modes as a Companion Actor in Journey of Digital Situational Learning Environment and its Effect on Students' Learning Performance [43]	QT	ZENBO, from ASUS	Direct (1 robot) (Group)	high school students (ages 15)	Taiwan	101	N.S.	English	Pre-test; post-test; questionnaire
27	Effects of a Pair Programming Educational Robot-Based Approach on Students' Interdisciplinary Learning of Computational Thinking and Language Learning [44]	QT	Board-game with programmable robot (coding educational robots)	Mediated (1 robot) (Group)	Grade 6 students	Singapore	15	N.S.	Mandarin Chinese	Pre-test; Post-test
						Taiwan	15	N.S.	English	Language-learning anxiety scale

(*continued*)

Table 1. (*continued*)

N.	Title	Type of Study	Social Robot	Interaction	Type of Sample	Sample Nationality	Sample Size	Mother Tongue	Language (Robots as Tutors in Language Learning)	Analysis methods used
28	Learning Chinese as a Second Language by Educational Robots Integrating the Operation of Conditional Logic in Computational Thinking and the Usage of the Causal Sentences [45]	QT	Kebbi robot by Nuwa Robotics (coding educational robots)	Mediated (1 robot) (Group)	Grade 5 students (ages 12)	Singapore	56	N.S.	Chinese	Pre-test and Post-test of Chinese Proficiency; e Pre-test and Post-test of the Computer Programming Self-efficacy
29	Improvement of Japanese adults' English speaking skills via experiences speaking to a robot [46]	QT	CommU by VSTONE	Direct (+ tablet) (1 robot) (1 subject)	University students (age 18–22)	Japan	9	Japanese	English	Pre-test; post-test
30	Are Tutor Robots for Everyone? The Influence of Attitudes, Anxiety, and Personality on Robot-Led Language Learning [47]	QT	NAO	Direct (1 robot) (1 subject)	Young adult (age 18–26)	Turkey	102	Turkish	English	Pre-test; post-test; (Negative Attitudes Toward Robots; L2 Anxiety; Personality Traits)

(*continued*)

Table 1. (continued)

N.	Title	Type of Study	Social Robot	Interaction	Type of Sample	Sample Nationality	Sample Size	Mother Tongue	Language (Robots as Tutors in Language Learning)	Analysis methods used
31	When Even a Robot Tutor Zooms: A Study of Embodiment, Attitudes, and Impressions [48]	QT	NAO	Direct (Video call Zoom) (1 robot) (1 subject)	Young adult (age 18–35)	Turkey	100	Turkish	English	Pre-test; Post-test; (Negative Attitudes Toward Robots; Impressions of the Robot Tutor; L2 Anxiety; Personality Traits)
32	Social Robot Tutoring for Child Second Language Learning [49]	QT	NAO	Direct (+ touchscreen placed Horizontally) (1 robot) (1 subject)	Primary school (ages 8)	United Kingdom	67	English	French	Pre-test; Post-test; Retention test
33	Joining-in-type Humanoid Robot Assisted Language Learning System [50]	QT	NAO	Direct (2 robot) (1 subject)	University students (Age 18–24)	Japan	51	Japanese	English	Video Recordings; eye tracking system; (EUDICO Linguistic Annotator (ELAN)); Questionnaire
34	Measuring Effect of Repetitive Queries and Implicit Learning with Joining-in Type Robot Assisted Language Learning System [51]	QT	NAO	Direct (2 robot) (1 subject)	University students (Age 18–24)	Japan	37	Japanese	English	Uses the expression correctly or not; BLUE (index for evaluating the quality of machine translation)
35	Social Robots for (Second) Language Learning in (Migrant) Primary School Children [9]	QT	NAO	Direct (+ tablet) (1 robot) (1 subject)	Primary school (age 4–6)	Netherlands	63	N.S.	Dutch	Pre-test; Post-test; Delayed post-test

(continued)

Table 1. (*continued*)

N.	Title	Type of Study	Social Robot	Interaction	Type of Sample	Sample Nationality	Sample Size	Mother Tongue	Language (Robots as Tutors in Language Learning)	Analysis methods used
36	Customized Robot-Assisted Language Learning to Support Immigrants at Work [52]	QT	NAO	Direct (+ tablet) (1 robot) (1 subject)	Immigrants (age 22–62)	Finland	10	N.S.	Finnish	Observation method; interviews
37	Teaching Turkish-Dutch kindergartners Dutch vocabulary with a social robot: Does the robot's use of Turkish translations benefit children's Dutch vocabulary learning? [53]	QT	NAO	Direct (+ tablet) (1 robot) (1 subject)	Primary school (Age 4–6)	Netherlands	67	Turkish	Dutch	Pre-test; Post-test; Delayed post-test
38	Robots or Agents – Neither Helps You More or Less During Second Language Acquisition [54]	QT	NAO	Direct (Virtual NAO) (1 robot) (1 subject)	Volunteers (age 15–53)	N.S	130	N.S.	German	Pre-test; Post-test
39	A toy or a friend? Children's anthropomorphic beliefs about robots and how these relate to second-language word learning [55]	QT	NAO	Direct (+ tablet) (1 robot) (1 subject)	Preschool (Age 5)	Netherlands	104	Dutch	English	Pre-test; Post-test

(*continued*)

Bilingualism and Second Language Learning through the Use of Social Robots   131

Table 1. (*continued*)

N.	Title	Type of Study	Social Robot	Interaction	Type of Sample	Sample Nationality	Sample Size	Mother Tongue	Language (Robots as Tutors in Language Learning)	Analysis methods used
40	Individual Differences in Children's (Language) Learning Skills Moderate Effects of Robot-Assisted Second Language Learning [13]	QT	NAO	Direct (1 robot) (1 subject)	Preschool (age 5)	Netherlands	193	Dutch	English	Pre-test Translation Task; Post-test Translation Tasks; Post-test Comprehension Task
41	Investigating the Effects of a Robot Peer on L2 Word Learning [7]	QT	NAO	Direct (+ tablet) (1 robot) (1 subject)	Preschool (age 5)	Netherlands	67	Dutch	English	Pre-test; Post-test; Delayed post-test
42	Using Self-Determination Theory in Social Robots to Increase Motivation in L2 Word Learning [56]	QT	NAO	Direct (+ tablet) (1 robot) (1 subject)	Primary school (Age 5–6)	Netherlands	49	Dutch	English	Pre-test; post-test; Delayed post-test
43	Child-Robot Interactions for Second Language Tutoring to Preschool Children [17]	QT	NAO	Direct (1 robot) (1 subject)	Preschool (Age 3)	Netherlands	85	Dutch	English	N.S

(*continued*)

Table 1. (*continued*)

N.	Title	Type of Study	Social Robot	Interaction	Type of Sample	Sample Nationality	Sample Size	Mother Tongue	Language (Robots as Tutors in Language Learning)	Analysis methods used
44	Foreign Language Tutoring for Young Adults with Severe Learning Problems [57]	QT	NAO	Direct (+ tablet) (1 robot) (1 subject)	young adults with severe learning problems (Age 17–35)	Netherlands	33	Dutch	English	video recording; response time recording on the tablet; interview
45	Second Language Tutoring using Social Robots: A Large-Scale Study [58]	QT	NAO	Direct (+ Tablet) (1 robot) (1 subject)	Primary school (Age 6)	Netherlands	194	Dutch	English	Pre-test; Post-test
46	Using a Robot Peer to Encourage the Production of Spatial Concepts in a Second Language [59]	QT	NAO	Direct (interactive table displays) (1 robot) (1 subject)	School (Age 6)	United Kingdom	25	English	French	Pre-test; Post-test

Notes. QT: quantitative study; QL: qualitative study; N.S.: Not Specified.

2.1 Article Selection

The purpose of this work was to summarize the research available on the topic produced in the last ten years. Only those articles were selected in which the real interaction between a social robot and a human in a learning context is assessed. Both quantitative and qualitative studies were considered. Book chapters, systematic reviews, meta-analyzes and other articles with no real measures were excluded. Participant characteristics or types of exposure were not inclusion/exclusion criteria. Even the type of social robot.

Finally, we were interested in inserting all the articles that contained an interaction with a humanoid robot. Specifically, the number of robots interacting simultaneously with human and whether or not this interaction was also mediated by the use of a tablet.

3 Results

3.1 Included Studies

A total of 46 articles were included in this description of the current state of the art (see Table 2). Of these, 80.95% consisted of quantitative studies, 6.52% from qualitative studies and 6.52% from both types. In 95.65% of cases, the interaction with the social robot was direct, and only in 4.34% of cases the interaction was mediated by other support.

During the robot interaction activity, no technological support was used in 56.52% of cases. While a tablet was used in 36.95, an interactive table showing images in 4.34% and a Personal Computer in 2.17% of the articles. In 69.56% of the studies the interaction occurred between the robot and participant, while in 15.21% of the articles a social robot was used in a group setting. Furthermore, the results showed that 10.86% of the study predicted the interaction between a robot and two people, and 4.34% of cases, two social robots that interacted simultaneously with one person.

Regarding the background of the sample, we examined two aspects: nationality and age. Specifically, 30.43% of the studies were conducted in the Netherlands, 8.69% in Sweden, and 6.52% in Japan, with the same percentage in Taiwan and Turkey. Besides, 4.34% of the studies were conducted in Singapore and the same percentage in Iran. Only the same 2.17% was respectively carried out in Cyprus, Holland, Macedonia, U.S.A., U.K., and Finland. However, the nationality of the sample was not specified in 17.39% of the articles.

In addition, the samples were mainly composed of adults (32.60%), primary school children (26.02%), preschool children (19.56%), high school students (10.86%), and 10.86% was composed by university students.

The 50% of the selected articles the mother tongue of the participants was not specified and for the migrant samples, was not possible to identify a single mother tongue. Furthermore, in 28.26% of cases, the mother tongue was Dutch, in 8.69% it was Turkish, and while 6.52% spoke Japanese. With the same percentage of 2.17% followed by Swedish, Slovak and English.

Considering instead the learning of a second language thanks to the support of a social robot, we find that the articles are distributed as follows: 56.52% provided for the learning of English, 15.21% was the Swedish and with the same percentage of 4.34% we find learning of the French language, the Dutch language, and the Chinese language. In conclusion, only 2.17% of cases, introduced the following languages: Italian, Norwegian, Spanish, Pontic dialect, Finnish, German and Slovak.

Table 2. Summary of the main results of the scoping review (N = 46).

	%	n
Included Studies		
Database		
Scopus	100	46
Sample nationality		
Netherlands	30.43	14
Sweden	8.69	4
Turkey	6.52	3
Taiwan	6.52	3
Japan	6.52	3
Iran	4.34	2
Singapore	4.43	2
Algeria	2.17	1
Cyprus	2.17	1
Holland	2.17	1
Macedonia	2.17	1
USA	2.17	1
UK	2.17	1
Finland	2.17	1
Not Specified	17.39	8
Sample language (mother tongue)		
Dutch	28.26	13
Turkish	8.69	4
Japanese	6.52	3
Swedish	2.17	1
Slovak	2.17	1
English	2.17	1
Not Specified	50	23

(*continued*)

Table 2. (*continued*)

	%	n
Sample second language		
English	56.52	26
Swedish	15.21	7
Chinese	4.34	2
French	4.34	2
Dutch	4.34	2
Italian	2.17	1
Norwegian	2.17	1
Spanish	2.17	1
Pontic dialect	2.17	1
Finnish	2.17	1
German	2.17	1
Slovak	2.17	1
Age of the sample		
Preschool	19.56	9
Primary School	26.02	12
High School	10.86	5
University	10.86	5
Adult	32.60	15
Social Robots		
Social Robots used		
NAO	67.39	31
Furhat	17.39	8
Zembo	4.34	2
EMYS	2.17	1
TEGA	2.17	1
Kebbi	2.17	1
CommU	2.17	1
Educative Robot	2.17	1
Type of Interaction		
1Robot – 1 Human	69.56	32
2Robot – 1 Human	4.34	2

(*continued*)

Table 2. (*continued*)

	%	n
1Robot – 1Group	15.21	7
1Robot – 2Humans	10.86	5
Use of other support		
Tablet	36.95	17
PC	2.17	1
Interactive Table	4.34	2
Nothing	56.52	26
Contact with the robot		
Direct	95.65	44
Mediated	4.34	2
Type of the studies (n = 46)		
Contact with the robot		
Quantitative	86.95	40
Qualitative	6.52	3
Mixed (quantitative and qualitative)	6.52	3

Table 2 shows the main results, nationality, mother tongue, second language, age of the sample, type of social robot used, type of interaction between the robot and the subject, which supports were used, contact with the robot and the type of study.

3.2 Social Robots Used in Second Language Learning

Different social robots were used in the selected articles. Concerning the type of social robot used, the NAO robot from Softbank Robotics was used in 67.39% of the studies. The robotic head Furhat was used in 17.39% and ZEMBO robot in 4.34% of the studies. EMYs, Tega, Kebbi, CommU robots and unspecified educational robots were used in 2.17% of cases.

Figure 2 shows the type of robot used for second language learning and distribution over years 2012 to 2022.

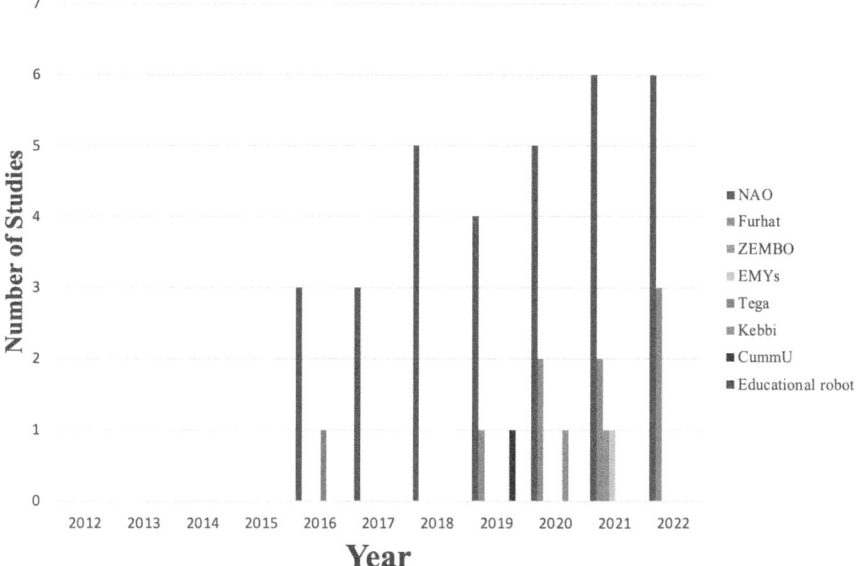

Fig. 2. Social robots used in second language learning from 2012 to 2022.

4 Discussion and Conclusion

The main focus of this scoping review is not intended to be systematic but descriptive of the topic. It should show, also considering the limitations, the state of the art of learning thanks to social robots, while specifically, it aimed to investigate the literature on learning a second language with the use and support of social robots.

In detail, results show that there has been an increase in articles on the "Robot-Assisted Language Learning (RALL)" topic from 2016 to 2022. The interest in this matter has increased exponentially in the last three years, while from 2012 to 2015 no studies have been identified on the topic. Specifically, 2022 shows the publication of ten articles on the scientific topic.

Most of the studies have used the NAO social robot, which is a humanoid robot with 25 degrees of freedom allowing for very harmonic motility, manufactured by Softbank Robotics. However, in northern Europe, especially in recent years, studies have focused more on the Furhat robotic head. Although this robot is devoid of the body, and therefore its use affects the evaluation of the language aspects linked to iconic gestures, this robot has proved particularly effective for the detailed mouth movements. This allows the robot, during the tutoring sessions, to pay more attention to the scanning of individual phonemes.

Regarding both the studies conducted with the NAO robot and the studies with Furhat robot, there was more attention from the participants than in the control group where the lesson was conducted by a human teacher.

In conclusion, also taking into account its limitations, this study showed how the topic of second language learning in adults and children can be supported by social robots. Obviously for a tool to be used is essential that it is mainly accepted, although as suggested by David et al. [60] if their acceptability were proven, this would not make their introduction automatically acceptable and unjustified. We know that the perception of robotic social support in the clinical and educational field is full of skepticism, especially among professionals [61]. However, recent studies on the argument have concluded that frequent use in the context of use has decreased initial skepticism and led to the intended use [62]. From the results of this scoping review it is evident that since 2016 and especially in the last year, the focus on the theme of second language learning with the support of the social robot is very usual. This may suggest that research on Human-Robot interaction is also effective in this field.

In the future, the aim will be to assess the use of social robots for second language learning in large samples of typically developing children and those with special educational needs. This remains a largely unexplored field.

References

1. Al Hakim, V.G., Yang, S.-H., Liyanawatta, M., Wang, J.-H., Chen, G.-D.: Robots in situated learning classrooms with immediate feedback mechanisms to improve students' learning performance. Comput. Educ. **182**, 104483 (2022)
2. Alemi, M., Meghdari, A., Ghazisaedy, M.: Employing humanoid robots for teaching English language in Iranian junior high-schools. Int. J. Humanoid Rob. **11**(03), 1450022 (2014)
3. Alemi, M., Meghdari, A., Basiri, N.M., Taheri, A.: The effect of applying humanoid robots as teacher assistants to help Iranian autistic pupils learn English as a foreign language. In: International Conference on Social Robotics, pp. 1–10 (2015)
4. Bartneck, C., Forlizzi, J.: A design-centred framework for social human-robot interaction. In: 13th IEEE International Workshop on Robot and Human Interactive Communication, ROMAN 2004, pp. 591–594 (2004)
5. Sarrica, M., Brondi, S., Fortunati, L.: How many facets does a 'social robot' have? A review of scientific and popular definitions online. Inf. Technol. People **33**, 1–21 (2019)
6. Woods, S.: Exploring the design space of robots: children's perspectives. Interact. Comput. **18**, 1390–1418 (2006)
7. van den Berghe, R., van der Ven, S., Verhagen, J., Oudgenoeg-Paz, O., Papadopoulos, F., Leseman, P.: Investigating the effects of a robot peer on L2 word learning. In: Companion of the 2018 ACM/IEEE International Conference on Human-Robot Interaction, pp. 267–268 (2018)
8. Randall, N.: A survey of robot-assisted language learning (RALL). ACM Trans. Hum.-Robot Interact. (THRI) **9**(1), 1–36 (2019)
9. Konijn, E.A., Jansen, B., Mondaca Bustos, V., Hobbelink, V.L.N.F., Preciado Vanegas, D.: Social robots for (Second) language learning in (Migrant) primary school children. Int. J. Soc. Robot. **14**(3), 827–843 (2022)
10. Belpaeme, T., et al.: Guidelines for designing social robots as second language tutors. Int. J. Soc. Robot. **10**(3), 325–341 (2018)
11. Conti, D., Cirasa, C., Di Nuovo, S., Di Nuovo, A.: 'Robot, tell me a tale!': a social robot as tool for teachers in kindergarten. Interact. Stud. **21**(2), 220–242 (2020)
12. Golonka, E.M., Bowles, A.R., Frank, V.M., Richardson, D.L., Freynik, S.: Technologies for foreign language learning: a review of technology types and their effectiveness. Comput. Assist. Lang. Learn. **27**(1), 70–105 (2014)
13. Van den Berghe, R., et al.: Individual differences in children's (language) learning skills moderate effects of robot-assisted second language learning. Front. Robot. AI **8**, 259 (2021)

14. Konijn, E.A., Hoorn, J.F.: Parasocial interaction and beyond: media personae and affective bonding. In: The International Encyclopedia of Media Effects, pp. 1–15 (2017)
15. Cumbal, R., Lopes, J., Engwall, O.: Detection of listener uncertainty in robot-led second language conversation practice. In: Proceedings of the 2020 International Conference on Multimodal Interaction, pp. 625–629 (2020)
16. De Carolis, B., Palestra, G., Della Penna, C., Cianciotta, M., Cervelione, A.: Social robots supporting the inclusion of unaccompanied migrant children: teaching the meaning of culture-related gestures. J. e-Learn. Knowl. Soc. **15**(2) (2019)
17. Vogt, P., De Haas, M., De Jong, C., Baxter, P., Krahmer, E.: Child-robot interactions for second language tutoring to preschool children. Front. Hum. Neurosci. **11**, 73 (2017)
18. Fuglerud, K.S., Solheim, I.: The use of social robots for supporting language training of children (2018)
19. Aldeberan Robotics: Aldebaran Robotics documentation (2020). http://doc.aldebaran.com/2-1/family/robots/index_robots.html#all-robots
20. Kanero, J., Geçkin, V., Oranç, C., Mamus, E., Küntay, A.C., Göksun, T.: Social robots for early language learning: current evidence and future directions. Child Dev. Perspect. **12**, 146–151 (2018)
21. Engwall, O., Cumbal, R., Lopes, J., Ljung, M., Månsson, L.: Identification of low-engaged learners in robot-led second language conversations with adults. ACM Trans. Hum.-Robot Interact. (THRI) **11**(2), 1–33 (2022)
22. De Haas, M., Vogt, P., Krahmer, E.: The effects of feedback on children's engagement and learning outcomes in robot-assisted second language learning. Front. Robot. AI **7**, 101 (2020)
23. de Haas, M., et al.: Engagement in longitudinal child-robot language learning interactions: Disentangling robot and task engagement. Int. J. Child-Comput. Interact. **33**, 100501 (2022)
24. de Wit, J., Brandse, A., Krahmer, E., Vogt, P.: Varied human-like gestures for social robots: investigating the effects on children's engagement and language learning. In: 2020 15th ACM/IEEE International Conference on Human-Robot Interaction (HRI), pp. 359–367 (2020)
25. Gillet, S., Cumbal, R., Pereira, A., Lopes, J., Engwall, O., Leite, I.: Robot gaze can mediate participation imbalance in groups with different skill levels. In: Proceedings of the 2021 ACM/IEEE International Conference on Human-Robot Interaction, pp. 303–311 (2021)
26. Pham, M.T., Rajić, A., Greig, J.D., Sargeant, J.M., Papadopoulos, A., McEwen, S.A.: A scoping review of scoping reviews: advancing the approach and enhancing the consistency. Res. Synth. Methods **5**(4), 371–385 (2014)
27. Daudt, H.M.L., van Mossel, C., Scott, S.J.: Enhancing the scoping study methodology: a large, inter-professional team's experience with Arksey and O'Malley's framework. BMC Med. Res. Methodol. **13**(1), 1–9 (2013)
28. Moher, D., Liberati, A., Tetzlaff, J., Altman, D.G., Group*, P.: Preferred reporting items for systematic reviews and meta-analyses: the PRISMA statement. Ann. Internal Med. **151**(4), 264–269 (2009)
29. Alemi, M., Bahramipour, S.: An innovative approach of incorporating a humanoid robot into teaching EFL learners with intellectual disabilities. Asian-Pac. J. Second Foreign Lang. Educ. **4**(1), 1–22 (2019)
30. Arar, C., Belazoui, A., Telli, A.: Adoption of social robots as pedagogical aids for efficient learning of second language vocabulary to children. J. e-Learn. Knowl. Soc. **17**(3), 119–126 (2021)
31. Banaeian, H., Gilanlioglu, I.: Influence of the NAO robot as a teaching assistant on university students' vocabulary learning and attitudes. Australas. J. Educ. Technol. **37**(3), 71–87 (2021)
32. Beňuš, Š., Sabo, R., Trnka, M.: Teaching L1 and L2 communication skills with a robotic head. In: 2019 17th International Conference on Emerging eLearning Technologies and Applications (ICETA), pp. 69–75 (2019)

33. Cumbal, R., Lopes, J., Engwall, O.: Uncertainty in robot assisted second language conversation practice. In: Companion of the 2020 ACM/IEEE International Conference on Human-Robot Interaction, pp. 171–173 (2020)
34. de Haas, M., Vogt, P., Krahmer, E.: When preschoolers interact with an educational robot, does robot feedback influence engagement? Multimodal Technol. Interact. **5**(12), 77 (2021)
35. de Wit, J., et al.: The effect of a robot's gestures and adaptive tutoring on children's acquisition of second language vocabularies. In: 2018 13th ACM/IEEE International Conference on Human-Robot Interaction (HRI), pp. 50–58 (2018)
36. De Wit, J., et al.: Designing and evaluating iconic gestures for child-robot second language learning. Interact. Comput. **33**(6), 596–626 (2021)
37. Demir-Lira, Ö.E., et al.: L2 vocabulary teaching by social robots: the role of gestures and on-screen cues as scaffolds. Front. Educ. **5**, 599636 (2020)
38. Engwall, O., Lopes, J.: Interaction and collaboration in robot-assisted language learning for adults. Comput. Assist. Lang. Learn. **35**(5–6), 1273–1309 (2022)
39. Engwall, O., Lopes, J., Åhlund, A.: Robot interaction styles for conversation practice in second language learning. Int. J. Soc. Robot. **13**(2), 251–276 (2021)
40. Engwall, O., et al.: Learner and teacher perspectives on robot-led L2 conversation practice. In: ReCALL, pp. 1–16 (2022)
41. Gkinos, M., Velentza, A.-M., Fachantidis, N.: Utilization of socially assistive robot's activity for teaching pontic dialect. In: International Conference on Human-Computer Interaction, pp. 486–505 (2022)
42. Gordon, G., et al.: Affective personalization of a social robot tutor for children's second language skills. In: Proceedings of the AAAI Conference on Artificial Intelligence, vol. 30, no. 1 (2016)
43. Al Hakim, V.G., Yang, S.-H., Wang, J.-H., Yen, C.C., Yeh, L., Chen, G.-D.: Robot with embodied interactive modes as a companion actor in journey of digital situational learning environment and its effect on students' learning performance. In: Proceedings of the 29th International Conference on Computers in Education, pp. 441–450 (2021)
44. Hsu, T.-C., Chang, C., Wu, L.-K., Looi, C.-K.: Effects of a pair programming educational robot-based approach on students' interdisciplinary learning of computational thinking and language learning. Front. Psychol. **13** (2022)
45. Hsu, T.-C., Wong, L.-H., Aw, G.P.: Learning Chinese as a second language by educational robots integrating the operation of conditional logic in computational thinking and the usage of the causal sentences. In: 2020 IEEE 20th International Conference on Advanced Learning Technologies (ICALT), pp. 236–237 (2020)
46. Iio, T., et al.: Improvement of Japanese adults' English speaking skills via experiences speaking to a robot. J. Comput. Assist. Learn. **35**(2), 228–245 (2019)
47. Kanero, J., Oranç, C., Koşkulu, S., Kumkale, G.T., Göksun, T., Küntay, A.C.: Are tutor robots for everyone? The influence of attitudes, anxiety, and personality on robot-led language learning. Int. J. Soc. Robot. **14**(2), 297–312 (2022)
48. Kanero, J., Tunalı, E.T., Oranç, C., Göksun, T., Küntay, A.C.: When even a robot tutor Zooms: a study of embodiment, attitudes, and impressions. Front. Robot. AI **8**, 169 (2021)
49. Kennedy, J., Baxter, P., Senft, E., Belpaeme, T.: Social robot tutoring for child second language learning. In: 2016 11th ACM/IEEE International Conference on Human-Robot Interaction (HRI), pp. 231–238 (2016)
50. Khalifa, A., Kato, T., Yamamoto, S.: Joining-in-type humanoid robot assisted language learning system. In: Proceedings of the Tenth International Conference on Language Resources and Evaluation (LREC 2016), pp. 245–249 (2016)
51. Khalifa, A., Kato, T., Yamamoto, S.: Measuring effect of repetitive queries and implicit learning with joining-in-type robot assisted language learning system. In: SLaTE, pp. 13–17 (2017)

52. Kouri, S., Köpman, E., Ahtinen, A., Ramirez Millan, V.: Customized robot-assisted language learning to support immigrants at work: findings and insights from a qualitative user experience study. In: Proceedings of the 8th International Conference on Human-Agent Interaction (2020), pp. 212–220
53. Leeuwestein, H., et al.: Teaching Turkish-Dutch kindergartners Dutch vocabulary with a social robot: does the robot's use of Turkish translations benefit children's Dutch vocabulary learning? J. Comput. Assist. Learn. **37**(3), 603–620 (2021)
54. Rosenthal-von der Pütten, A.M., Straßmann, C., Krämer, N.C.: Robots or agents– neither helps you more or less during second language acquisition. In: International Conference on Intelligent Virtual Agents, pp. 256–268 (2016)
55. van den Berghe, R., et al.: A toy or a friend? Children's anthropomorphic beliefs about robots and how these relate to second-language word learning. J. Comput. Assist. Learn. **37**(2), 396–410 (2021)
56. Van Minkelen, P., et al.: Using self-determination theory in social robots to increase motivation in L2 word learning. In: Proceedings of the 2020 ACM/IEEE International Conference on Human-Robot Interaction, pp. 369–377 (2020)
57. Vogt, P., Dunk, S., Poos, P.: Foreign language tutoring for young adults with severe learning problems. In: Proceedings of the Companion of the 2017 ACM/IEEE International Conference on Human-Robot Interaction, pp. 317–318 (2017)
58. Vogt, P., et al.: Second language tutoring using social robots: a large-scale study. In: 2019 14th ACM/IEEE International Conference on Human-Robot Interaction (HRI), pp. 497–505 (2019)
59. Wallbridge, C.D., et al.: Using a robot peer to encourage the production of spatial concepts in a second language. In: Proceedings of the 6th International Conference on Human-Agent Interaction, pp. 54–60 (2018)
60. David, D., Thérouanne, P., Milhabet, I.: The acceptability of social robots: a scoping review of the recent literature. Comput. Hum. Behav. **137**, 107419 (2022)
61. Conti, D., Di Nuovo, S., Buono, S., Di Nuovo, A.: Robots in education and care of children with developmental disabilities: a study on acceptance by experienced and future professionals. Int. J. Soc. Robot. **9**, 51–62 (2017)
62. Conti, D., Trubia, G., Buono, S., Di Nuovo, S., Di Nuovo, A.: An empirical study on integrating a small humanoid robot to support the therapy of children with Autism Spectrum Disorder and Intellectual Disability. Interact. Stud. Soc. Behav. Commun. Biol. Artif. Syst. **2**(2), 177–211 (2021)

Reading Profile in Deaf Adults

Francesca Vizzi[1(✉)], Pierluigi Zoccolotti[2,3], Marika Iaia[1], Paola Angelelli[1], and Chiara Valeria Marinelli[4]

[1] Lab of Applied Psychology and Intervention, Department of Human and Social Sciences, University of Salento, Lecce, Italy
francesca.vizzi@unisalento.it
[2] Department of Psychology, University of Rome La Sapienza, Rome, Italy
[3] ISTC Institute for Cognitive Sciences and Technologies, CNR, Rome, Italy
[4] Learning Science Hub, Department of Humanities, University of Foggia, Foggia, Italy
Chiaravaleria.marinelli@unifg.it

Abstract. We examined the reading profile of deaf subjects, focusing on psycholinguistic variables and considering the impact of the global factor, to determine whether phonological, lexical, and semantic effects would differ in some way for these individuals in comparison to hearing individuals in reading. Thirteen deaf young adults proficient in both oral lipreading and sign language were compared to a group of hearing subjects matched for gender, age, and education. Deaf participants had longer vocal reaction times in reading aloud single words with respect to hearing subjects. However, they showed a similar reading profile to controls, being affected by psycholinguistic variables in a very similar way. Deaf individuals did not show a multiplicative effect as a function of word difficulty in their reading slowness but only a constant delay. Overall, the deficit shown by deaf participants was relatively limited and not associated with specific cognitive processes. This finding is in keeping with the idea that at least some individuals with a severe hearing impairment may reach reasonably high levels of word reading.

Keywords: deafness · global factor · lexical reading · sublexical reading

1 Introduction

Oral language skills are a fundamental component of literacy acquisition, which can be affected in deaf people for a variety of reasons (Perfetti & Sandak, 2000; Musselman, 2000). In fact, exposure to spoken language is usually delayed in this population (Bertone & Volpato, 2009), because it takes time to learn to lip-read and to make use of any acoustic residuals through hearing aids. The phonological deficit and language delay may have consequences on learning to read and write. Indeed, even in hearing children, the presence of a language delay produces difficulties in written language acquisition and text comprehension (Angelelli et al., 2016; Chilosi et al., 2009).

Deaf subjects report less adequate spelling skills than hearing subjects with the same age and years of education (Williams & Mayer, 2015). Moreover, in most cases, difficulties are found even after some periods of rehabilitation (Bertone & Volpato,

2009). The written productions of deaf subjects present peculiar traits (Caselli et al., 2006; Chesi, 2006): the text is characterized by the formulation of short and telegraphic sentences and a poor vocabulary.

The errors found concern the nominal domain, in particular the systematic omission of indefinite articles, while in the verbal domain difficulties are mainly reported in ordering the subject and verb (Franchi & Musola, 2010). Errors and omissions in the use of free morphology are also reported, especially in the use of pronouns and prepositions (Chesi, 2006).

The difficulty deaf people have in understanding and using these words correctly is mainly due to their length (number of letters), their atonic nature, the absence of semantic content, and the fact that they are not essential within speech, characteristics that make these words difficult to identify through lip-reading. Importantly, the deficit in the use of syntax is not limited to production, but deaf children have also difficulties in solving visually presented syntactic contrasts (such as, active-passive, singular- plural, etc.); Bishop, 1983).

A study conducted by our group on the same adults with prelingual deafness examined in the present study showed that these difficulties persist even after years of schooling (Vizzi et al., 2022). In fact, the analysis of the written productions of adults with prelingual deafness showed a deficit in many aspects of written language, not only in the use of morphosyntactic rules but also an ineffective use of informative vocabulary (Vizzi et al., 2022). Their written texts were shorter, with fewer adjectives and subordinates, less informative and with a higher number of phonological and morphosyntactic errors compared to controls. Also, the psycholinguistic characteristics of words written by the deaf individuals highlighted the linguistic poverty of this population. They overused words acquired earlier in life and with a greater number of orthographic neighbours with respect to control subjects.

Deaf children's reading skills also appear to be worse than those of hearing peers (Geers, 2003; Geers & Hayes, 2011; Harris & Terlektsi, 2010; Johnson & Goswami, 2010; Kyle & Harris, 2006; Moeller et al., 2007). Although the use of hearing cochlear implants has significantly improved reading skills in deaf children, they still show lower performance (Mayer et al., 2016). Deaf subjects have a lower perception of phonoacoustic details of language (Brown & Bacon, 2010; Pisoni et al., 2008; Tomblin et al., 2015): they access phonology using multiple compensation strategies, not always effective (Leybaert, 1993; Marschark & Harris, 1996). The difficulty in accessing the acoustic input leads to a consequent poor phonological competence (Lyxell et al., 2008; Pisoni et al., 2008), that in turn may affect reading (and spelling) acquisition.

However, large inter-individual differences have been reported, such that a proportion of deaf subjects read at the same level as hearing subjects (e.g., Belanger et al., 2012). Deaf individuals can achieve adequate reading, despite poor phonological processing, through lexical processing (Mayberry et al., 2011; Strong & Prinz, 2000) or the use of contextual information. In fact, on average deaf people present a lexical structure quite similar to that of hearing individuals (McEvoy et al., 1999). fMRI studies confirm this hypothesis: activation in the visual word shape area (VWFA) is similar in deaf and hearing individuals, but the former show less activation in the temporoparietal cortex, which is responsible for phonological processing (Glezer et al, 2018). They also show reduced resting-state connectivity between the VWFA and the auditory language area in the left anterior superior temporal gyrus (Wang et al., 2014). Furthermore, deaf individuals showed sensitivity to orthographic information but not to phonological information in the inferior frontal gyrus (Glezer et al., 2018).

Deaf individuals have a less efficient perception of the photoacoustic details of language (Brown & Bacon, 2010; Pisoni et al., 2008; Tomblin et al., 2015): they access phonology using multiple compensatory strategies, which are not always effective (Leybaert, 1993; Marschark & Harris, 1996). Difficulty in accessing acoustic input leads to poor phonological competence (Lyxell et al., 2008; Pisoni et al., 2008), which in turn may affect reading (and spelling) acquisition.

Behavioural studies have reported that many deaf readers ignore function and low-frequency words and focus on the keywords in a text to derive the overall meaning of the sentence they are reading (Domínguez and Alegrìa, 2010; Domínguez et al., 2014). Eye movement studies seem to confirm this hypothesis (Bélanger and Rayner 2015): eye movements when reading meaningful texts are similar to those of hearing subjects, but with fewer regressions (i.e., 15–20% of movements) and word refixations and more functional word skipping (Bélanger and Rayner, 2015). This pattern indicates a tendency to focus on critical lexical items and context (Mayberry et al., 2011; Strong & Prinz, 2000). It should be noted that the increased use of contextual information in deaf individuals (as originally proposed by Fischler, 1985) is mostly present in low- achieving deaf individuals (Bélanger and Rayner, 2013).

The "word-processing efficiency hypothesis" (Bélanger and Rayner, 2015) proposes that the few deaf individuals who perform as well as hearing individuals have a wider visual span than controls with equivalent reading skills. Thus, some (though not all) deaf individuals can optimize their spelling skills even in the presence of deficient phonological processing, to close the gap in reading and achieve a level of performance comparable to that of proficient hearing readers (Bélanger and Rayner, 2015). Therefore, there may be qualitative differences in the reading of deaf versus hearing individuals and greater inter-individual variability among deaf readers in the level of proficiency achieved in word recognition. Examining the psycholinguistic variables that influence the reading performance of deaf individuals could be useful for examining this hypothesis. However, only a few studies have examined which psycholinguistic word characteristics modulate reading in deaf people.

As described above, the main focus of previous research has been on phonological effects, while only a few studies have considered the role of frequency or contextual effects (e.g., Bélanger et al., 2013). In Italian (Barca et al., 2013), the language under investigation here, one study examined the lexicality effect in deaf individuals (using spoken language or sign language) and in control hearing subjects using a task that required to discriminate words from strings of letters. No difference was found between the deaf individuals who used spoken language and the controls, whereas the deaf individuals using sign language showed an advantage for words, perhaps indicating a lexical strategy in individuals skilled in this mode of communication.

In the present study, we examined the influence of psycholinguistic variables in the reading of deaf subjects to observe differences with the reading profile displayed by hearing subjects, taking individual variability into account. To this end, we examined the role of phonological, lexical and semantic variables in modulating vocal reaction times (RT) and accuracy in reading single words aloud. To explore sublexical processes, we examined the effects of length, contextual rules (e.g., letters such as c and g, which require the analysis of successive letters to be pronounced correctly, Barca et al., 2007) and frequency of bigrams; to explore lexical processing, the effects of word frequency and stress (in Italian, the correct reading of words with irregular stress requires lexical retrieval, Burani and Arduino, 2004), while for semantic processing, the effects of age of acquisition, imaginability and concreteness were examined.

In general, based on the literature reviewed, we expect lexical and semantic processing to be spared in deaf individuals, while some deficits can be expected in the case of sub-lexical (phonological) effects such as length, contextual rules, and bigram frequency. We examined young adults who had completed high school and were proficient in both oral lip-reading and Italian sign language. We focused on deaf individuals who had achieved a reasonably good level of oral (and sign) communication and consequently may have developed a compensatory strategy to manage their deafness.

Differences in specific experimental conditions, when two groups vary in the general level of performance, may depend on the combined effect of global differences in cognitive speed and the specific influence of a particular experimental manipulation. The examination of vocal RTs makes it possible to assess the possible contribution of a global factor in the reading times of deaf subjects. The presence of a general speed deficit can influence performance under different conditions, producing larger group differences in a 'slow' group than in a corresponding 'fast' control group (Faust et al., 1999). A deficit performance on the part of deaf subjects does not necessarily imply a subject-specific deficit but may represent the result of the influence of global components on performance in reading tasks. As the research reviewed has generally shown considerable group differences in the reading abilities of deaf and hearing subjects, we thought it would be interesting to examine whether at least some of these differences could be explained in terms of a global factor. For this purpose, the rate and quantity model (RAM, Faust et al., 1999) and the difference engine model (DEM, Myerson et al., 2003) were considered. These models provide complementary predictions on the detection of global components in reading performance (e.g., De Luca et al., 2017; Zoccolotti et al., 2008, 2018; Marinelli et al., 2011, 2013, 2014).

Overall, we compared deaf and hearing young adults in a single word reading aloud task with the aim of quantifying their reading deficit and describing which psycholinguistic factors, if any, best characterized their difficulty. For the first time, we tested for the possible presence of a global factor in deaf readers. Finally, we also examined whether deaf and hearing individuals differed in terms of text comprehension skills.

2 Method

2.1 Participants

Participants were 13 deaf young adults (7M, 6F, mean age = 36.64 years; SD = 9.91) and 13 control subjects. All participants had a high educational qualification, i.e., second-level high school diploma or professional qualification, and an adequate performance on the SPM Raven test (Raven, 1996).

Deaf individuals had a hearing impairment ≥ 70 db; 66% of participants had congenital deafness and 34% acquired, with an average age of the diagnosis of 21 months (SD = 15.6). They did not have any other sensory, psychiatric or neurological deficits, except deafness. Nine individuals had hearing parents while four had both deaf parents. Participants with hearing parents used the Italian vocal language within the family context but also had good knowledge of Italian Sign Language (ISL). Participants with deaf parents early acquired ISL but also had good lipreading skills. As for the use of hearing aids, 50% of the sample stated that they did not use them at all due to physical discomforts of various kinds; 44% of the subjects stated that they used hearing aids assiduously; the remaining 6% stated that they used the aids sporadically. None of the subjects had had cochlear implantation.

Hearing control subjects were matched one by one with the deaf individuals for gender, age and educational qualifications. As expected, groups did not differ for gender ($\chi 2 < 0$), age and educational level (ts about 0).

2.2 Materials

Reading Comprehension Examination

Reading comprehension was evaluated through the Advanced 3 MT test (Cornoldi et al., 2017). In this test, the participant reads a meaningful text without a time limit and responds to 10 multiple-choice questions concerning the passage.

Reading Examination

Vocal RTs were recorded in reading the whole set of words of Varless 2 (Burani et al., 2015; http://www.istc.cnr.it/grouppage/varless2), a database of 626 morphologically simple Italian nouns studied for several psycholinguistic variables. Based on previous studies, several different sub-lists were obtained from the Varless 2 database, examining frequency (Barca et al., 2007), stress assignment (Marinelli, 2010), N-size (Marinelli et al., in preparation), age of acquisition (Mazzotta et al., 2005), word imageability and frequency (Mazzotta et al., 2005), length (De Luca et al. 2008), contextual rules (Barca et al., 2007). Sub-list conditions means were used only to test global components in the data, while analyses on the effect of psycholinguistic variables were carried on the whole Varless 2 database.

Words were individually presented in a computerized reading aloud test, through the SuperLab software. Words were presented in the centre of a computer screen after a fixation point lasting 750 ms. Each letter (font Verdana 42) subtended 0.4 cm horizontally (corresponding to 0.4 deg of visual angle at the 57 cm distance used). The participants read each word aloud as quickly and as accurately as possible; the onset of the vocal response was recorded. Words disappeared after the subject's response. The next word appeared after a 250 ms inter-trial interval. The reading task was preceded by 3 stimuli of practice and was divided in 5 blocks, to avoid attentional drops.

The experimenter manually scored errors with the support of an audio-recorder. Note that pronunciation defects were not penalized in deaf subjects, but only errors. Self-corrections were considered errors. Vocal RTs of incorrect responses were not analysed. False responses and invalid trials (i.e., RTs lower than 300 ms or higher than 3000 ms) were excluded from the analyses (0.12% for controls and 2.25% for deaf participants, respectively; $t(25) = 2.95, p < .01$).

2.3 Procedure

Test instructions were given both in Italian and in ISL, as well as information about the experimental procedure. Written informed consent was obtained from all participants for inclusion in the study. The study was conducted according to the principles of the Helsinki Declaration.

3 Results

3.1 Analysis of Global Factor

These analyses were limited to vocal RTs as predicted by the RAM (Faust et al., 1999) and DEM (Myerson et al., 2003). According to the DEM, the condition means were plotted against the standard deviations of the same conditions separately for the two groups of subjects (Myerson et al., 2003). The model allows isolating a cognitive-decisional compartment (that corresponds to the central cognitive processing and might be affected in a multiplicative way by task difficulty) from a sensory-motor compartment (that adds to the individual performance the "constant" time necessary for sensory processing and motor programming and may be estimated through the intercept on the x-axis). To yield a sufficient number of condition means, we calculated means and SDs based on several sub-lists (as presented in the Method section) derived from the Varless 2. Note that these condition means were used only for detecting global components while the actual effect of the psycholinguistic variables was tested on the whole Varless 2 database.

In Fig. 1, condition means are plotted against the standard deviations of the same conditions separately for the two groups of subjects (as envisaged by the DEM model, Myerson et al., 2003). The fit of the linear regression is reasonably high ($r = .83$) with an intercept on the x-axis of 496.6 and a slope of .59, indicating that variability increases as a function of condition's difficulty. These two values are compatible with a previous meta-analysis on reading data (Zoccolotti et al., 2018); also note that reading aloud tasks tend to produce higher slopes and higher intercepts (Zoccolotti et al., 2018) than most other speeded tasks (Myerson et al., 2003). Overall, deaf participants were slower than controls but their inter-individual variability in RTs grew by the same factor as it occurred in the hearing participants. Thus, deaf participants were not only slower than hearing control subjects, but also more variable, coherently with the law of RTs that states that the spread of the distribution grows as a function of the mean (Wagonmakers & Brown, 2007).

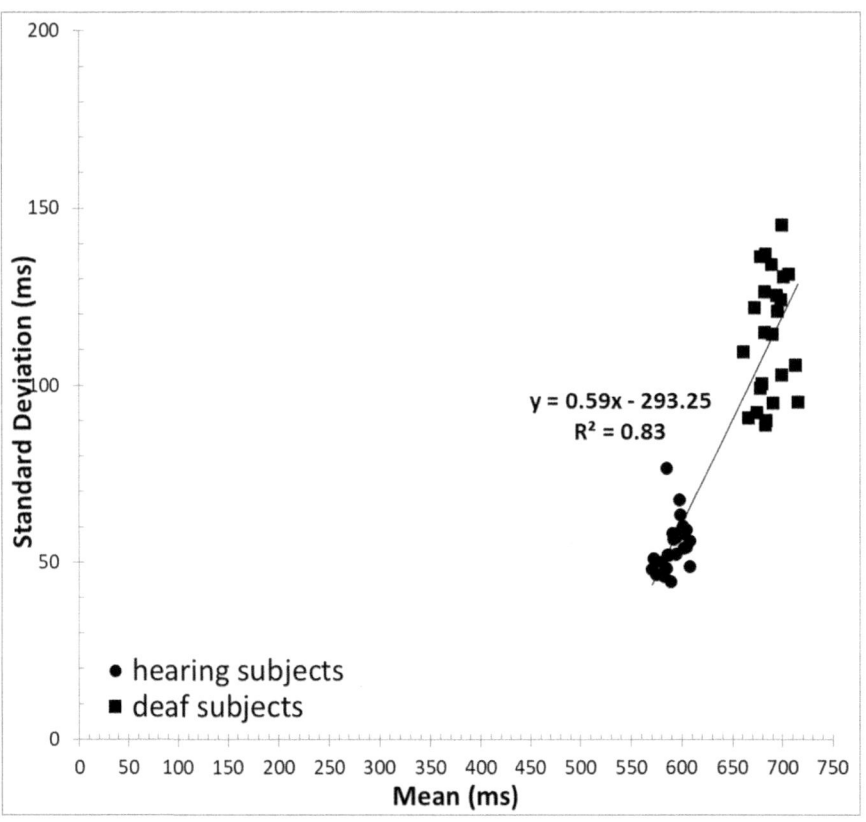

Fig. 1. Condition means (in ms) are plotted against the standard deviations of the corresponding conditions. Data of deaf and control subjects are separately presented.

As the condition means of the two groups did not overlap, in order to get a more continuous distribution we replicated the means versus standard deviations plot also using performance on single words in the database, averaging across deaf and hearing subjects, respectively. The relevant data are presented in Fig. 2. The fit of the linear regression is moderate ($r^2 = .42$) with an intercept on the x-axis of 441.4 and a slope of .65, confirming a general tendency for variability to increase as a function of the condition's difficulty.

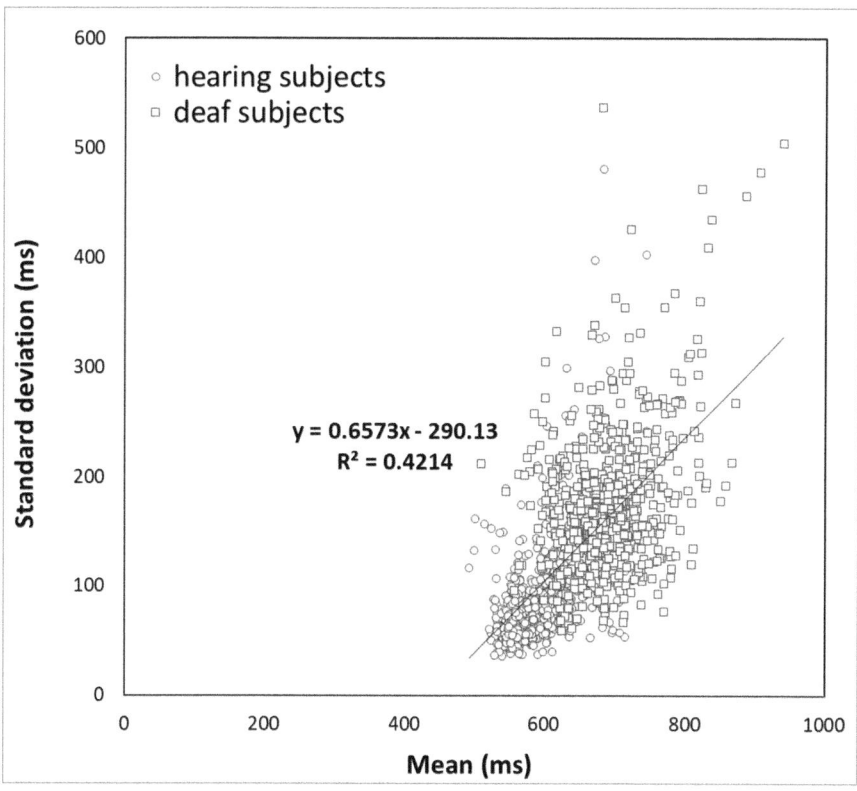

Fig. 2. Mean for individual words (in ms) are plotted against standard deviations. Data of deaf and control subjects are separately presented.

Next, we tested whether the slowness of deaf individuals could be ascribed to the presence of a global factor, by means of a Brinley plot. To this purpose, the prediction of RAM (Faust et al., 1999) of a linear relationship between the condition means of the two groups was examined. The resulting Brinley plot is presented in Fig. 3. The dotted diagonal line in the graph indicates the reference for identical performance in the two groups. Inspection of the figure indicates a linear relationship accounting for all conditions (r = .51). The intercept of the linear fit is 135.51, indicating that deaf subjects were about 136 ms slower than controls. However, their slowness did not vary in a multiplicative way with the difficulty of experimental conditions. In fact, as shown in Fig. 3, the slope was close to unity (b = .93) and the regression line was nearly parallel to the diagonal dotted line, indicating that both groups were modulated in a similar way by condition difficulty (as due to the influence of psycholinguistic variables).

Overall, data confirmed that deaf children read slower than hearing controls across conditions. However, this slowness was not affected by a multiplicative factor and both groups were modulated in a similar way by condition difficulty (i.e., as an effect of psycholinguistic variables). Rather the difference could be explained in terms of constant value (intercept). Based on the RAM, the slowness in reading of deaf individuals does

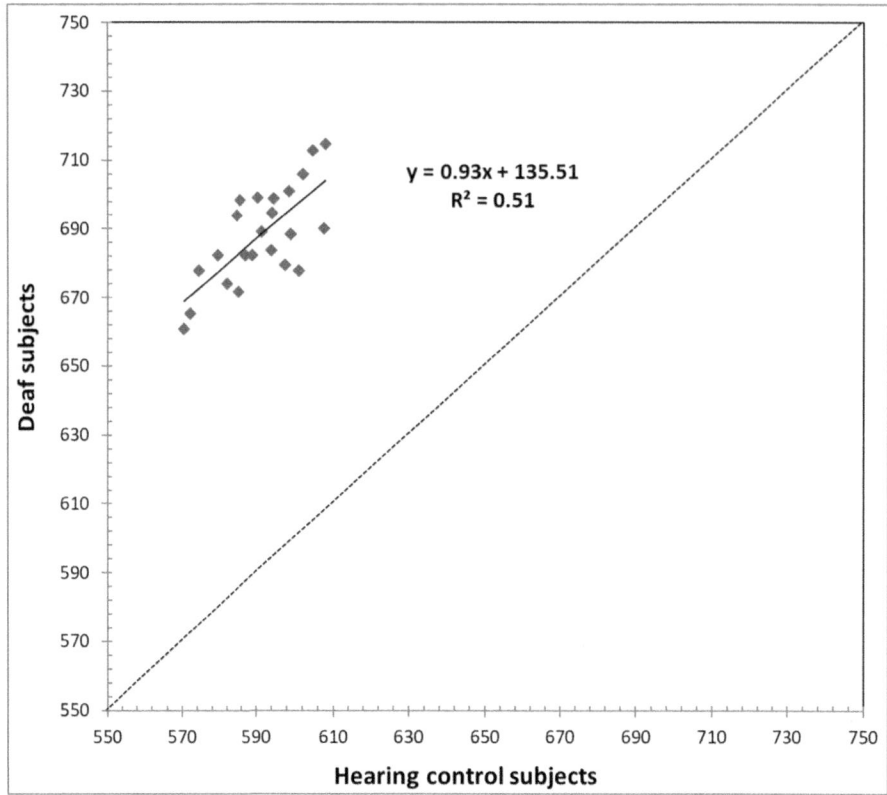

Fig. 3. Condition means (in ms) of deaf and control subjects are plotted against each other. The dotted diagonal line indicates the reference for identical performance in the two groups.

not depend upon the influence of a global (multiplicative) factor. For this reason, we did not proceed with the transformation of raw data in z score as suggested by RAM model in case of the existence of a global factor affecting performances (Faust et al., 1999).

3.2 Analysis of Psycholinguistic Effects

Next, we examined the possible role of psycholinguistic variables in influencing reading accuracy and speed in reading single words.

Accuracy data indicated a nearly flawless performance from hearing control subjects (99.88% of accuracy, SD = 0.97). Performance of deaf individuals was lower (t = 20.7, p < .0001), but still rather accurate (95.29%; SD = 5.43). The presence of a ceiling effect did not allow further analyses on accuracy data. Thus, statistical analyses focused on RT data only.

We run a linear mixed effect model analysis on the vocal RTs in reading the whole set of 626 words. *Group* (deaf and control subjects), *word length* (number of letters), *contextual rules* (presence or absence of contextual rules), *bigram frequency* (natural logarithmic of mean values computed according to Colfis database, Bertinetto et al., 2005), *word frequency* (natural logarithmic of values according to Colfis database, Bertinetto et al., 2005), *stress* (on the penultimate vs antepenultimate syllable) as well as *age of acquisition*, *imageability* and *concreteness* (rating according to Varless 2 database; Burani et al., 2015) were entered as fixed factors, while *items* and *participants* as random factors. We added in the model also the interaction between the group factor and all aforesaid fixed factors to check whether or not these psycholinguistic variables affected the two groups differently.

Results showed the significance of the main effect of *group* (F (1,24) = 8.09, p < 0.01; β = 93.12): deaf participants had longer vocal RTs than the control group (690 vs 597 ms, respectively; diff = 93.1). Also, the main effect of *length* was significant (F (1,617) = 4.37, p < .05; β = 2.41) indicating that RTs slowed by an average of 3.5 ms per each additional letter (mean RT latencies were: 627, 639, 645, 654, and 645 ms for 4-, 5-, 6-, 7-, 8- and 9-letter words, respectively). The *word frequency* effect was significant (F (1,617) = 8.77, p < .01; β = −3.19): low frequency words (i.e., −1 SD from the frequency average) were read on average in 649 ms, medium frequency words in 644 ms, and high frequency words (i.e., +1 SD from average) were read in 639 ms. Also, the age of acquisition effect was significant (F (1,617) = 5.68, p < .05; β = 5.01): words acquired earlier in life (−1 SD) were read with shorter RTs (on average 638 ms) than words with a mean age of acquisition or late acquired words (+1 SD), which on average had RTs of 644 ms and 650 ms, respectively. The *concreteness* effect approached significance (F (1,617). = 3.15, p = .076; β = 3.58): RTs tended to be shorter in reading more concrete words (mean 640 ms) than medium and low concrete words (read on average in 644 and 648 ms, respectively). The effects of *Contextual rules*, *imageability*, *stress* and *bigram frequency* factors were not significant (Fs about 1).

Critically for the purpose of the present study, the *group* factor did not interact with any psycholinguistic variable examined, indicating that the psycholinguistic variables affected reading speed in a similar way in the two groups. Random effects of items and participants were significant (LRT = 377 and 4868 respectively, p < .0001).

3.3 Reading Comprehension

Performance in text comprehension was compared in the two groups of participants by t test analysis. Deaf subjects had a lower accuracy in text comprehension (52.3%; SD = 2.62) compared to control participants (83.13%; SD = 1.18; t (25) = 3.54, p < .001).

4 Discussion

Overall, the results indicated that as a group deaf young adults were slower and also less accurate than controls closely matched on gender, age and educational level. Deaf subjects reached a moderately good accuracy in reading (95.29%), even though their performance was lower with respect to that of hearing control participants, for whom the errors were nearly absent. Note that the presence of a ceiling effect in the accuracy data did not allow investigating whether, in reading accuracy, deaf participants were modulated by psycholinguistic variables in a different way with respect to hearing subjects. Different experimental designs are necessary if one wants to examine differences in terms of reading accuracy.

Deaf participants were also slower in reading with respect to hearing subjects (ca. 93 ms). However, their reading performance was modulated by the same variables affecting unimpaired readers. In fact, reading speed of both groups was affected by some lexical, sublexical and semantic variables examined, such as word length, word frequency and age of acquisition, as expected (Barca et al., 2002). However, none of these effects interacted with the group factor, indicating that the impact of the psycholinguistic variables considered was similar in the two groups.

The application of the RAM model (Faust et al., 1996) on vocal RTs highlighted the absence of a global factor affecting reading of deaf individuals. According to the RAM model, general "cognitive speed" and level of processing required to perform a given task (or "difficulty") interact multiplicatively to produce actual reading performance. In the present data, the differences between the two groups grew linearly as a function of condition difficulty, but the slope of the linear regression was near unity, indicating the absence of a multiplicative difference between the two groups as a function of condition difficulty. This highlights that group differences were "genuine", i.e., not due to an overadditivity effect (or global factor). This finding highlights the qualitative difference between the reading slowness of deaf individuals and that of other clinical samples, such as dyslexic children (for a review see Zoccolotti et al., 2019), for which overadditivity accounts for a large proportion of the reading slowness. Across conditions, deaf subjects were slower in reading compared to hearing participants. However, this group difference did not grow numerically as a function of condition difficulty, but it was constant.

It is not entirely clear how this constant value should be interpreted. On logical grounds, it may be thought to indicate the longer time spent for planning the articulatory movement by deaf participants compared to controls. Indeed, the quality of phonological output was generally poor and a lenient scoring system was adopted so as not to penalize the pronunciation defects of deaf subjects. However, it should be noted that, if this interpretation were correct, one would expect that, in the plot matching condition means and standard deviations, the x- intercept would be slightly longer in the case of the RT means of deaf individuals as compared to that of control subjects (Myerson et al., 2003). This pattern could not be detected in the present data and a single regression line accounted reasonably well for the data of both groups in the plot based on the condition means as well as in that based on single word items. However, the group difference was indeed small, amounting to ca. 35 ms in terms of group means. Therefore, it is possible that the plot analysis was simply not sensitive enough to detect such a small difference. Ideally, one should have a larger spread of condition means to obtain a reliable estimate of the intercept on the x axis separately for the two groups of individuals. At any rate, what seems clear, based on models of RTs, such as RAM (Faust et al., 1999) and DEM (Myerson et al., 2003), is that the present data are not in keeping with the idea that central, or decisional, components of the reading process are impaired in deaf individuals.

Results showed a marked difference between deaf and control subjects in comprehension skills: deaf participants had a lower performance in the task of comprehending a written text than hearing control subjects, consistently with previous results (e.g., Wauters et al., 2006). It does not seem likely that the comprehension difficulty of deaf subjects can be entirely explained by problems in word decoding as these were comparatively small as compared to the comprehension deficit. On the contrary, it has been proposed that general linguistic difficulties may contribute to this outcome (Musselman, 2000). Further, it is possible that difficulties in comprehending syntactic contrasts may also contribute in dampening performance in text comprehension (Bishop, 1983).

Overall, the present findings highlight that the reading skills of deaf young adults were lower than those of a closely matched control group. In particular, as a group, they were slower and less accurate in reading single words aloud. However, the group difference in reading speed was quantitatively small (ca. 93 ms) and the RTs of deaf individuals were influenced by psycholinguistic variables in a similar way as those of the control subjects. Furthermore, the group difference in reading speed was constant, i.e., it did not vary as a function of condition difficulty. Based on DEM (Myerson et al., 2003), this indicates that the source of the effect does not involve the central, or decisional, components of the reading process.

It should be noted that the deaf young adults examined here had completed high school and were proficient in using both oral communication and ISL. Therefore, it seems important that the interpretation of the present findings keeps into consideration these characteristics of the examined sample. Thus, it may be posited that at least a proportion of deaf individuals may reach a level of performance similar, or only slightly inferior, to that of matched hearing subjects. In conclusion, at least in a sample of young adults with good academic achievement and both oral and sign language communication skills, it appears that the deficit in reading decoding is comparatively small. By contrast, deaf individuals were markedly affected in the comprehension of a text, indicating that additional factors presumably play a role in this case. It appears important to extend these findings to a larger group of deaf individuals with a wider spectrum of communication skills.

References

Angelelli, P., et al.: Spelling impairments in Italian dyslexic children with and without a history of early language delay. Are there any differences? Front. Psychol. Educ. Psychol. **7**, 527 (2016)

Barca, L., Burani, C., Arduino, L.S.: Word naming times and psycholinguistic norms for Italian nouns. Behav. Res. Methods Instrum. Comput. **34**, 424–434 (2002)

Barca, L., Ellis, A.W., Burani, C.: Context-sensitive rules and word naming in Italian children. Read. Writ. **20**, 495–509 (2007)

Barca, L., Pezzulo, G., Castrataro, M., Rinaldi, P., Caselli, M.C.: Visual word recognition in deaf readers: lexicality is modulated by communication mode. PLoS ONE **8**(3), e59080 (2013)

Bertinetto, P.M., et al.: CoLFIS (Corpus e Lessico di Frequenza dell'Italiano Scritto) [Corpus and Frequency Lexicon of Written Italian] (2005). http://www.istc.cnr.it/grouppage/databases

Bélanger, N.N., Baum, S.R., Mayberry, R.I.: Reading difficulties in adult deaf readers of French: phonological codes, not guilty! Sci. Stud. Read. **16**, 263–285 (2012)

Bélanger, N.N., Slattery, T.J., Mayberry, R.I., Rayner, K.: Skilled deaf readers have an enhanced perceptual span in reading. Psychol. Sci. **23**, 816–823 (2012)

Bélanger, N.N., Rayner, K.: Frequency and predictability effects in eye fixations for skilled and less-skilled deaf readers. Vis. Cogn. **21**, 477–497 (2013)

Bélanger, N.N., Mayberry, R.I., Rayner, K.: Orthographic and phonological preview benefits: Parafoveal processing in skilled and less-skilled deaf readers. Q. J. Exp. Psychol. **66**, 2237–2252 (2013)

Bélanger, N.N., Rayner, K.: What eye movements reveal about deaf readers. Curr. Dir. Psychol. Sci. **24**, 220–226 (2015)

Bertone, C., Volpato, F.: Oral language and sign language: possible approaches for deaf people's language development. Cadernos de Saúde **2**, 51–62 (2009)

Bishop, D.V.M.: Comprehension of English syntax by profoundly deaf children. J. Child Psychol. Psychiatry **24**, 415–434 (1983)

Blythe, H.I., Dickins, J.H., Kennedy, C.R., Liversedge, S.P.: Phonological processing during silent reading in teenagers who are deaf/hard of hearing: an eye movement investigation. Dev. Sci. **21**, e12643 (2018)

Brown, C.A., Bacon, S.P.: Fundamental frequency and speech intelligibility in background noise. Hear. Res. **266**, 52–59 (2010)

Burani, C., Arduino, L.S., Marinelli, C.V., Barca, L.: Variabili lessicali e sub-lessicali_2: valori per 626 nomi dell'italiano (2015). http://www.istc.cnr.it/grouppage/varless2

Burani, C., Arduino, L.S.: Stress regularity or consistency? Reading aloud Italian polysyllables with different stress patterns. Brain Lang. **90**(1–3), 318–325 (2004)

Caselli, M.C., Maragna, S., Volterra, V.: Linguaggio e Sordità. Gesti. segni e parole nello sviluppo e nell'educazione. Il Mulino, Bologna (2006)

Chesi, C.: Il linguaggio verbale non standard dei bambini sordi. Edizioni Universitarie Romane, Roma (2006)

Chilosi, A.M., et al.: Reading and spelling disabilities in children with and without a history of early language delay: a neuropsychological and linguistic study. Child Neuropsychol. **15**, 582–604 (2009)

Conrad, R.: The Deaf Schoolchild. Harper and Row, London (1979)

Cornoldi, C., Pra Baldi, A., Giofrè, D.: Prove MT Avanzate-3-Clinica. La valutazione delle abilità di Lettura, Comprensione, Scrittura e Matematica per il biennio della Scuola Secondaria di II Grado. Erikson (2017)

De Luca, M., Barca, L., Burani, C., Zoccolotti, P.: The effect of word length and other sublexical, lexical and semantic variables on developmental reading deficit. Cogn. Behav. Neurol. **21**, 227–235 (2008)

De Luca, M., Marinelli, C.V., Spinelli, D., Zoccolotti, P.: Slowing in reading and picture naming: the effects of aging and developmental dyslexia. Exp. Brain Res. **235**(10), 3093–3109 (2017). https://doi.org/10.1007/s00221-017-5041-1

Domìnguez, A.B., Alegrìa, J.: Reading mechanisms in orally educated deaf adults. J. Deaf Stud. Deaf Educ. **15**, 136–148 (2010)

Domínguez, A.B., Carrillo, M.S., del Mar Perez, M., Alegría, J.: Analysis of reading strategies in deaf adults as a function of their language and meta-phonological skills. Res. Dev. Disabil. **35**, 1439–1456 (2014)

Emmorey, K., Midgley, K.J., Kohen, C.B., Sehyr, Z.S., Holcomb, P.J.: The N170 ERP component differs in laterality, distribution, and association with continuous reading measures for deaf and hearing readers. Neuropsychologia **106**, 298–309 (2017)

Faust, M.E., Balota, D.A., Spieler, D.H., Ferraro, F.R.: Individual differences in information-processing rate and amount: implications for group differences in response latency. Psychol. Bull. **125**, 777–799 (1999)

Fischler, I.: Word recognition, use of context, and reading skill among deaf college students. Read. Res. Q. **20**, 203–218 (1985)

Franchi, E., Musola, D.: Acquisizione dell'italiano e sordità. Omaggio a Bruna Radelli. Libreria Editrice Cafoscarina (2010)

Geers, A.: Predictors of reading skill development in children with early cochlear implantation. Ear Hear. **24**, 59S-68S (2003)

Geers, A.E., Hayes, H.: Reading, writing, and phonological processing skills of adolescents with 10 or more years of cochlear implant experience. Ear Hear. **32**, 49S-59S (2011)

Glezer, L.S., et al.: Orthographic and phonological selectivity across the reading system in deaf skilled readers. Neuropsychologia **117**, 500–512 (2018)

Gutierrez-Sigut, E., Vergara-Martínez, M., Perea, M.: Early use of phonological codes in deaf readers: an ERP study. Neuropsychologia **106**, 261–279 (2017)

Gutierrez-Sigut, E., Vergara-Martínez, M., Marcet, A., Perea, M.: Automatic use of phonological codes during word recognition in deaf signers of Spanish Sign Language. FEAST Formal Exp. Adv. Sign Language Theory **1**, 1–15 (2018)

Harris, M.Y., Terlektsi, E.: Reading and spelling abilities of deaf adolescents with cochlear implants and hearing aids. J. Deaf Stud. Deaf Educ. **16**, 24–34 (2010)

Johnson, C., Goswami, U.: Phonological awareness, vocabulary, and reading in deaf children with cochlear implants. J. Speech Lang. Hear. Res. **53**, 237–261 (2010)

Kyle, F.E., Harris, M.: Concurrent correlates and predictors of reading and spelling achievement in Deaf and hearing school children. J. Deaf Stud. Deaf Educ. **11**, 273–289 (2006)

Leybaert, J.: Reading in the deaf: the roles of phonological codes. In: En, M., Marschark, D., Clark (eds.) Psychological Perspectives in Deafness, pp. 203–227 (1993)

Lyxell, B., et al.: Cognitive development in children with cochlear implants: relations to reading and communication. Int. J. Audiol. **47**, 47–52 (2008)

Marcet, A., Perea, M.: Is nevtral NEUTRAL? Visual similarity effects in the early phases of written-word recognition. Psychon. Bull. Rev. **24**, 1180–1185 (2017)

Marcet, A., Perea, M.: Can I order a burger at rnacdonalds.com? Visual similarity effects of multi-letter combinations at the early stages of word recognition. J. Exp. Psychol. Learn. Memory Cogn. **44**, 699 (2018)

Marinelli, C.V.: Reading and spelling in skilled and dyslexic children: a cross-linguistic perspective. Doctoral dissertation in Cognitive Neuroscience. Sapienza University, Rome, Italy (2010)

Marinelli, C.V., Angelelli, P., Di Filippo, G., Zoccolotti, P.: Is developmental dyslexia modality specific? A visual-acoustic comparison on Italian dyslexics. Neuropsychologia **49**, 1718–1729 (2011)

Marinelli, C.V., Traficante, D., Zoccolotti, P., Burani, C.: Orthographic neighbourhood-size effects on the reading aloud of Italian children with and without dyslexia. Sci. Stud. Read. **17**, 333–349 (2013)

Marinelli, C.V., Trenta, M., Benassi, M., Burani, C., Zoccolotti, P.: Psycholinguistic factors affecting the error profile in a regular orthography (in preparation)

Marschark, M., Harris, M.: Success and failure in learning to read: the special case (?) of deaf children. In: Reading Comprehension Difficulties: Processes and Intervention, vol. 12, pp. 279–300 (1996)

Mayberry, R.I., del Giudice, A.A., Lieberman, A.M.: Reading achievement in relation to phonological coding and awareness in deaf readers: a meta-analysis. J. Deaf Stud. Deaf Educ. **16**, 164–188 (2011)

Mayer, C., Watson, L., Archbold, S., Ng, Z.Y., Mulla, I.: Reading and writing skills of deaf pupils with cochlear implants. Deaf. Educ. Int. **18**, 71–86 (2016)

Mazzotta, S., Barca, L., Marcolini, S., Stella, G., Burani, C.: Frequenza, immaginabilità ed età di acquisizione delle parole: in che misura influenzano la lettura dei bambini italiani? Psicologica clinica dello sviluppo **2**, 247–266 (2005)

McEvoy, C., Marschark, M., Nelson, D.L.: Comparing the mental lexicons of deaf and hearing individuals. J. Educ. Psychol. **91**, 312 (1999)

Moeller, M.P., Tomblin, J.B., Yoshinaga-Itano, C., McDonald Connor, C., Jerger, S.: Current state of knowledge: language and literacy of children with hearing impairment. Ear Hear. **28**, 740–753 (2007)

Moreno-Pérez, F.J., Saldaña, D., Rodríguez-Ortiz, I.R.: Reading efficiency of deaf and hearing people in Spanish. J. Deaf Stud. Deaf Educ. **20**, 374–384 (2015)

Musselman, C.: How do children who can't hear learn to read an alphabetic script? A review of the literature on reading and deafness. J. Deaf Stud. Deaf Educ. **5**, 11–31 (2000)

Myerson, J., Hale, S., Zheng, Y., Jenkins, L., Widaman, K.F.: The difference engine: a model of diversity in speeded cognition. Psychon. Bull. Rev. **10**, 262–288 (2003)

Paizi, D., De Luca, M., Zoccolotti, P., Burani, C.: A comprehensive evaluation of lexical reading in Italian developmental dyslexics. J. Res. Reading **36**, 303–329 (2013)

Perfetti, C.A., Sandak, R.: Reading optimally builds on spoken language implications for deaf readers. J. Deaf Stud. Deaf Educ. **5**, 32–50 (2000)

Perry, C., Ziegler, J.C., Zorzi, M.: Nested incremental modeling in the development of computational theories: the CDP+ model of reading aloud. Psychol. Rev. **114**, 273–315 (2007)

Pisoni, D.B., Kronenberger, W., Conway, C.M., Horn, D.L., Karpicke, J., Henning, S.: Efficacy and effectiveness of cochlear implants in deaf children. In: Marschark, M., Hauser, P. (eds.) Deaf Cognition: Foundations and Outcomes. Oxford University Press, New York (2008)

Sánchez, E., García-Rodicio, H.: Re-lectura del estudio PISA: qué y cómo se evalúa e interpreta el rendimiento de los alumnos en la lectura. Revista de Educación **1**, 195–226 (2006)

Strong, M., Prinz, P.M.: Is American Sign Language related to English literacy? In: Chamberlain, C., Morford, J., Mayberry, R. (eds.) Language Acquisition by Eye, pp. 131–141. Erlbaum, Hillsdale (2000)

Tomblin, J.B., Harrison, M., Ambrose, S.E., Walker, E., A., Oleson, J.J., Moeller, M.P.: Language outcomes in young children with mild to severe hearing loss. Ear Hearing **36**, 76S–91S (2015)

Transler, C., Reitsma, P.: Phonological coding in the reading of deaf children: Pseudohomophone effects in lexical decision. Br. J. Dev. Psychol. **23**, 525–542 (2005)

Wang, X., Caramazza, A., Peelen, M.V., Han, Z., Bi, Y.: Reading without speech sounds: VWFA and its connectivity in the congenitally deaf. Cereb. Cortex **25**, 2416–2426 (2014)

Wagenmakers, E.J., Brown, S.: On the linear relation between the mean and the standard deviation of a response time distribution. Psychol. Rev. **114**, 830–841 (2007)

Wauters, L.N., Van Bon, W.H.J., Tellings, A.E.J.M.: Reading comprehension of Dutch deaf children. Reading Writing **19**, 49–76 (2006)

Williams, C., Mayer, C.: Writing in young deaf children. Rev. Educ. Res. **85**, 630–666 (2015)

Vizzi, F., Angelelli, P., Iaia, M., Risser, A.H., Marinelli, C.V.: Writing composition ability and spelling competence in deaf subjects: a psycholinguistic analysis of the source of difficulties. Reading Writing **36**, 1–26 (2022)

Zoccolotti, P., De Luca, M., Judica, A., Spinelli, D.: Isolating global and specific factors in developmental dyslexia: a study based on the rate and amount model (RAM). Exp. Brain Res. **186**, 551–560 (2008)

Zoccolotti, P., De Luca, M., Di Filippo, G., Marinelli, C.V., Spinelli, D.: Reading and lexical decision tasks generate different patterns of individual variability as a function of condition difficulty. Psychon. Bull. Rev. **25**, 1161–1169 (2018)

Zoccolotti, P., Marinelli, C.V., Martelli, M., Spinelli, D., De Luca, M.: Psycholinguistic factors and global components in developmental dyslexia. In: Sulpizio, S., Barca, L., Primativo, S., Arduino, L.S. (eds.) Word Recognition, Morphology and Lexical Reading. Essays in Honour of Cristina Burani. College Publications (2019)

Game-Based Learning and Innovative Teaching Environments

Comparison of Traditional and Virtual Reality Learning in Children with ADHD

Alessandro Frolli[1(✉)], Sonia Ciotola[2], Clara Esposito[2], Francesco Cerciello[2], Angelo Rega[3], and M. C. Ricci[1]

[1] Disability Research Centre University of International Studies in Rome, 00147 Rome, Italy
{alessandro.frolli,m.ricci}@unint.eu
[2] FINDS - Italian Neuroscience and Developmental Disorders Foundation, 81040 Caserta, Italy
{sonia.ciotola,clara.esposito,
francesco.cerciello}@fondazionefinds.it
[3] Department of Psychology, University of Naples, 80100 Naples, Italy
angelo.rega@unina.it

Abstract. The DSM-5 defines ADHD as a chronic neurologic-based behavior disorder characterized by a persistent pattern of inattention and/or hyperactivity and impulsivity. Hyperactivity and inattention interfere with cognitive functioning and participation in various activities, including school ones. The symptoms of ADHD are hypothesized to cause learning deficits in school, particularly in learning to write, read and calculate. The various treatment hypotheses include behavioral interventions and pharmacological support. Recent technological advances have shown the usefulness and potential of virtual reality (VR) as a hypothesis for intervention with neurodevelopmental disorder. In this regard, the aim of this study was to evaluate the effectiveness of use as children with ADHD. In a previous study we have already validated our idea by investigating how virtual reality has enabled faster learning in ADHD subjects than traditional training. After expanding the sample, in this study we compared two training courses (one traditional and one via VR), developed for learning history in children with ADHD. After having subjected the participants to the classical training and to the one with VR, our results exceeded a better learning than the starting condition. Furthermore, our analysis found that the group that performed the VR training performed better than the group that did the traditional training. Our study suggests that VR technology helps effective ADHD symptom management by promoting improvement in traditional treatment and learning options.

Keywords: Virtual reality · Attention deficit hyperactivity disorder · Children · Learning · Motivation · Embodied cognition

1 Introduction

Among the neurodevelopmental disorders, one of the most common is attention deficit hyperactivity disorder (ADHD) [1]. This disorder is chronic with a neurological basis characterized by a persistent pattern of inattention and / or hyperactivity and impulsivity which, compared to typically developing children of the same age, are more inappropriate or disruptive. The onset of hyperactivity occurs at the age of 3 or 4 years, with hyperactivity and inattention combining which normally appear at age 5 to 8. In 2013, the diagnostic criteria were revised with the DSM-5 [2]; in fact, in this diagnostic manual, the list of symptoms doesn't change, but rather: the age of onset of the disorder, the diagnostic category in which it is currently included, the transition from the concept of "subtype" to the concept of "clinical manifestation" and finally, the possibility of comorbidity between ADHD and Autistic Spectrum Disorder (ASD) [2].

In DSM IV [3] the symptoms had to be present before 7 years of age, while with DSM 5 the age of onset must be before 12 and not before 7 years of age.

Many ADHD patients have comorbid disorders such as depression, disruptive behavior disorders, which must be addressed in the treatment plan. The treatment of ADHD is based on a combination of interventions, academic, cognitive behavioral, and in the most severe cases with psychopharmacological interventions that produce excellent response rates [4]. Hyperactivity and inattention through self-control difficulties interfere with the child's psychological development and hinder the carrying out of common daily activities. [5].

At school, these children pay no attention and work in a disorganized way. They also appear restless and very unpredictable in relationships. They disregard teachers' instructions on homework and tend to become bullies in the classroom. When impulsivity and hyperactivity appear, they can make decisions without reasoning, or not respect them, they can start a conversation or a game, generate difficulties in delaying gratification and inhibiting emotional reactions. This is mainly explained as a neurodevelopmental disorder of the prefrontal lobe, which affects the development of executive functions in childhood. It includes inhibitory control, working memory, cognitive flexibility, planning, performance of goal-oriented behaviors, as well as monitoring of personal behavior [1–6]. Between different technological systems, the potential of Virtual Reality (VR) in children with ADHD is highlighted. VR includes the use of external tools that provide sensory information (mainly visual, auditory, and haptic) to interact with the virtual environment; internal tools, which allow the collection of information on the movement and position of the user with respect to his interaction with the system (for example, through gloves, trackers, exoskeletons or a mouse); systems for reproducing graphic images created by the virtual environment; and software and databases that model objects in the virtual world, using their shape, texture or movement [7, 8]. VR is an "embodied technology" [8] that provides the feeling of presence and immersion [9]. This helps to improve the movements, actions and emotions adapted to the context. VR is generally understood as a technology that generates a virtual immersion in a digital environment, thanks to a computerized graphic simulation that allows users to immerse themselves in an interactive three-dimensional world in which different types of sensory and emotional experiences meet. Yantong's study on the feasibility of virtual reality in school-age children with ADHD during learning has shown that the use of virtual reality-based tools marks an essential turning point in the diagnosis of ADHD [10]. In recent years, VR has acquired great importance in the educational field. VR is generally understood as a technology that generates a virtual immersion in a digital environment, thanks to a computerized graphic simulation that allows users to immerse themselves in an interactive three-dimensional world in which different types of sensory experiences meet. and emotional and it is precisely because of its immersive, imaginative and interactive characteristics that VR in education is becoming so popular Its implementation allows the student to be placed in different environments with a realism that could never be achieved with a textbook; avoiding, at the same time, some elements that could hinder learning, including hyperactivity and inattention [11].

About that, the aim of this study was to evaluate the effectiveness of using VR based interventions in children with ADHD. In a previous study, we have already validated our idea by examining how VR compared to traditional training can promote faster learning in ADHD subjects compared to traditional training [2]. Since the sample of our previous study was small, in this study we decided to expand the sample and compare two trainings developed for story learning in children with ADHD: one involved the use of specific teaching procedures provided by a specialized educator, and one was developed through the use of VR and interactive videos. We wanted to verify which of the two forms of teaching allowed a better quality of learning and whether it could guarantee an increase in motivation. Specifically, the hypothesis tested in the work is that the intervention based on the use of VR allows better acquisition and an increase in student motivation.

2 Material and Methods

2.1 Participants

The sample considered in this study is made up of 144 subjects aged between 9 and 10, selected from 12 schools in the province of Caserta (Italy). The inclusion criteria were as follows: a) aged between 9 and 10 years, b) absence of a specific learning disorder (SLD), c) absence of other childhood neuropsychiatric pathologies presenting as comorbidities, d) IQ between 85 and 105, e) middle-high socio-cultural class of parents. After considering the possibility of inclusion in the sample, we divided the subjects into two experimental groups of 72 subjects each. All subjects received a diagnosis of ADHD through a formalized neuropsychological assessment consisting of the following tests: WISC-IV, MT Test, AC-MT Test administered to children and CRS-R scale administer to teachers.

The subdivision was performed randomly (randomized): subjects in both groups had the same inclusion criteria and did not have different sociocultural factors. The two groups underwent two different treatments, as explained in the next section. The first experimental group consisted of 72 subjects with a mean age of 9.20 years (SD = 0.32) and a mean IQ of 100.20 (SD = 3.5), including 62 males and 10 females. The second experimental group consisted of 72 subjects with a mean age of 9.30 (SD = 0.50) and a mean IQ of 99.9 (SD = 3.7), including 60 men and 12 women. The data were collected at the Laboratory of Neuroscience, Learning Processes and Immersive VR of the University of International Studies of Rome by qualified psychologists in collaboration with the Regional Education Office (USR).

2.2 Protocol Evaluation

The protocol used to assess the inclusion criteria consists of the following tests: Wechsler Intelligent Scale for Children [12], AC-MT Test [13], MT Test [14] and Conners Rating Scale (CRS) [15].

WISC IV. Is the fourth version of the Wechsler Intelligent Scale for Children available in Italy since 2012. It is a clinical tool that allows to evaluate the cognitive abilities of children and young people aged 6 years and 16 years and 11 months.

It is possible to obtain an assessment of intelligence with the calculation of the Intellectual Quotient (IQ), clinical information to conduct neuropsychological assessments and in-depth studies in specific areas, such as Specific Learning Disorders (SLD) and Attention Deficit Disorder / Hyperactivity (ADHD) and estimating cognitive functioning prior to traumatic events, such as: brain damage or other pathologies. Furthermore, with the administration of Wisc IV it is possible to have a guide to plan treatments for the enhancement and recovery of cognitive functions, monitor their progress and make placement decisions in specific clinical and educational facilities. The WISC-IV is made up of 15 subtests: 10 main and 5 supplementary, which allow to obtain 4 indices: verbal comprehension index (VCI), visual-perceptual reasoning (PRI), working memory (WMI) and information processing speed (PSI), which make up the intellectual quotient (IQ).

AC-MT Test. Test used to evaluate the learning and processing difficulties of mathematical calculation.

The test is divided into some tests: written calculation, calculation in mind, back numbering, dictation of numbers and retrieval of numerical facts.

MT Test. Test that allows you to evaluate reading skills by taking as a reference three parameters: speed, correctness and understanding. Different songs are used for each parameter.

The correctness and speed test allows you to evaluate whether the student reads aloud correctly, what mistakes he makes and what the pace of his reading is.

The comprehension test allows to ascertain whether the child, when he reads a passage alone, is able to understand the meanings that the written message transmits. Through this test it is also possible to evaluate the decoding ability and the linguistic competence of the student.

CRS. CRS is a diagnostic test for ADHD. It consists of a self-administered version for parents and teachers, and one for adolescents. It is a scale that measures symptoms such as inattention and lack of control of impulses; asks questions about things like behavior, work or schoolwork, and social life. They can also show how these symptoms affect things like grades, work, family life, and relationships. The main symptoms investigated are: Hyperactivity, difficulty paying attention, problems keeping friends, emotional problems, impulsivity, nervousness, compulsions. The score is expressed on a scale from 0 (no symptoms) to 3 (severe symptoms).

2.3 Procedures

As previously mentioned, all the subjects, after having received the diagnosis of ADHD through a formalized neuropsychological evaluation, were randomly assigned (randomized) to two groups in order to perform two different learning trainings.

The first, he conducted a training on learning history using traditional methods: the topic to be learned was read individually by the instructor and a feedback procedure was used to support the read status. The second group, composed of 72 subjects, instead trained the learning of history through virtual reality. In this procedure, some videos of the subject under study were presented in 3D using a special viewer. At the end of the study, a review was performed using a questionnaire consisting of 10 questions, and token economy was then used for each correct answer, with term reinforcement provided after 7 positive answers.

At T0, all children engaged in individual learning and, at the end of the first trimester, completed a 90-question progress questionnaire to assess basic levels of individual learning. Data collection was conducted over a period of approximately six months and lasted. For 4 months the two groups carried out the two trainings aimed at learning history. At T1 (early May), all children answered a new questionnaire with 90 items on historical topics covered during the 4 months of training. Therefore, it is possible to evaluate differences if there were differences in the percentage of correct answers between T0 and T1 if there were differences in the percentage of correct answers.

3 Results

Data analyzes were performed using SPSS 26.0 statistical data collection software. Significance was accepted at 5%.

We then compared G1 and G2 at T0 and T1 to assess whether there were improvements after learning training (within time variable) and then compared both groups at T1 (between groups) to see which of the two treatments could provide better acquisition. We therefore conducted a 2*2 mixed univariate ANOVA: Factor within groups = time (T0 and T1) and factor between groups = group (G1 and G2). Level ($p < 0.05$). We called G1 (group 1, which did not undergo traditional learning training) and G2 (group 2, which underwent virtual reality learning training). We called T0 the measurement before the learning training and T1 the measurement 4 months after the learning training was conducted.

We used Student's T-test, a parametric statistical test that can be used when the two groups being compared are independent. Specifically, we used the T-test for independent samples with two-sided significance to make comparisons between the groups (correct response values) at T0 and to check whether both groups were homogeneous before the implementation of the learning training

The results showed a non-significance of the scores ($t(102) = 2.088$; $p = 0.039$); this result indicates that the two groups at T0 (before the learning training) were homogeneous (Table 1).

The comparison between the two groups by ANOVA showed the following results:
Time * group interaction is significant [$F(1,102) = 862.005$, $p < 0.05$]. This data indicates that there is a significant interaction between the time and the type of treatment.

More specifically, both treatments have a positive effect on correct responses, but this is most significant for the intervention with virtual reality (G2) after training (T1) (Table 2).

Table 1. Comparison of the two groups at T0

Groups	T0		t	p
	Means	SD		
1	57.31	1.96	2,077	0.037
2	57.72	2.11		

Table 2. Effect of the time * group interaction

Time	Group 1		Group 2		F	p
	Means	SD	Means	SD		
T0	57.31	1.96	57.72	2.11		
T1	68.12	3.15	79.01	2.31	871.006	< 0.05*

* Statistical significance $p < 0.05$

4 Discussion

Emerging technologies (including VR) are contributing to the expansion of our knowledge and providing new solutions to various problems.

The development of VR has enabled the use of new training and intervention tools that appear to be more effective and promising than traditional tools. For example, the environments of VR offer the possibility of simulating real situations; with VR it is also possible to create environments that are difficult to experience in everyday life [16]. The use of VR has shown positive results in recent years in the context of inclusive education and especially for people with special educational needs (BES), including ADHD. Some authors have studied the relationship between the use of virtual content and the increase of interest, motivation, and selective and sustained attention [17]. The reduction of some symptoms related to ADHD, such as hyperactivity, inattention and impulsivity, and intolerance of waiting, has been studied through the use of serious games specifically designed for educational purposes. Some studies have shown the potential of VR in treating and improving attention without distraction; others have shown that ADHD children were better able to complete attention tasks through the use of virtual reality than with traditional techniques. Rizzo et al. had designed a VR classroom to assess attention performance. In their study, participants used an HMD to complete tasks while visual and auditory stimuli were presented. Because participants with ADHD make many errors and excessive body movements in their tasks, other studies have shown that virtual reality plays an important role in improving these conditions and reducing symptoms and behavioral problems [18]. However, most studies of virtual reality in ADHD populations have focused on the assessment of attention in a virtual classroom environment rather than the learning process [17]. With our study, we aimed to propose two innovations compared to previous studies: first, we proposed learning history training through the use of VR that focused on the assessment of the learning process, and second, we included a substantial number of children with ADHD. The aim of this study was to assess the impact of the use of VR on the learning of children with ADHD affected, through a comparison with individual learning Training with the educator. Our results showed, considering a larger sample, how participants showed better learning outcomes in both VR training and one-on-one training with the educator compared to the baseline condition. Moreover, it was found that G2 (training on VR) showed better results than G1 (training with the instructor). In particular, it was found that these children's motivation to learn increased, especially intrinsic motivation related to the material used and active participation in the learning context, which was significantly greater in the G2 group. Thus, the training of VR was characterized mainly by active participation and direct involvement in the learning experience.

Virtual reality has the ability to clarify some of the cognitive processes, including attention, memory and executive function [19], furthermore, the studies by Adams et al. [20] and Díaz-Orueta et al. [21] have confirmed these results and have suggested that the VRC-CPT test is a suitable tool for children with ADHD symptoms. VR combined with interactive tests, providing specific stimuli, can remove distractions and hold patients' attention and concentration for a long time and also be useful in the rehabilitation of ADHD children. Numerous studies have confirmed the benefits of virtual reality in cognitive performance, such as working memory, executive function and attention [22]. At present, the application of virtual reality technology to clinical practice is still in its infancy. The content and indices of the VR test still need to be expanded and improved. The health guidelines list the possible side effects of virtual reality ranging from headaches, seizures, nausea, fatigue, sleepiness, disorientation, apathy, and dizziness. These symptoms are related to computer disease or virtual reality disease, which can endanger health and safety as well as the effectiveness of virtual reality. Cybersickness as a complex problem is the psychological response to exposure to VR environments studies have indicated that computer disease is a barrier to the use of training or rehabilitation tools in virtual reality environments [23] Therefore, computer disease can be prevented or managed by understanding its causes and the factors that influence its incidence). Depending on the type of VR system, the purpose of the activities and the characteristics of the individual user, a number of steps can be taken to correct or manage the side effects of VR. Studies have indicated several methods of preventing cyber disease, adapting and customizing according to user needs, a more natural user interface (UI), and using haptic interfaces, making the head-mounted display (HMD) lighter as well as ensuring moderate use of a VR system [22].

5 Conclusion and Limitations

The results suggest that the technology of VR can be useful in interventions for children with ADHD, as it provides stable and controlled stimuli to achieve consistent progress, while being flexible as it is adapted to the needs of the patients.

In addition, they provide safe learning environments that minimize errors, time, and costs, and improve user motivation through pleasant and easy-to-use environments.

A large body of evidence also suggests that the technology of VR could complement and enhance traditional treatment options, thereby promoting their effectiveness in treating ADHD symptoms. However, limitations of our study include the limited generalizability of the results, as no follow-up was conducted to maintain the acquired knowledge.

References

1. Romero-Ayuso, D. et al.: Effectiveness of virtual Reality-based interventions for children and adolescents with ADHD: A systematic review and meta-analysis. Children **8**, 70 (2021)
2. American Psychiatric Association: Diagnostic and Statistical Manual of Mental Disorders. 5th ed. Arlington, VA: American Psychiatric Association (2013)
3. American Psychiatric Association: Diagnostic and statistical manual of mental disorders: DSM-IV-TR, 4ª edn. (2000)
4. Tsujii, N., et al.: Efficacy and safety of medication for attention-deficit hyperactivity disorder in children and adolescents with common comorbidities: a systematic review. Neurol Ther. 2021. https://doi.org/10.1007/s40120-021-00249-0
5. Baragash, R.S., Al-Samarraie, H., Moody, L., et al.: Augmented reality and functional skills acquisition among individuals with special needs: a Meta-analysis of group design studies. J. Spec. Educ. Technol. **35**(3), 382–397 (2020)
6. Barkley, R.A.: Behavioral inhibition, sustained attention, and executive functions: constructing a unifying theory of ADHD. Psychol. Bull. **121**, 65–94 (1997)
7. Guyatt, G.H., et al.: GRADE guidelines: 1. introduction-GRANDE evidence profiles and summary of findings tables. J. Clin Epidemiol. **64**, 383–394 (2011)
8. Cochrane: Cochrane handbook for systematic reviews of interventions (2020). https://handbook-5-1.cochrane.org/. Accessed 8 Dec 2020
9. Shamseer, L., et al.: CONSORT extension for reporting N-of-1 trials (CENT) 2015: explanation and elaboration. BMJ **350**, h1793 (2015)
10. Fang, Y., Han, D., Luo, H.: A virtual reality application for assessment for attention deficit hyperactivity disorder in schoolaged children. Neuropsychiatr. Dis. Treat. **15**, 1517–1523 (2019)
11. Villena-Taranilla, R., Tirado-Olivares, S., Cózar-Gutiérrez, R., González-Calero, J.A.: Effects of virtual reality on learning outcomes in K-6 education: a meta- analysis. Educ. Res. Rev. **34**, 100434 (2022)
12. Orsini, A., Pizzuti, L., Picone, L.: Wechsler intelligence scale for children IV Edizione Italiana. Firenze: Giunti OS (2012a)
13. Cornoldi, C., Cornoldi, C., Lucangeli, D., Bellina, M.: AC-MT 6-11. Test di valutazione delle abilità di calcolo e soluzione dei problemi. Gruppo MT. Con CD-ROM. Edizioni Erickson (2012)
14. Cornoldi, C., Colpo, G., Carretti, B., Gola, M.L., Saponaro, C., Viola, F.: Prove MT-Kit scuola: classi 1–2 primaria: dalla valutazione degli apprendimenti di lettura e comprensione al potenziamento. Giunti Edu (2017)
15. Conners, C.K.: Conners 3rd Edition (Conners 3). Ad. it. di C. Primi e D. Maschietto, Giunti Psychometrics, Firenze 2017 (2008)
16. Willcutt, E.G., Pennington, B.F., Boada, R., et al.: A comparison of the cognitive deficits in reading disability and attentiondeficit/hyperactivity disorder. J. Abnorm. Psychol. **110**, 157–172 (2001)

17. Yeh, S.C., Tsai, C.F., Fan, Y.C., et al.: An innovative ADHD assessment system using virtual reality, pp. 78–83 (2012)
18. Gongsook, P., Herrlich, M., Malaka, R., et al.: Time simulator in virtual reality for children with attention deficit hyperactivity disorder, pp. 490–493. ICEC (2012)
19. Rose, F.D., Brooks, B.M., Rizzo, A.A.: Virtual reality in brain damage rehabilitation: review. Cyberpsychol. Behav. **8**, 241–262 (2005)
20. Adams, R., Finn, P., Moes, E., Flannery, K., Rizzo, A.S.: Distractibility in attention/deficit/hyperactivity disorder (ADHD): the virtual reality classroom. Child Neuropsychol. **15**, 120–135 (2009)
21. Díaz-Orueta, U., Garcia-López, C., Crespo-Eguílaz, N., Sánchez-Carpintero, R., Climent, G., Narbona, J.: AULA virtual reality test as an attention measure: convergent validity with conners' continuous performance test. Child Neuropsychol. **20**, 328–342 (2014)
22. Bashiri, A., Ghazisaeedi, M., Shahmoradi, L.: The opportunities of virtual reality in the rehabilitation of children with attention deficit hyperactivity disorder: a literature review. Korean J. Pediatr. **60**(11), 337 (2017). https://doi.org/10.3345/kjp.2017.60.11.337

Exploratory Study of the Effects of Digital Storytelling Using Tangible User Interfaces on Acquired Knowledge About a Story in a Group of Primary School Children

Francesco Sulla[1(✉)], Stefania Fantinelli[1], Clarissa Lella[2], Ciro Esposito[1], and Raffaele Di Fuccio[1]

[1] University of Foggia, Foggia, Italy
francesco.sulla@unifg.it
[2] University of Naples 'Federico II', Naples, Italy

1 Introduction

Technology is becoming an increasingly important part of our lives, and the field of Education is no exception.

Information and Communication Technology (ICT) solutions are even more present in teachers' daily job with pupils since the COVID-19 pandemic, and their effect on teaching and learning is relevant (e.g., Schleicher, 2020; Sulla et al., 2022). Digital technologies allow new ways of teaching, and may change "what people learn, how people learn, where people learn and when they learn. Technology can enable teachers and students to access specialized materials well beyond textbooks, in multiple formats and in ways that can bridge time and space" (OECD, 2020). In particular, studies show that in the field of digital learning and teaching methodologies the application of gaming in learning practices is increasingly more popular and the positive effects are considerable (Christopoulos & Sprangers, 2021), also with children (Limone & Toto, 2021). Indeed, when working with children, games represent a powerful tool for sustaining their education. However, the educational power of digital technology for children has typically been limited by the fact that users explore and manipulate abstract two-dimensional screen-based representations, and not real physical objects. This can be overcome by using the technology of Tangible User Interfaces (Krestanova et al., 2021). Ishii and Ullmer (1997) defined Tangible User Interfaces (TUIs) as tools that mediate between the physical and digital worlds, providing an extension of the digital world. This extension allows an experiential and manipulative approach in the physical world. The element that allows TUIs to be differentiated from the other interfaces concerns their ability to produce a change of state in the digital world through the manipulation of physical objects (Fishkin, 2004). The relevance of Tangible User Interfaces consists in their ability of mediating between the analogic and digital worlds supporting a hybrid approach (Antle and Wise, 2013). TUIs combine the use of the sensory and concrete

---

F. Sulla and S. Fantinelli—These authors contributed equally to this work.

aspects, which is typical of Montessori materials, with the practicality and popularity of technology, generating something new and innovative.

The relevance of TUIs is supported in the literature by the theory of Embodied Cognition. This theory assumes that cognition and corporeality are intrinsically connected (Wilson, 2002). From the theories of Embodied Cognition, it has generated a specific field of pedagogy and it is named 'embodied pedagogy'. Education based on this vision aims at the involvement of the body and the senses through multimodal learning experiences to stimulate cognitive development in students (Alibali & Nathan, 2012). This way of schooling is implicitly supported by the thought of personalities such as: Piaget, Froebel and Montessori. Following the principles of constructivism, they encourage children to do more hands-on work and to use tangible materials, allowing them to learn independently (Zuckerman, 2010).

The Tangible User Interfaces, thus described, can influence several aspects of teaching (Di Fuccio, 2022).

Firstly, the creation of tools based on the logic of TUIs allows ample space to design community activities. TUIs can be designed to create a learning environment where it is possible to foster collaboration among students, share control among collaborators and enable simultaneous interaction. This feature assumes a real relevance, due to the positive role attributed to curricula based on peer education and students collaboration (Liu et al., 2016; Topping, 2005).

Secondly, TUIs support the use of gamification mechanisms. When applied to education, the gamification can change the approach to study. It transforms what for many is perceived as a constraint into something that is enjoyable to do. This is possible through gamification mechanisms that generate intrinsic motivation, produce the flow phenomenon, generate positive competitiveness, and exploit a language that is familiar to young people (Bruke, 2014; Csíkszentmihályi, 1990; Maestri et al., 2018).

Thirdly, TUIs enable the realisation of multisensory storytelling activities exploiting the positive effects of multisensorial approach and storytelling. In children's development, storytelling offers many psychological and educational benefits. Storytelling enhances imagination, improves vocabulary, and refines communication skills. Early exposure to storytelling shows benefits in terms of acquisition of increased vocabulary skills, production, comprehension, and improvement in sustained attention skills (Vally et al., 2015). In addition, oral storytelling stimulates the development of language comprehension, emotional well-being, empathy, sense of responsibility, sense of identity, imagination, creativity and literacy skills (Curenton et al., 2008; Haven, 2007; Griffin et al., 2004; Reese et al., 2010; Reese et al., 2010; Van Puyenbroeck & Maes, 2008).

Multisensory education has also been extensively discussed in the literature, particularly for its ability to generate inclusive didactics. Furthermore, it has positive effects in case of individuals diagnosed with sensory disabilities, autism or with special educational needs (SEN) (Kamei-Hannan et al., 2022; Somma et al., 2021; Novakovic et al., 2019; Starcic et al., 2013).

TUIs can be a valuable tool to support sensory stimulation (Ponticorvo et al.; 2018). The manipulative properties of TUIs support pupils with poor motor skills and learning difficulties. TUIs stimulate the inclusion of pupils with SEN in classroom activities by changing social dynamics, generating new forms of cooperation, reducing the isolation of students with disabilities, facilitating collaboration, and increasing the participation of students with special needs (Starcic et al., 2013). Moreover, the use of gamification is well accepted by children with autism. It shows significant effects in increasing their learning abilities by encouraging interaction (Navan & Khaleghi 2020).

All these elements show the possible effect of TUIs for inclusive education. Indeed, TUIs give the chance to adapt teaching to the learning characteristics of each pupil without falling into stigmatisation. Tangible User Interfaces can support creating activities that are suitable for everyone, not only in terms of contents, but also in the way they are administered.

2 Method

A mixed methodology has been implemented, triangulating qualitative and quantitative data collection methods, that can be described in three different phases:

1. Online focus-groups aimed at the co-design of the educational tool;
2. Data collection through the storytelling TUI tool;
3. Questionnaire after implementation (acceptability and usability);
4. Qualitative feedback through structured interviews with teachers.

2.1 Participants and Procedure

The first step is characterised by an exploratory objective: to explore the TUI technology as an educational tool and expand the vision of the topic as much as possible, thanks to the collective dimension of opinions raised by participants in focus groups.

There have been three main areas of discussion: problems and difficulties in learning and education at schools; strengths and weaknesses of frequently used educational tools for students with learning disabilities/difficulties and special educational needs; exploring whether TUI could enhance learning in students with learning disabilities/difficulties and special educational needs.

Participants were secondary school teachers recruited during the Italian teacher specific needs traineeship, it was an online course; 25 parallel focus groups were conducted with 188 participants.

The second phase of research involved 39 primary school students with a mean age of 8.4 years (SD = 0.87). Among them, 5 have special educational needs (SEN), of which 4 have a diagnosis of a specific learning disorder.

The choice to collect data on a sample attending primary schools derives from the opinions expressed by teachers during the focus groups preliminary to the construction of the instrument with the TUI.

The sample was made up of two classes of the Istituto Omnicomprensivo Montero di Bisaccia, in Campobasso (Italy). The recruitment took place through the mediation of the head teacher, who was interested in the research and gave her availability and support throughout the data collection phase.

Since the participants are minors, before collecting the data, the parents of the pupils were asked to give their informed consent in accordance with Law no. 219 of 22 December 2017 on the processing of data for research purposes.

To evaluate the effects of the tool, two different study conditions were developed.

In the first condition, that was the *experimental condition*, the students participated in a lesson during which they listened to a story using the TUI-based tool (Story1). In this condition, the teacher was required to have a supporting role during the lesson, collaborating with the experimenter in explaining the activity and maintaining order in the classroom.

In the second condition, that was the *control condition*, the students participated in a traditional lesson, in which they listened to a story without the use of any type of technology (Story2). In this case, the teacher was invited to carry out the lesson in a standard way, as they usually do. The only difference would have been the presence in the classroom of the experimenter who acted in the role of observer.

To investigate the effect of the use of TUI on learning, in terms of acquired knowledge about a story, each of the two classes (Class1 and Class2) was subjected to each of the two conditions.

Specifically, Class1 was subjected first to the experimental condition with Story1 and then to the control condition with Story2. Instead, Class2 was first subjected to the control condition with Story2 and then to the experimental condition with Story1.

2.2 Materials

2.2.1 Technological Tools

The study applied a system based on the paradigm of tangible user interfaces (TUI) set on the classrooms involved in the study. The system includes two components: a software and a hardware.

The software side is an application made with the editor created in the framework of the BlueArrow project (Limone & Di Fuccio, 2021) funded in the programme Erasmus+. The authoring system is made for the creation of digital storytellings that applies the tangible user interface approach, providing an easy interface for the development of an application. The tool is freely available on the BlueArrow's website (https://www.bluearrowproject.eu/wp/o3/) and use a software called STELTviewer (Miglino et al., 2013; Di Fuccio et al., 2016). The Blue Arrow's editor allows the development of interactive stories, with different scenes: each scene requires a correct answer. The player replies to the system using the tangible object, one of them is connected with the right answer. Two stories in Italian were applied in this study called "La piccola avventura di Teo (The little Teo's adventure)" and "Una strana conchiglia (A strange seashell)". The authors developed the stories with a parallel scheme, then the order in which the narrator's request was made follows a pre-established order, identical for both stories. The stimuli presented to the user that refers to the right answer covers different senses: olfactory, manipulative/tactile, visual and auditory.

The scheme of right tangible answers for the two stories is the following:

- A tangible object representing the main character in the story
- A tangible object representing a hobby of the main character
- An olfactory stimulus
- A sound stimulus
- A tactile stimulus

- A tangible coloured card
- An olfactory stimulus
- A sound stimulus
- A tangible object representing a character in the story

The stories are as exercises of the STELT viewer application[1] that runs on AndroidOS.

The hardware of the application are the tangible objects itself and the digital component of the system.

The tangible objects, powered with NFC tags for their recognitions, are: 1 starting card, 2 dolls, 2 puppets, 2 balls of wool, 1 seashell, 1 beach bucket, 4 olfactory jars, 4 cylindrical sound boxes, 3 coloured cards, 2 tactile jars (Fig. 1).

a)   b)

Fig. 1. a) objects used for the Story1; b) objects used for the Story2

The digital side of the application runs on an Android smartphone Redmi Note 8 Pro mirrored in a personal computer with a WindowsOS and displayed in an interactive whiteboard available in the classes. The smartphone played as the system that recognizes the tangible objects, exploiting the NFC antenna inside the phone. The user interacts with the system by taking the object he/she considers the right answer and placing it on the back of the smartphone, that sends the recognition of the object to the application, allowing the physical interaction with the story. It recalls the same methodology applied by Ponticorvo et al. (2018).

2.2.2 Questionnaires

The tools used for data collection during the experimental condition were: Observation grids compiled by the experimenter acting as observer; Questionnaire on the content of the story, to evaluate the knowledge acquired on the story just heard; System Usability Scale (SUS; Brooke, 1996) to evaluate the usability of the tool based on TUI; Questionnaire to collect information on the acceptability, experience of use and inclusiveness of the activity; and Structured interview addressed to teachers to collect their opinions and observations on the use of TUI in the classroom.

---

[1] https://play.google.com/store/apps/details?id=it.smarted.steltviewer&hl=es_co.

As far as the control condition is concerned, the tools used during the control condition were: Observation grids compiled by the experimenter acting as observer; Questionnaire on the content of the story, to evaluate the knowledge acquired on the story just heard; and Questionnaire to collect pupils' opinion on the lesson.

All the tools used are described in detail in the next paragraph.

3 Results

3.1 Qualitative Analyses and Results of Focus Groups

All the focus groups have been transcribed and analysed with a bottom up approach in order to depict the recurrent and significant themes raised by participants, the interviewer's questions grid served as frame to create macro categories for the specific themes; in the following table are reported the four macro categories with themes and few related examples.

Macro category	Main Theme	Example
Difficulties in the school setting of students with Specific Learning Disabilities (SLD)	Difficulty in maths, technical, logical or scientific subjects	*"Difficoltà nelle materie tecniche, […] tutte le materie che predispongono a fare calcoli."* [Difficulties in technical subjects…all subjects that foreseen doing the math] *"Per quanto riguarda il DSA, ho notato che le maggiori difficoltà le trovano nelle materie scientifiche economiche, soprattutto in matematica."* [Talking about pupils with learning disabilities, I've noticed that the subjects they struggled the most with are those in the scientific-economic area, especially maths]
Teachers' difficulties in teaching	The need for specific and individualised learning methods	*"Spesso c'è la tendenza a non tarare l'intervento sullo studente proponendo una metodologia standard a tutti, mentre dovrebbe essere studiata quella che è più adatta al singolo studente."* [Often there's a tendency not to tailor the intervention on the students' needs and to use standard methods instead, whereas it would be better to find the best (strategy) for each student]

(continued)

(continued)

Macro category	Main Theme	Example
Educational and learning tools already known for students with SLD	Mind maps	*"Facciamo le mappe concettuali, così per loro è più facile orientarsi e ricordare le cose principali."* [We make mind maps, so that it easier for them to remember the main concepts]
Applicability of Tangible User Interfaces (TUI) as educational tool	Motivation; creation of link between abstract and concrete concepts; storing capability	*"le TUI mi piacciono perché si associa l'aspetto concreto, questo è attivante per la persona, dà anche una sensazione di potenza."* [I like TUIs because they give you the chance to do an association to the concrete side (of a concept), this is activating for the person (that uses it), it also gives you a feeling of power] *"Possono impattare anche sulla motivazione, perché magari, avere un qualcosa di interessante che stimoli anche il gioco, può coinvolgere lo studente [...] permette di associare lo studio ad un'attività piacevole e non ad un'attività pesante"* [they may have an impact on motivation, because having something interesting that the student link to a playful activity may engage them (…) it allows to link studying to a pleasant activity instead of a boring one]

Participants across several focus groups agreed regarding the feasibility of TUI as an educational tool especially suitable for the use into primary schools; this led to the tool design and planning and to the second implementation phase.

3.2 Observation

With regard to the second phase, from the observation conducted in the classroom, in the two conditions, the following main elements emerged:

1) During the experimental condition, the participants were respectful of their turn and maintained an excellent level of attention to the activity. In some cases, they tried to help comrades who were in difficulty, warning them if they were oriented towards the choice of the wrong object.

2) The stimuli towards which the participants showed greater enthusiasm were the olfactory ones and the smells. For these stimuli, collaboration was greater, there was greater confrontation between pupils in choosing the right object and more time was taken to make a decision.
3) Compared to the experimental condition, in the control condition, the pupils were more distracted from the surrounding environment.
4) By focusing on pupils with SEN, they showed the same level of participation as their peers and were included in the decision-making processes necessary to choose the right object.

3.3 Questionnaire on the Story Content

In the third phase, data on the knowledge acquired was collected through ad hoc questions related to the content of the stories. The questions were structured in a parallel way for the two stories, that is, while requiring a different answer in terms of content, they were structured in a similar way to limit the differences. The questionnaire on the acquired knowledge required the pupils to answer 10 open-ended questions, such as: "Who is the protagonist of the story?", "How was Teo/Lisa described?".

For each answer a score was assigned based on the following criteria: 0 in case of missing or totally wrong answer; 0.5 in the event of an answer that is not entirely correct, incomplete or imprecise; 1 in case of correct answer.

The total score out of 10 was calculated for each pupil, given by the sum of the scores attributed to the individual questions, and for each class, the mean was calculated for each of the two conditions. As reported in Table 1, the data collected show Class1 obtained on average a higher score in the control condition than in the experimental condition with TUI. In contrast, Class2 showed higher scores in the TUI condition than in the control condition.

One of the possible explanations for this difference could be linked to a technical problem that occurred during the experimental condition in Class1. The problem concerned the speed with which the story resumed immediately after identifying the object responding to the delivery and it may have affected the ability to understand the history of the pupils. This same limitation in the functionality of the prototype was instead eliminated in the experimental condition with Class2, adding a time frame before the story resumed in the narrative, after identifying the correct object.

Based on this consideration, a one-tailed Student's t test was performed to compare the means of the two conditions (experimental and control). The test was performed both on the data obtained from the whole sample (including both Class1 and Class2), and on the data obtained only from Class2.

The t test showed that the means of the experimental condition and the control condition did not differ significantly, neither considering the whole sample ($p = .42$), nor considering only Class2 ($p = .15$) (see Table 1).

This means that the condition with TUI is not associated with better outcomes in terms of understanding, compared to the traditional condition. Therefore, the results indicate that lessons with TUI and traditional lessons have an equivalent effect on pupils' learning.

Table 1. Means and standard deviations for each condition and t-test results

	Class1 TUI condition	Class1 control condition	Class2 TUI condition	Class2 control condition	Total sample TUI condition	Total sample control condition
M	5.75	6.12	6.92	6.27	6.34	6.20
SD	1.76	1.61	1.40	1.79	1.58	1.70
p-value (t test)	/		.15		.42	

3.4 Usability

The usability data of the tool were collected through the *System Usability Scale* (SUS; Brooke, 1996), which was translated using the back translation technique. Originally, it was intended to be administered at the end of usability tests on old computers, today it is used in a variety of contexts. It consists of 10 statements, for each statement the participants must provide a degree of agreement on a 5-point Likert scale, ranging from 1 (disagree) to 5 (completely agree). The SUS has its own scoring protocol that allows each subject to have a score that varies between a minimum of "0" and a maximum of "100." The mean of the global values obtained by the SUS represents the average level of satisfaction of the sample.

In the specific case of the following study, the SUS was administered to a sample of 35 children, since the scoring of the SUS is only possible having completed the questionnaire in full, the incomplete questionnaires were eliminated: this reduced the sample from 35 to 32 subjects. The mean of the scores obtained by the sample is 79.27 with a standard deviation of 22.19.

Through the reading tables of the SUS scores proposed by Sauro and Lewis (2016), it is possible to place each score within specific percentile ranges.

With regard to the sample considered, out of 32 subjects 26 obtained a score higher than 68, that is a score higher than that obtained by 50% of the subjects on which the normative data were collected.

Of the subjects with above average scores, 10 achieved a SUS score greater than 96% of the subjects on whom the normative data was collected, showing a high level of usability of the tool (see Fig. 2).

3.5 Acceptability and Experience of Use

To evaluate the acceptability of the activity and the experience of use, the pupils were asked to answer a questionnaire containing questions such as "how much did you like this activity?", "Were you bored during this activity?", To each statement the subjects were asked to answer on a four-step scale ranging from 1 (not at all) to 5 (very much). These are questions created ad hoc for this study, given the lack of validated tools in the literature that would allow us to evaluate these dimensions.

The answers given generally showed high levels of satisfaction with the instrument based on the TUI.

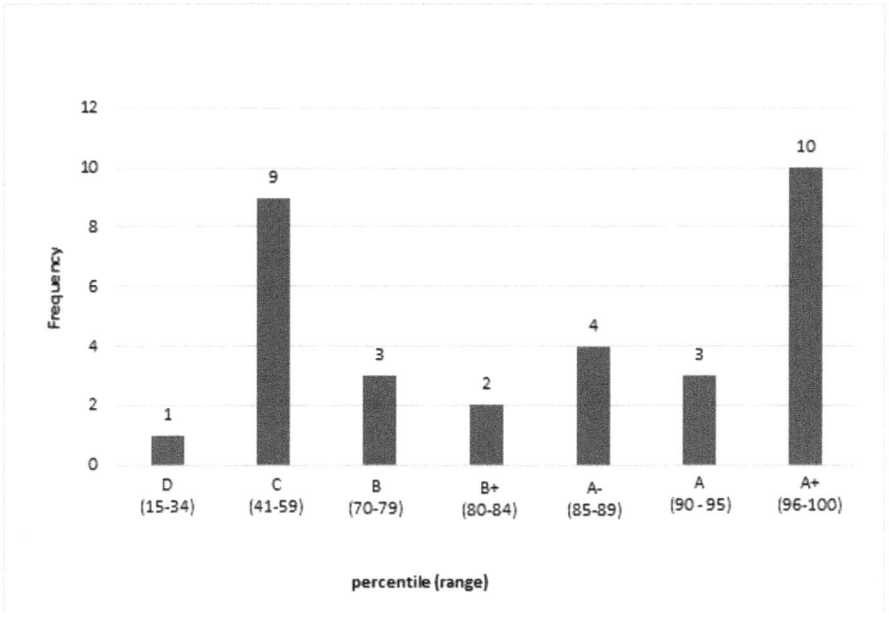

Fig. 2. Frequency of SUS results in percentile

97% of subjects reported that they wanted to repeat a lesson with the TUI and 97.5% reported that they liked the activity very much.

75% of the pupils reported that they were not bored at all and 72.2% that they were not distracted at all, suggesting that this type of activity is perceived as highly attractive and capable of sustaining attention.

In addition, 80% of respondents reported being able to stay focused from very to very much.

Finally, the answers given regarding the TUI lesson and regarding the traditional lesson were compared.

The results show that while for the first two questions, the pupils scored higher in the traditional condition. The remaining three questions, on the other hand, move more in favour of the lesson with the TUI (see Table 2).

3.6 Inclusivity

The questions used to collect data on the inclusive potential of the activity were extracted from the *Questionnaire to detect the inclusive quality of the school*, developed and validated in Italy by Ferrara and Pedone (2018).

This tool, in its integral form, allows an evaluation in two macro-areas and in seven dimensions. Among the factors considered we find: inclusive cultures, inclusive policies, inclusive practices, support for pupils, elements of inclusion in teaching and working with others.

Given the purposes of this study, only the items that referred to the inclusiveness of teaching and working with others were selected.

Table 2. Comparison between the lesson with TUI and the traditional lesson.

Questions	Lesson with TUI	Traditional lesson
How did you like this lesson?	4,22	4,83
Were you able to stay focused during the lesson?	3,92	4,31
How bored did you get during this lesson?	1,54	1,61
Did you get distracted during the lesson?	1,62	1,64
Did you have a hard time answering questions about the story?	1,70	2,42

As proposed by the authors, each answer was assigned a value in the following way: very much = 5, enough = 4, little = 3, not at all = 2, I need more information = 1.

The results of the study show that all the averages of the answers for each question, except for the questions "During the lesson we were encouraged to collaborate with classmates" and "During the lesson we shared what we knew among us pupils" obtained a score between 4 and 5; The only two questions whose average score does not fall within the 4–5 range fall instead into the 3–4 one, i.e. they correspond to an answer that is somewhere between "enough" and "a lot". Furthermore, even the average score obtained by each subject is between 4 and 5, this means that on average each subject has answered each question with a score that goes towards the highest inclusivity scores.

Furthermore, another interesting fact regarding the inclusive potential of the activity derives from the answers given by the pupils to the question "what did you like most about this activity?". To this question, the answer that received a higher percentage of choice was precisely "working with others", chosen by 80.6% of respondents.

3.7 Interviews with Teachers

Finally, in the fourth phase, the (three) teachers who participated in the realisation of the activities were offered to participate in structured interviews. The interviews covered three main aspects: the evaluation of the teaching experience with the TUI; whether, and how, TUI can foster inclusivity; the possible limits of TUI use in the school setting.

Overall, the opinion expressed by the teachers on the experience with the TUI was positive. All three interviewees highlighted the attractive potential of TUI and their ability to make learning fun, and their impact on the motivation and attention of learners.

In terms of inclusion, the proposed activity was considered suitable for everyone, in particular for students with Specific Learning Disabilities (SLDs), given the ability to make them keep a constant focus on the storytelling.

Furthermore, in all the interviews there was agreement on the fact that a pro of TUI lies in the fact that they can make abstract ideas/concepts concrete, which is an aspect that usually traditional teaching methods do not have.

As for the limits and perplexities, they mostly concerned the possibility that the alleged positive effects could be reduced or disappear in the case of prolonged exposure to this type of experience. According to the teachers, the novelty element could play an essential role in decreasing the usefulness of this type of tool.

4 Discussion

The current investigation aimed at evaluating the effects of multisensory digital storytelling using tangible user interfaces on learning, in terms of acquired knowledge about a story, compared to traditional storytelling. While it was not found a statistically significant difference between the two conditions (indicating that lessons with TUI and traditional lessons have an equivalent effect on pupils' learning), data on usability and acceptability of the TUI-based tool showed a great appreciation by both teachers and students. The latter also declared they had fun and got distracted very little during the lesson. The stimuli towards which the participants showed greater enthusiasm were the olfactory ones and the smells, which are the sensory elements less stimulated during traditional teaching. Elements of the storytelling that were related to hearing and sight, more stimulated in traditional lessons, obtained lower scores – meaning lower appreciation. The role of fun and enjoyment is seen in the literature as a natural and important part of the learning process for children. For example, in a field study, Long (2007) found that the most common motivation for participating in a game-based coding experience was to have fun, and her study results suggested that having fun while learning results in a higher learning effort to be committed. Other studies reported an improvement in their attitudes towards the taught subjects and positive change in learning outcomes (e.g., Apter et al., 2020; Papavlasopoulou et al., 2018, Sáez-López et al., 2016). Even though our results did not show any differences in pupils' rate of right responses right after the experimental condition, a difference might be seen in content retention in the long run. However, the study design does not permit to collect data in this regard. Future studies using a longitudinal design should focus on the effect of TUI-based tools in learning retention rates. Longitudinal studies would also permit to assess whether the greater engagement to the lesson that was found in this study would diminish with time; and whether the 'wow-effect' of an unusual tool for teaching would diminish too, maybe in favour of a greater focus on academic content.

Looking at this study with a critical eye, it is possible to identify other limitations that can, however, be considered as a starting point for future study projects in the same field. The pandemic situation and the rules in force in schools connected to it, impacted both on the possibility of recruiting a larger sample and on some aspects of the activity carried out in the classroom, such as, for example, the inability to make use of taste or the fact that the use of face masks could have had an impact on non-verbal communication between students and therefore on group dynamics. Future studies should use a larger sample and a more controlled setting in order to increase the generalizability of the results.

Another element to take into consideration is the presence of the teacher in the classroom during the administration to the pupils of the questionnaires regarding the activity. Several times the pupils asked the experimenter to be reassured that the teacher would not have read their answers. This may imply that especially the items on attention and concentration during the lesson could have been partly influenced from the pupils' concern of making a bad impression on the teacher.

Another limitation might have been the fact that some of the items of the System Usability Scale resulted to be difficult to understand by some of the pupils, even after the experimenter and teachers' explanations. Future studies should adapt and validate SUS in a children sample.

5 Conclusions

Taking into consideration the results that emerged from this study, we may consider the two teaching methods investigated as equivalent in terms of learning potential, intended as the pupils' ability to acquire knowledge when listening to a story. This makes the multisensory digital storytelling based on TUIs a valid alternative to traditional methods, with the addition of a stimulation of the senses of touch and smell, that are usually not stimulated at all. The appreciation shown by the pupils towards this experience highlights how TUIs can actually be a support to the possibility of building knowledge in different ways – following a Montessori approach.

Data on usability and acceptability of the TUI-based tool showed a great appreciation by both teachers and students. These elements should not be ignored, seeing that a teaching tool, albeit attractive, needs to have characteristics that make it easily usable by the user it is intended for.

The last element to consider concerns the elements that emerged from the questionnaire on inclusion, it should not be forgotten that one of the objectives of this study is to investigate the possible effect of the multisensory storytelling tool on inclusion, especially on the inclusion of subjects with SEN. The questions on inclusion highlighted how this type of activity fostered teamwork and collaboration among pupils.

All these elements can be considered the starting point for further studies rather than an arrival point.

The one proposed through the multisensory storytelling tool is just one of the possible variations through which the potential of technologies based on TUI can be exploited. The results of this study have an exploratory scope, their effective relevance lies in considering them the starting point for investigating new ways of teaching, which can be, at the same time, useful with respect to the teaching objective par excellence, which is to learn but, at the same time, they can also be well-liked by all pupils and become a means by which to encourage the creation of an inclusive environment for all.

References

Alibali, M.W., Nathan, M.J.: Embodiment in mathematics teaching and learning: evidence from learners' and teachers' gestures. J. Learn. Sci. **21**(2), 247–286 (2012)

Antle, A.N., Wise, A.F.: Getting down to details: using theories of cognition and learning to inform tangible user interface design. Interact. Comput. **25**(1), 1–20 (2013)

Apter, B., Sulla, F., Swinson, J.: A review of recent large-scale systematic UK classroom observations, method and findings, utility and impact. Educ. Psychol. Pract. (2020). https://doi.org/10.1080/02667363.2020.1802233

Brooke, J.: SUS-A quick and dirty usability scale. Usability Eval. Ind. **189**(194), 4–7 (1996)

Bruke, B.: Gamify: How Gamification Motivates People to Do Extraordinary Things. Routledge, New York (2014)

Christopoulos, A., Sprangers, P.: Integration of educational technology during the Covid-19 pandemic: an analysis of teacher and student receptions. Cogent Educ. **8**(1), 1964690 (2021)

Csìkszentmihalyi, M., Csikzentmihaly, M.: Flow: The Psychology of Optimal Experience, vol. 1990. Harper & Row, New York (1990)

Curenton, S.M., Craig, M.J., Flanigan, N.: Use of decontextualized talk across story contexts: How oral storytelling and emergent reading can scaffold children's development. Early Educ. Dev. **19**(1), 161–187 (2008)

Di Fuccio, R.: I sensi nel digitale. Le Tangible User Interfaces innovano la pratica pedagogica. Progedit, Bari (2022)

Di Fuccio, R. , Ponticorvo, M., Ferrara, F., Miglino, O.: Digital and multisensory storytelling: narration with smell, taste and touch. In: European Conference on Technology Enhanced Learning, pp. 509–512. Springer, Cham (2016). https://doi.org/10.1007/978-3-319-45153-4_51

Ferrara, G., Pedone, F.: L'inclusione vista dagli alunni: costruzione e validazione del questionario per rilevare la qualità inclusiva della scuola. L'Integrazione Scolastica e Sociale **17**(4), 357–374 (2018)

Fishkin, K.P.: A taxonomy for and analysis of tangible interfaces. Pers. Ubiquit. Comput. **8**(5), 347–358 (2004)

Griffin, T.M., Hemphill, L., Camp, L., Wolf, D.P.: Oral discourse in the preschool years and later literacy skills. First Lang. **24**(2), 123–147 (2004)

Haven, K.: Story Proof: The Science Behind the Startling Power of Story. Greenwood Publishing Group (2007)

Ishii, H., Ullmer, B.: Tangible bits: towards seamless interfaces between people, bits and atoms. In: Proceedings of the ACM SIGCHI Conference on Human factors in computing systems, pp. 234–241 (1997)

Kamei-Hannan, C., Chang, Y.C., Fryling, M.: Using a multisensory storytelling approach to improve language and comprehension: a pilot study. Br. J. Vis. Impair. **40**(2), 175–186 (2022)

Krestanova, A., Cerny, M., Augustynek, M.: Development and technical design of tangible user interfaces in wide-field areas of application. Sensors **21**(13), 4258 (2021)

Limone, P., Toto, G.A.: Psychological and emotional effects of digital technology on children in Covid-19 pandemic. Brain Sci. **11**(9), 1126 (2021)

Limone, P., Di Fuccio, R.: teleXbe-2021–The balance distance and face-to-face learning: a field for the discussion of scientific evidence. In: Technology Enhanced Learning Environments for Blended Education-The Italian e-Learning Conference 2021, vol. 3025, pp. 1–5. Ceur (2021)

Liu, C.C., Lu, K.H., Wu, L.Y., Tsai, C.C.: The impact of peer review on creative self-efficacy and learning performance in Web 2.0 learning activities. J. Educ. Technol. Soc. **19**(2), 286–297 (2016)

Long, J.: Just For Fun: using programming games in software programming training and education. J. Inf. Technol. Edu. Res. **6**(1), 279–290 (2007)

Maestri, A., Polsinelli, P., Sassoon, J.: Giochi da prendere sul serio: gamification, storytelling e game design. FrancoAngeli (2018)

Miglino, O., Di Ferdinando, A., Schembri, M., Caretti, M., Rega, A., Ricci, C.: STELT (smart technologies to enhance learning and teaching): a toolkit devoted to produce augmented reality applications for learning teaching and playing. Sistemi Intelligenti **25**(2), 397–404 (2013)

Navan, A.A., Khaleghi, A.: Using gamification to improve the education quality of children with autism. Revista científica **37**, 90–106 (2020)

Novakovic, N., Milovancevic, M.P., Dejanovic, S.D., Aleksic, B.: Effects of Snoezelen—Multisensory environment on CARS scale in adolescents and adults with autism spectrum disorder. Res. Dev. Disabil. **89**, 51–58 (2019)

OECD: Learning remotely when schools close: how well are students and schools prepared? Insights from PISA (OECD policy responses to coronavirus, COVID-19). Organisation for Economic Co-operation and development (2020)

Papavlasopoulou, S., Sharma, K., Giannakos, M.N.: How do you feel about learning to code? Investigating the effect of children's attitudes towards coding using eye-tracking. Int. J. Child-Comput. Interact. **17**, 50–60 (2018)

Ponticorvo, M., Di Fuccio, R., Ferrara, F., Rega, A., Miglino, O.: Multisensory educational materials: five senses to learn. In: International Conference in Methodologies and intelligent Systems for Technology Enhanced Learning, pp. 45–52. Springer, Cham (2018). https://doi.org/10.1007/978-3-319-98872-6_6

Reese, E., Suggate, S., Long, J., Schaughency, E.: Children's oral narrative and reading skills in the first 3 years of reading instruction. Read. Writ. **23**(6), 627–644 (2010)

Reese, E., Yan, C., Jack, F., Hayne, H.: Emerging identities: narrative and self from early childhood to early adolescence. In: Narrative development in adolescence, pp. 23–43. Springer, Boston, MA (2010). https://doi.org/10.1007/978-0-387-89825-4_2

Sáez-López, J.M., Román-González, M., Vázquez-Cano, E.: Visual programming languages integrated across the curriculum in elementary school: A two year case study using "Scratch" in five schools. Comput. Educ. **97**, 129–141 (2016)

Sauro, J., Lewis, J.R.: Quantifying the User Experience: Practical Statistics for User Research. Morgan Kaufmann (2016)

Schleicher, A.: The Impact of COVID-19 on Education: Insights from "Education at a Glance 2020". OECD Publishing (2020)

Somma, F., Di Fuccio, R., Lattanzio, L., Ferretti, F.: Multisensorial tangible user interface for immersive storytelling: a usability pilot study with a visually impaired child. In: teleXbe (2021)

Starcic, A.I., Cotic, M., Zajc, M.: Design-based research on the use of a tangible user interface for geometry teaching in an inclusive classroom. Br. J. Edu. Technol. **44**(5), 729–744 (2013)

Sulla, F., Ragni, B., D'Angelo, M., Rollo, D.: Teachers' emotions, technostress, and burnout in distance learning during the COVID-19 pandemic. In: Proceedings of the Third Workshop on Technology Enhanced Learning Environments for Blended Education, 10–11 June 2022, Foggia, Italy (2022)

Topping, K.J.: Trends in peer learning. Educ. Psychol. **25**(6), 631–645 (2005)

Vally, Z., Murray, L., Tomlinson, M., Cooper, P.J.: The impact of dialogic book-sharing training on infant language and attention: a randomized controlled trial in a deprived South African community. J. Child Psychol. Psychiatry **56**(8), 865–873 (2015)

Van Puyenbroeck, J., Maes, B.: A review of critical, person-centred and clinical approaches to reminiscence work for people with intellectual disabilities. Int. J. Disabil. Dev. Educ. **55**(1), 43–60 (2008)

Wilson, M.: Six views of embodied cognition. Psychon. Bull. Rev. **9**(4), 625–636 (2002)

Zuckerman, O.: Designing digital objects for learning: lessons from Froebel and Montessori. Int. J. Arts Technol. **3**(1), 124–135 (2010)

Virtual Reality and Learning in Children with SEN

Alessandro Frolli[1(✉)], Clara Esposito[2], Francesco Cerciello[2], Sonia Ciotola[2], Angelo Rega[3], and M. C. Ricci[1]

[1] Disability Research Centre University of International Studies in Rome, 00147 Rome, Italy
{alessandro.frolli,m.ricci}@unint.eu
[2] FINDS-Italian Neuroscience and Developmental Disorders Foundation, 81040 Caserta, Italy
{clara.esposito,francesco.cerciello,
sonia.ciotola}@fondazionefinds.it
[3] Dipartimento di psicologia e scienze della salute, Pegaso University, Naples, Italy
angelo.rega@unipegaso.it

Abstract. Virtual reality (VR) and its use in education has long been discussed, one of the main challenges is that VR was unaffordable for educational institutes. However VR has evolved since then, the technology is up to date, cheaper and more accessible than it has ever been. This paper presents a study that examines the benefits of VR educational applications in comparison to the traditional learning application. We evaluate the impact of this analysis on a population on students with Special Education Needs (SEN) in learning History. We selected 150 subjects aged between 9 and 10 selected from 12 schools in the province of Caserta. By analyzing the results we have found that the participants in both VR-training and individual training with the educator showed better learning than the starting condition. Furthermore, we highlighted how the group with training in VR achieved better results than the group that had followed a traditional training.

With this study, we have highlighted how students are intrinsically motivated when learning takes place using VR, and the result obtained is manifested in terms of higher learning than less motivated students (who followed traditional training).

Keywords: Virtual reality · Children · Learning · Motivation · Special education needs · Socio-cultural disadvantage

1 Introduction

The rise of the digital revolution has changed and characterized our society in the last decade. This revolution has disrupted entire industries and job markets, leading individuals to either upgrade or transfer their skills in order to continue within their designated fields or transition to new workplace contexts. The labor market expects its employees to apply their knowledge to real-world settings, analyze and solve problems, connect decisions to actions, and be innovative and creative. In addition, the COVID-19 pandemic has exacerbated changes in the education landscape by enforcing an online and remote environment; physical distancing and other precautions require a shift to greater use of disruptive digital technologies augmented reality (e.g. virtual and augmented reality). This situation has shed a light on how technology is now crucial to enhance the performance and how is it essential. The confluence of these factors has led to a need for both individuals and higher education institutions to upgrade and adapt to new digital techniques and modalities book [1]. The school system often responds inadequately to the needs of the new generations and are scarcely able to understand the need of a teaching based on skills. In fact, we often see a school that continues to deal with knowledge, neglecting the know-how and, above all, the ability to contextualize both knowledge and know-how. The core of a regenerated school should be the ability to arouse motivation and interest in learning by transforming the mere notional knowledge into skills, creativity and problem-solving strategies. In this technological are we can see a school system based on conceptualizing and with a teaching plan based on the goal reaching. The school system is based of performance and sometime this causes differences between pupils. In the school world, these typical kind of issues are included in the Law 53/2003 (Ministerial Directive). These pupils are called SEN that means Special Educational Needs. For them, over the years, an ad hoc intervention has been designed that allows teachers to create a personalized teaching plan using specific tools because each child should have the opportunity to develop his/her potential to the fullest. Special Education Needs (SEN) refers to particular educational needs that students may manifest even for short periods only: "for biological, physiological, psychological or social reasons, which it is necessary that schools offer adequate and personalized responses. The SEN also includes students with problems related to social, economic, emotional, or difficulties due to lack of knowledge of Italian or students with problematic parents (not followed by the family, parents not present, depressed, separated or divorced, etc.). Technological tools have been proposed to help the needs of different student populations [2] like notebooks, tablets or mobile phones with specific app have replaced the classic paper notebooks, online classrooms and a personalized learning approach have been used to adapt education both to the difficulties of an historical period and to the specific preferences of each student [3]. Numerous studies over the past two decades have shown the advantages of using virtual and augmented reality in the classroom. One of their main strengths is that they transform the teacher's role from a provider of knowledge to a facilitator who helps students explore and learn [4]. This greatly complements constructivist learning theory because students feel empowered and engaged because they are in control of the learning process [5, 6]. Students can experientially learn and progress at their own rythm as they explore virtual environments and avoid situations where students fall behind in class and catch up the rest of the class [7]. Furthermore, virtual reality can help any type of students learn abstract concepts because they can experience and visualize these concepts in a virtual environment [8, 9]. In contrast with the traditional learning process which is usually language based, conceptual, and abstract, a virtual reality learning environment fosters active learning and helps students grasp abstract knowledge [10]. Low-spatial ability learners particularly benefit from virtual reality because the visualizations help lower the extraneous cognitive load of the learning objectives [11]. Virtual reality allows the user to comprehend systems or objects that are of widely different scales. In fact, VR learning environments can be customized to allow children to focus on their strengths rather than their weaknesses and complete tasks. It also offers the possibility to control the learning process. Therefore, in this study, we selected SEN children with sociocultural disadvantage. Meeting the needs of these children, developing skills and using the appropriate educational environment as a basis for the selection of materials and organizational goals. It is important to remember that the performance of these children varies greatly from individual to individual [12–14].

2 Materials and Methods

2.1 Participants

The sample consists of 150 subjects aged between 9 and 10 years old selected from 12 schools in the province of Caserta. The inclusion criteria were as follows: a) Age between 9 and 10 years, b) Absence of a SLD, c) Absence of other childhood neuropsychiatric conditions present in comorbidity, d) IQ between 85 and 100, c) SES score ≤ 1, that was indicative of socio-cultural disadvantage. After evaluating the possibility of inclusion in the sample, we divided the subjects into two groups consisting of 75 subjects each one. All subjects were at a social and cultural disadvantage and classified as SEN. This disadvantage condition was detected through the administration of SES. This condition of disadvantage was detected through a questionnaire administered Social Economic Scale (SES) to teachers who reported the socio-cultural condition and the environment of each individual pupil. Questionnaire scores ranged from 1 (very low condition) to level 3 (very high level). The average score obtained by Gr1 was 1.62 (SD = 0.54), while the average score obtained by Gr2 was 1.42 (SD = 0.59). The division into the two experimental groups was randomized: the subjects of both groups had the same inclusion criteria. The two groups have undergone two different types of treatment, as will be discussed in the next paragraph. The first experimental group consists of 75 subjects with an average age of 9.37 (SD = 0.39) of which 42 males and 33 females. The second experimental group consists of 75 subjects with an average age of 9.48 (SD = 0.34) of which 43 males and 32 females. Therefore, there were no age differences in the two groups. The data were collected at the laboratory of neuroscience, learning processes and Immersive VR of the university of international studies of Rome by psychologists qualified in collaboration with the regional school office (USR) and with the Federico II University of Naples and the university of studies of Campania Luigi Vanvitelli.

2.2 Evaluation Protocol

The protocol used to assess the inclusion criteria consists of the following tests Raven matrices [16] and Scale for socio-economic level assessment (SES) [15] and MT, AC-MT 6–11 [17] and BVSCO-II [18] to screen some specific learning difficulties:

SES. Self-administered questionnaire that makes it possible to collect information on the educational and occupational level of the parents and to indicate the position of the person or family within the social system. The socio-demographic questionnaire was completed to obtain an index of socio-economic level (SES calculated using the Hollingshead index) and other demographic and lifestyle variables for each pair of parents. The SES is a cultural and economic index calculated as a weighted average between the educational level and work of both parents [15].

Raven Matrices (CPM-Colored Progressive Matrices): Raven's progressive matrices measure non-verbal intelligence throughout the entire range of intellectual development, from childhood to maturity, regardless of cultural level. They are used within children between the ages of 3 and 11. Our protocol included only matrices A and B, extracted from standard test, with an additional test (AB) of 12 elements. Each sub-test required completing a series of figures with the missing one, comparing them to a model and judging their progress by an increasing degree of difficulty [16].

MT Tests: Test battery used to evaluate correctness, speed of reading and comprehension of the written text, which are considered basic skills transversal to the different school disciplines, ranging from the beginning of primary school up to the end of secondary school. Each stage requires 6 tests, which are administered in 2 phases during the year. These tests measure basic skills transversal to different school subjects. One test measures reading ability, and the other test measures reading comprehension. There are two reading comprehension tests, which evaluate the ability to comprehend written material. These tests require the subject to read aloud short text and measure their speed and accuracy. A child's text comprehension test looks at his or her ability to understand a text. In this test, children are asked to read a text and answer questions about it [17].

AC-MT Tests: Test battery for evaluating numerical and calculation skills in children aged 6 to 11 years. It allows collecting information related to four different indices: two refer to the accuracy variable (but are collected through an individual and a collective phase). These two indices allow evaluating the accuracy of the answers. However, the test does not evaluate how automated such competence is. The third index (speediness) evaluates the calculation speed, or the also called total time/latency time [18].

BVSCO: Comprehensive tool to evaluate all the aspects involved in the learning path of writing: graphism, spelling competence and the production of written text. The battery estimates the skills of the child for the entire school career of primary and secondary school grade. It is based on the spelling learning model, which provides that the child initially acquires the transformation mechanisms of the alphabetic phase and subsequently those relating to the spelling and lexical phase [19].

2.3 Procedure and Tasks

The subjects of this study were divided into two groups according to the type of learning training carried out. The first group performed training in history learning according to traditional methods: the subject was read by the student individually with the educator and the memorization was supported by a feedback process. At the end of the study, a questionnaire consisting of 10 questions was checked and a token economy was used for each correct answer reinforcing after 7 positive answers. The second group performed a training to learn History through the use of VR. This procedure involved some videos of the topic to be studied in 3D using a dedicated viewer. At the end of the exposure of the video was also carried out an assessment by a questionnaire and token as well. At T0, all the children had completed individual learning. At the end of the first four months, they completed a history questionnaire composed by 90 items to assess the starting level during individual learning. During 4 months (September-December) children who were divided into two groups, performed the two trainings for the learning of History. At T1 (beginning of January) all the children carried out a new questionnaire composed by 90 items with History topics studied during the 4 months of training. It was possible to assess between T0 and T1 whether there were differences in the percentage of correct answers.

2.4 Methods

Data analysis was performed using the SPSS 26.0 statistical survey software. Significance at the level of 5% ($p < 0.05$) has been accepted. We named G1 (Group 1 that did a traditional learning training) and G2 (Group 2 that did a learning training with virtual reality). We named T0 the measure of the learning training and T1 the measure of the learning training taken after 4 months. We used the student's t test, a parametric statistical test that can be used when two groups in comparison are independent of each other. Specifically, we used the t Test to be able to make comparisons between groups (scores of correct answers) at T0 and to check whether both groups were homogeneous before doing the learning training.

3 Results

The results showed that the scores ($t = -0.51$, $p = 0.88$) were not significant; this indicates that the two groups at T0 (before learning training) were homogeneous (Table 1).

Table 1. Comparison of two groups at T0

Groups	T0		t	p
	Means	SD		
1	49.12	1.87	−0.51	0.88
2	49.16	1.88		

We then compared Gr1 and Gr2 at T0 and T1 to assess whether there were improvements after learning training (variable within-time) and then compared both groups at T1 (variable between-group) to see which of the two treatments could allow a better acquisition. (Fig. 1). Therefore, we performed a two-way mixed ANOVA analysis 2*2: factor within the groups = time (T0 and T1) and factor between groups = group (Gr1 and Gr2). (Table 2).

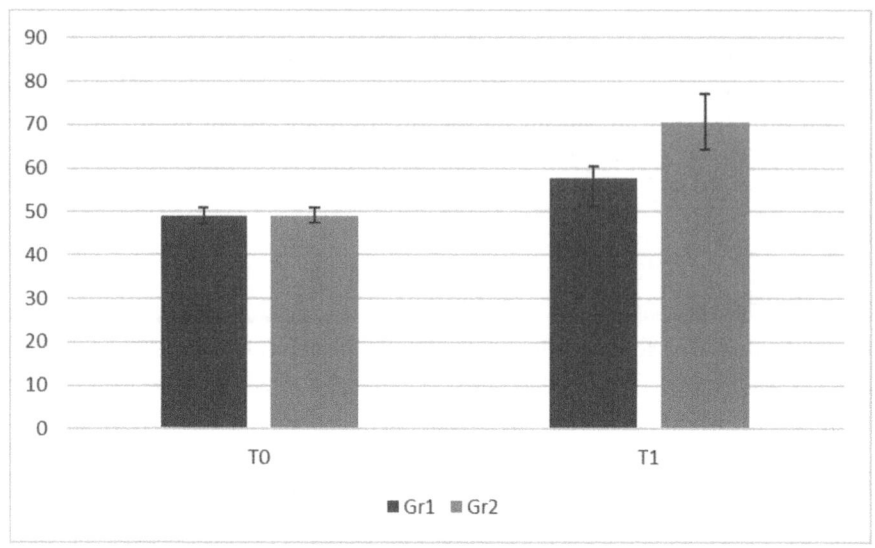

Fig. 1. Comparison of two groups between T0 and T1.

This analysis showed the following results:

Table 2. Interaction time*group.

Time	Group 1		Group 2		F	p
	Means	SD	Means	SD		
T0	49.12	1.87	49.16	1.88		
T1	57.72	2.64	70.56	6.4	71.794	< 0.05*

* *Statistical significance $p < 0.05$*

Interaction time*group is significant ($F 71.794$, $p<0.05$). This data indicates that there is a significant interaction between time and the type of treatment. More specifically, both treatments have a positive effect on the correct responses, but this is more significant for training with VR (Gr2) after training (T1) (Table 2 and Fig. 1).

4 Discussions

In this study we have analyzed both the educational applications such as the traditional one and the innovative one with the use of VR. We reported motivations for using VR technologies in education, as well as the issues and limitations associated with doing so. Our initial analysis into the applications and motivations of VR in education provided by authors in current scientific literature yielded some surprising findings [13]. Currently, VR apps are mostly used for training and simulation purposes. This means that there's a need for more studies on whether head-mounted displays make learning easier and more immersive. These tools are gain significant traction in education due to their ability to immerse learners in different scenarios. Many studies have found that new technologies like VR can improve education by increasing the learning possibilities. [20]. Considering the potential improvement of learning using VR, it is clear why researchers, organizations and educators are looking at this technology in recent times, trying to add an extra dimension to the class compared to both teaching and learning. Recently, virtual reality (VR) is increasingly being used in formal education as a tool for cognitive training and inquiry-based learning [21–23], while serving as an intervention tool for psychiatric disorders such as depression, anxiety, phobias, and anxiety [24]. Multiple research papers indicate that virtual reality technologies have potential as tools for special education. These studies mention students with physical disabilities and neurodevelopmental disorders who find unique applications for VR in their education. Additionally, publishing these studies indicate potential to improve cognitive difficulties, such as autism and ADHD, using VR [25–27]. However, VR-focused literature within the SEN involves little children from a worse sociocultural environment. Therefore, our study aims to implement VR within this specific category of social background [28, 29]. With this study we propose a novelty respect the VR using in the learning of history in a specific category of subjects (SEN).

The purpose of this study was to examine the impact of VR use on the learning of children with special educational needs by comparing teachers' individual learning training. Our results showed that participants learned better in both the VR training and the individual training with the educator than in the initial situation. Furthermore, it turns out that Gr2 (trained with VR) achieves better results than Gr1 (trained with Educator). In particular, we found that these children showed an increase in motivation to learn, especially intrinsic motivation related to the materials used and active participation in the learning environment, especially in Gr2. Indeed, VR training characterized by active participation and direct participation in the learning experience proved beneficial in increasing motivation, as highlighted in the same thread. We also observed how motivation changed in group 1 and group 2. Children who were trained by the use oh VR appeared very motivated, and this factor influenced positively the history learning.

5 Conclusions and Limitations

We set out to evaluate the differences in VR and traditional applications within the area of education. In order to accomplish this task, we had to make sure that both applications are being evaluated on the same terms in order to reach the most trustworthy and unbiased results.

Our analysis showed that students are intrinsically motivated, and the result is manifested in terms of higher learning than less motivated students (who followed a traditional training). Also based on previous literature, it can be hypothesized that if students are intrinsically motivated, cognitive resources are also more strongly included, which may lead to greater learning success. Educators tend to use VR solutions only in specific situations that require realistic simulations or for educational purposes. We also discovered that little of the work analyzed was actually grounded in solid pedagogical reasoning.

Additionally, many studies are driven by intrinsic factors, including the belief that students are motivated by the novelty of VR technology; this factor is likely to decrease with continued use. Our analysis into the reported issues and limitations of VR systems also yielded interesting results, with problems pertaining to cost, training and software and hardware usability accounting for much of the data. Particularly prevalent was the occurrence of software usability issues; occurring nearly twice as frequently as most of the other issue reported. Moreover, a limitation of our study in in the lack of follow-up on the maintenance of acquired knowledge that limits the generalization of the study.

References

1. Peisachovich, E.H., Dubrowski, A., Da Silva, C., Kapralos, B., Klein, J.E., Rahmanov, Z.: Using simulation-based methods to support demonstration of competencies required by microcredential courses. Cureus. **13**(8), e16908 (2021). https://doi.org/10.7759/cureus.16908. PMID:34513481;PMCID:PMC8418224
2. Collins, A., Halverson, R.: Rethinking Education in the Age of Technology: The Digital Revolution and Schooling in America. Teachers college press, vol. 192 (2018)
3. Di Natale, A.F., Repetto, C., Riva, G.: Immersive virtual reality in K-12 and higher education: a 10-year systematic review of empirical research. Br. J. Educ. Technol. **51**(6), 20062033 (2020)
4. Youngblut, C.: Educational uses of virtual reality technology. No. IDA-D-2128. Institute for Defense Analyses Alexandria VA (1998)
5. Dede, C.: Planning for neomillennial learning styles. Educ. Q. **28**(1), 7–12 (2005)
6. Antonietti, A., et al.: Virtual reality and hypermedia in learning to use a turning lathe. J. Comput. Assist. Learn. **17**(2), 142–155 (2001)
7. Jonassen, D.H., Peck, K.L., Wilson, B.G.: Learning with technology: a constructivist perspective (1999)
8. Sala, N.: Applications of virtual reality technologies in architecture and in engineering. Int. J. Space Technol. Manag. Innov. (IJSTMI) **3**(2), 78–88 (2013)
9. Rosenblum, L.J., Cross, R.A.: The challenge of virtual reality. Visual. Model., 325–399 (1997)
10. Ray, A.B., Deb, S.: Smartphone based virtual reality systems in classroom teaching—A study on the effects of learning outcome. Technology for Education (T4E). In: 2016 IEEE Eighth International Conference. IEEE (2016)
11. Lee, E.A.L., Wong, K.W., Fung, C.C.: How does desktop virtual reality enhance learning outcomes? A structural equation modeling approach. Comput. Educ. **55**(4), 1424–1442 (2010)
12. Goldin, C., Katz, L.F.: The race between education and technology. In: Inequality in the 21st Century. (1st edn.) Routledge, pp: 49–54 (2018)
13. Kavanagh, S., Luxton-Reilly, A., Wuensche, B., Plimmer, B.: A systematic review of virtual reality in education. Themes Sci. Technol. Educ. **10**(2), 85–119 (2017)
14. Boyles, B.: Virtual reality and augmented reality in education. Center For Teaching Excellence, United States Military Academy, West Point (2017)
15. Venuti, P., Senese, V.P.: Un questionario di autovalutazione degli stili parentali: uno studio su un campione ita-liano. G. Ital. Psicol. **34**(3), 677–698 (2007)
16. Raven, J.C.: Coloured Progressive Matrices Sets A, Ab, B. Manual Sections 1 & 2; Oxford Psychologists Press. Oxford (1995)
17. Cesare Cornoldi, Alvaro Pra, Baldi,David Giofrè, Prove MT Avanzate-3-Clinica, Giunti
18. Cornoldi C, Lucangeli D, Bellina M. AC-MT 6–11. Assessment test of calculation skills and problem solving. MT Group. Erickson Editions (2nd edn). Edizioni Erickson 2012
19. Cornoldi C., Re A., Tressoldi P.E., BVSCO-2 Valutazione della Scrittura e della Competenza Ortografica, Giunti (2013)

20. Kaye, A.T., Rumble, G.: Distance Teaching for Higher and Adult Education. (1st edn.) Routledge (2018)
21. Papanastasiou, G., Drigas, A., Skianis, C., Lytras, M., Papanastasiou, E.: Virtual and augmented reality effects on K-12, higher and tertiary education students' twenty-first century skills. Virtual Real. **23**, 425–436 (2019)
22. Daniela, L., Aierken, Y.: The educational perspective on virtual reality experiences of cultural heritage. In: Daniela, L. (ed.) New Perspectives on Virtual and Augmented Reality: Finding New Ways to Teach in a Transformed Learning Environment Taylor & Francis: Abingdon, UK, (2020). ISBN 9780367432119
23. Daniela, L., Lytras, M.D.: Editorial: themed issue on enhanced educational experience in virtual and augmented reality. Virtual Real. **23**, 325–327 (2019)
24. Cieślik, B., Mazurek, J., Rutkowski, S., Kiper, P., Turolla, A., Szczepańska-Gieracha, J.: Virtual reality in psychiatric disorders: a systematic review of reviews. Complementary Ther. Med. **52**, 102480 (2020)
25. Drigas, A., Mitsea, E., Skianis, C.: Neuro-linguistic programming, positive psychology & VR in special education. Sci. Electron. Arch. **15**, 30–39 (2022)
26. Bravou, V., Oikonomidou, D., Drigas, A.S.: Applications of virtual reality for autism inclusion. A review. Retos Nuevas Tend. Educ. Fís. Deporte Recreación **45**, 779–785 (2022)
27. Drigas, A., Mitsea, E., Skianis, C.: The role of clinical hypnosis and VR in special education. Int. J. Recent Contrib. Eng. Sci. IT (iJES) **9**, 4–17 (2021)
28. Makransky, G., Borre-Gude, S., Mayer, R.E.: Motivational and cognitive benefits of training in immersive virtual reality based on multiple assessments. J. Comput. Assist. Learn. **35**(6), 691–707 (2019)
29. Radianti, J., Majchrzak, T.A., Fromm, J., et al.: A systematic review of immersive virtual reality applications for higher education: design elements, lessons learned, and research agenda. Comput. Educ. **147**, 103778 (2020)

Game-Based Assessment: Between Goals and Psychometric Rigor

Gianluigi Serio[1(✉)], Michela Balsamo[2], and Leonardo Carlucci[1]

[1] Department of Humanities (DISTUM), University of Foggia, Foggia, Italy
gianluigi.serio@unifg.it
[2] "G. d'Annunzio" University of Chieti-Pescara, Chieti, Italy

Abstract. High-quality psychometric assessment is essential in several domains, e.g., in education, where it is used for evaluating students' knowledge and skill. However, traditional psychometric methods are often challenged due to various undesirable characteristics associated with their use in the real world (i.e., anxiety and social desirability bias). To overcome these limitations and to provide more meaningful and realistic assessment, a class of game-related assessments has been developed (Game-Based Assessments – GBAs). However, to develop reliable and scientifically based game tools, these new approaches require addressing interdisciplinary challenges, where the clear definition of the target constructs, the soundness of psychometric techniques, and specific aims (e.g., game-based assessment vs. game-based learning) are of capital importance. Psychometric topics, such as reliability, validity, and traditional data analysis techniques, as well as methodological and developmental aspects of GBAs, will be examined with particular attention to the benefits and challenges these new game-based approaches are posing. Furthermore, this paper focuses on digital GBAs that offer new evaluation possibilities through process data and computational psychometrics approaches. Finally, we discuss preliminary efforts by psychometricians and game designers to overcome the pitfalls inherent in developing game-based assessment approaches.

Keywords: Game-Based Assessment · Psychometrics · Game-Based Learning · Gamification · Gameful

1 How to Define Game-Based Assessment

Developing valid and reliable psychometric assessment tools capable of effectively achieving the set purposes is crucial for different application contexts (e.g., education, psychological and clinical assessments). Traditional psychometric methods are often challenged due to various undesirable characteristics associated with their use in the real world. For example, tests measuring cognitive abilities tend to get poor user reactions and are not well received due to their abstract and non-contextualized design [1, 2]. These tasks are often susceptible to factors unrelated to the capabilities they are designed to investigate [3–5]. Furthermore, self-report noncognitive measures are vulnerable to various biases related to a people' ability to reflect upon themselves accurately and their motivation to do so honestly [6]. Typical pencil and paper assessments can be perceived as repetitive and boring [7], resulting in a limited ability to motivate participants [8, 9]. Many of these instruments have been developed for clinical purposes. Therefore, they are too easy for typical populations, reducing their discriminatory power because of the ceiling effect [10].

To overcome these limitations and to offer more meaningful and realistic assessments, a class of game-related assessments, called game-based assessments (GBAs), has been increasingly developed. These approaches have gamefulness as their primary purpose: to create an evaluation environment characterized by a gameful experience. A gameful experience is a psychological state realized by the interaction between a system (characterized by aims, rules, and challenges) and the person. This psychological state arises from the synergy of three psychological characteristics: i) perceiving presented goals to be non-trivial and achievable, ii) being motivated to pursue those goals under arbitrary externally-imposed constraints, and iii) believing that one's actions within these constraints are volitional [11]. In short, game-based assessment is an assessment method in which participants are evaluated while involved in a gameful experience. It should be differentiated GBAs from gameful design, which refers to practices by assessment professionals using game mechanics or other game concepts to guide their decision-making in the design of a GBA [12, 13]. An assessment designer might set out to create a new interview, multiple-choice assessment, situational judgment test, or any other method while integrating aspects of games research and practice; in this way, the new assessment was gamefully designed [14, 15]. Differently, assessment gamification is a redesign strategy in which developers use concepts derived from game design to extant assessment methods. For example, a multiple-choice personality assessment might be gamified by converting it into a story, a type of gamification called "*storification*" [16].

In summary, GBAs might reflect the result of gamification, the development of new dedicated assessment games [17], as well as a practice-based assessment of commercial games and video games (i.e., game-based intelligence assessment) [18–20]. Here, we focus on digital GBAs from a psychometric perspective. The advancement of digital games and computerization technologies has allowed, among other things, the structuring of complex stimuli, that would be impracticable in traditional evaluation [18]. In general, computer technology can make evaluation scores more objective, in part because of its ability to record metrics, such as reaction time [3]. Furthermore, emerging technologies, such as immersive virtual environments, have great potential to strengthen scientific inquiry skills in several application contexts [21, 22]. Modern GBAs might study and try to use these potentials best.

In many cases, a GBA has game mechanics similar to those found in commercial video games, such as interactivity with objects of the environment and with other characters, the personalization of avatars, the rankings, the levels, and a story [15, 23]. However, unlike a GBA, commercial video games are not developed to meet the psychometric requirements for a reliable assessment [36]. Moreover, commercial video games limit access to process data and do not offer the opportunity to modify the underlying code (nevertheless, see [18]). Finally, conventional commercial video games generally involve complex behaviors, the progression of skills, and an increase in the degree of challenge [24]. In a GBA, these aspects contribute to generate a gameful experience but, at the same time, can result to manifold psychometric problems [25]. For example, the progressive nature of the game experience can lead to changes in the covariances of errors over time [12]. Furthermore, the traditional psychometric assumption of unidimensionality becomes less sustainable in a GBA because observed gaming behaviors likely reflecting multiple traits [18]. On the other hand, developing a GBA, too simple to satisfy classical psychometric properties, could mean not producing any added value compared to a traditional assessment. Indeed, GBAs distance themselves from simple transpositions of traditional assessments into computerized assessments, as the latter merely represent the use of computer interfaces to administer test materials relative to paper-based tests permitting more interactive question types and the possibility to create sophisticated tests which include adaptive elements about different levels of integration between technology and assessment [26]. For these reasons, developing a GBA requires complex management of the conflicts between game design elements (e.g., mechanics, dynamics, aesthetics) [13] and psychometric rigor [27].

A GBA can generate meaningful scores mainly through two approaches that differentiate theory-driven-GBAs from data-driven-GBAs [17]. In a theory-driven GBA, the gaming experience must generate specific metrics related to the investigated trait. Content validation is achieved with the help of subject matter experts who assess the relevance between game behavior and a specific trait. In addition, it is necessary to empirically test the validity, for example, between the data collected with the GBA and other validated tools that measure that specific trait (and a different trait). Instead, a post-hoc scoring model is developed into a data-driven GBA, for example, through computational psychometry approaches [28]. In this case, developers try to generate many metrics for different purposes. One option is to use unorganized data directly collected by the GBA to build multiple cluster player profiles with unsupervised machine-learning approaches. A second possibility could be to use labeled data in supervised machine learning approaches to predict skills and other aspects of interest [12, 17]. These types of assessment data mining are much more common in game-based learning (GBL) [17, 29, 30]. GBLs represent the use of games to support and improve teaching and learning processes, as well as to engage users, who are the students, who develop a sense of accomplishment [31–33]. GBAs and GBLs differ from each other both from a psychometric perspective and in purposes. For example, a GBL mainly aims to improve performance during the various phases of the game [31]. On the contrary, in a GBA, the user performance must remain constant; otherwise, this poses a reliability problem. Indeed, psychometric tests are based on the assumption that traits are stationary over time, while score increasing during the game would imply that what the GBA is measuring is unstable [12]. However, some assumptions of a GBA are useful to verify both direct measures of learning (i.e., knowledge) and indirect measures (i.e., involvement and usability) [31]. By quantitatively measuring how users interact with a GBA or a GBL could be useful in informing game designers on methods to maximize engagement (i.e., multidimensional approach to engagement) [34]. Finally, differentiating specific goals can contribute to select the appropriate game genres [35, 36]. One GBA project could come close to measure cognitive abilities through the gameplay of a first-person shooter, while another could approach it through puzzles. Instead, a design meant to measure a personality trait could be completely different [17]. Therefore, the conclusions from one

GBA probably do not generalize to GBAs, making goal settings and design processes critical in their development.

2 GBAs: Benefits and Challenges

An ever-increasing volume of recent literature is exploring the use of GBAs across various psychometric settings, including cognitive assessment [1, 3, 16], personality assessment [37, 38], and assessment of perceptual capabilities [39, 40], in various application contexts (i.e., education, health care, and employee selection) [1, 36, 41]. This rapid and widespread diffusion poses its basis in the numerous benefits that can derive from using GBAs [42]. Indeed, a GBA can increase motivation and reduce anxiety during the assessment [43, 44] by engaging participants in more immersive, authentic, and meaningful environments, characterized by greater interactivity as compared to traditional assessment [3, 45, 46]. Moreover, engagement in a GBA can determine general positive feelings encouraging the emergence of flow experiences [47, 48]. Indeed, users sense time passing faster when immersed in gameplay [49]. In contrast to a standardized test, which only produces product data, a GBA also captures, stores, and shares massive amounts of user data (i.e., process/trace/in-game data: mouse clicks, keystrokes, navigational behavior, time stamps) [50–52], through advanced systems and innovative technologies that go beyond the traditional "*one-shot*" assessment measures [53]. GBAs are more appropriate as compared to traditional evaluations in assessing "*real world*" skills considered fundamental in a different context (i.e., education and health care) [45], such as creativity, critical thinking, and teamwork. Indeed, in addition to large amounts of data, GBAs can rely on complex problem-solving simulations characterized by real-time interactive possibilities among participants [54]. Another important aspect is that GBAs can reduce participants' falsification behaviors through, for example, a stealth approach [55]. The stealth approach aims to measure performance by unobtrusively logging user behaviors rather than explicitly asking to self-report their thoughts and behaviors [45]. In this way, a GBA can reduce the bias of users to respond in certain ways (e.g., for promoting a positive image about themselves, which is the tendency called social desirability). GBAs can maintain a high commitment during the evaluation, which reduces the likelihood of some candidates dropping out in the process and also increases the time that data can be collected [56, 57]. These goals could be achieved through gaming mechanics (i.e., by providing in-game feedback such as a badge or virtual prize). Finally, GBAs could be used to improve and increase the accessibility of assessments, for example, for people with disability, although this field is still in its infancy [58, 59].

Despite the benefits of applying GBAs, some challenges require further research [30]. GBAs need broader scientific rigor in proving the validity of their use as assessments [37]. In this regard, whether the psychometric standards developed for traditional assessments are entirely satisfied, even for validating GBAs is questionable [60]. This issue is particularly relevant for process data, which require, for example, soft-computing approaches (computational psychometry) [54]. Furthermore, there is the question of how to treat confounding variables specific to GBAs, such as psychomotor factors and familiarity with computer technology or games [20]. For example, some research on the GBAs found that prior gaming experience affected participants' performance in achieving good test results [27, 61]. Another aspect is that GBAs contain irrelevant factors, such as objects in the environment, the interface, or colors, to increase engagement or to create a more ecological assessment compared to the traditional test. These elements can introduce errors and noise into assessments, negatively impacting GBAs' sensitivity and specificity [45, 53]. There is also a risk that GBAs can be too engaging for some types of assessment. For example, in a study by Delisle, Braun [62], office tasks were implemented in a fast-paced GBA to test a group of ADHD users. These tasks required functions that are typically impaired in ADHD. The results have shown that users could easily carry out these tasks, suggesting that the GBA helped the users mask core deficits of ADHD.

Therefore, certain game features can undermine the scientific validity of GBAs for specific constructs [45]. Similar results could also suggest how to organize activities or educational environments concerning students' particular needs. Finally, specific design choices (i.e., degree of linearity of a GBA) or individual features of gameful experiences [11] could significantly modify the assessment results. These issues will require many studies in which single elements of GBAs will be systematically manipulated, taking into account the specific purposes of the different GBAs (i.e., A/B tests which compare different configurations of one game element controlling for other factors) [25]. Reliable and shared guidelines are urgent because developing a GBA is typically very expensive [37] and, therefore, not necessarily more cost-effective than the traditional evaluation [63, 64]. Some of these challenges will be further explored in the following paragraphs.

3 Psychometric Qualities in GBAs

Assessing the psychometric qualities of a GBA is a topic that requires special attention because poor psychometric qualities can invalidate all GBA development work. Indeed, a GBA that does not meet certain psychometric standards will be a game that returns numbers [17]. First, a key requirement of a GBA is its reliability. Reliability typically refers to the internal consistency with which test items measure overall competency and is usually calculated as various forms of intercorrelation coefficients [30, 65]. Classically, Cronbach's alpha is used for such purposes. However, this measure of reliability is not particularly adequate because it underestimates reliability when the underlying latent construct is not one-dimensional [66]. Although other proposals have been previously made (i.e., Structural Equation Model – SEM; Item-Response Theory model – IRT) [67, 68], data-driven GBAs may have no analog psychometric possibilities [12]. It should be considered that a reliable assessment instrument gives the same results when it measures the same construct under identical conditions, considering the sources of measurement errors [31].

Using a test-retest method for GBAs' reliability would involve testing each participant multiple times using the same GBA, posing a potential issue arising from the practice effect, where a participant's scores could naturally improve over time when playing the same game [69]. A solution that could mitigate the effect of practice can come from calculating an overall learning difference, as participants are expected to exhibit an average improvement from one game iteration to the next. This strategy introduces a degree of error in the learning difference calculation but could help explain some of the natural improvements affecting participants' performance over time. A second strategy could be calculating the reliability between different items/quests or alternative forms of the same GBA that aim to measure distinct but related behaviors by comparing their scores. However, this requires a careful analysis of the game's attributes (i.e., the different levels of difficulty of the quests considered) because GBAs are typically dynamic and may involve changes depending on the user's game interaction [3]. A second psychometric aspect to consider in developing a GBA is its validity.

Game designers must include characteristics crucial to obtain evidence of target knowledge and skills in assessment situations [30]. In this development phase, the contribution of experts in the field of investigation is essential. One problem with construct validity in a GBA is that cognitive ability can also be measured even when this is undesirable, which happens when developers try to make the GBA more engaging by exploiting game mechanics that involve excessive cognitive effort. However, this is detrimental to accurately measuring the target trait of the assessment [70]. Also, it is possible to design a GBA to reduce cognitive effort compared to traditional assessments. For example, when reading requirements are reduced (i.e., the amount and level of difficulty of the text), the cognitive effort required to process the text is also reduced. Hence, cognitive ability can be employed in functions more relevant to the measured construct. In turn, these precautions can reduce construct-irrelevant variance in test scores [3]. Moreover, validity refers to the degree to which scores obtained via a GBA correlate with other assessments that measure the same construct (convergent validity) or are unrelated to different measures (divergent validity) [27]. It is necessary to include external users' results in the analysis, which, on a theoretical basis, have a relationship with the investigated trait (i.e., job or academic performance). Also, in this case, significant differences there will be depending on the specific purpose of the GBA. For example, in the case of gamification, it might be useful to calculate incremental predictive validity via hierarchical regression models [37].

Equity considers differences among participants in terms of educational, social, and other backgrounds [69]. In GBAs, the equity should be addressed carefully because assessment may work differently across sub-groups (e.g., males vs. females, skilled players vs. non-gamers). For example, the literature generally reports that, compared to females, males play all kinds of games more frequently and for longer duration [71]. Therefore, GBAs should minimize the influence of player skill or other relevant characteristics on measurement accuracy [27]. Sanchez, Langer [72] proposed the VGPu (Video Game Pursuit) and the IGW (Intimate with games) scales to investigate relevant attitudes toward video games. VGPu refers to individuals' competence and natural drive toward playing video games, as well as their prior experience interacting with them. Instead, IWG refers to the extent to which an individual finds it difficult to play and achieve competence in video games.

Other authors have attempted to more specifically quantify the subjective experience of gameplay [73, 74]. For example, Brockmyer et al. [73] used the Game Engagement Questionnaire (GEQ) to predict engagement in violent video games. Instead, the Game Play Questionnaire (GPQ) is a subjective measure of gaming experience developed by Ryan et al. [74]. Based on the theoretical framework of self-regulated learning (SRL), Ryan et al. [75] identified three factors that might influence players' enjoyment of video games: autonomy, competence, and intuitive controls. However, to accurately measure the gaming experience of a GBA, it would also need to quantify how many game elements are present, how those game elements interact with non-game elements, how effectively those game elements carry to gaming experiences, and probably a variety of dimensions hitherto not taken into consideration. Yohannis et al. [76] reviewed the game design literature, creating a list of nine common characteristics of games (i.e., players, environment, rules, challenges, interactions, goals, emotional experience, quantifiable outcome, and negotiable consequence). The complexity of the construct and the different definitions of the gaming experience [11] make its measurement enough ambiguous. Furthermore, as MacLeod et al. [77] argued, using self-report measures involves judgment and subjective inferences that may influence questionnaire scores.

Therefore, a second possibility is to infer player profiles through in-game data (i.e., exploration behavior, number of interactions with other characters or significant objects in the environment). Visualization, grouping, classification, and feature extraction methods are all examples of data mining approaches that can be applied to analyze these data. The aforementioned data processing possibilities must also be used very carefully in the development methodology of the GBA. For example, if the primary goal is assessment rather than learning, it may not be acceptable to provide high control to players [27], but, at the same time, this would limit the amount of data that can be used to make accurate predictions. The use of machine learning could also be invaluable for personalizing the gaming experience, for example, by modeling online data to individually set the challenges of specific games [39], an aspect particularly useful in the scope of the GBLs. However, machine learning algorithms need the availability of large and representative training datasets [54]. A second limitation of these approaches is that the results are difficult to interpret (i.e., black-box models), even if tools that exploit hybrid data modeling characteristics (i.e., Adaptive Neuro-Fuzzy Inference System – ANFIS) could be used to overcome this lack [78, 79]. Finally, including tutorials in GBAs is essential to compensate for user differences in familiarity with game controls and balance differential learning curves in video games. Nevertheless, many video games can take hours of play to master [80]. Each of the aspects taken into consideration can contribute to the standardization of the GBA, i.e., the definition of clearly specified procedures for the administration and the assignment of scores [31, 81].

4 Conclusions

The fluid nature of the multiple interacting aspects in GBAs poses significant challenges and deviations from standard assessment development practices [25]. GBAs are not necessarily effective in overcoming the limitations of traditional testing [82]. Rather, designing adequate assessments require theoretical knowledge of hitherto unexplored cognitive, emotional, and motivational mechanisms [83, 84] to successfully decide on appropriate structures, mechanics, and principles [85]. Furthermore, GBAs are more behaviorally complex than other traditional tests. Therefore, they can capture relevant behaviors beyond traditional assessments, involving the development of alternative assessments rather than a redesign that maintains the psychometric profile of the original measure [16]. While this might result in lower construct validity, at the same time, it may result in better prediction, especially through non-linear machine learning data analysis methods [86]. Game activities should be designed to provide players meaningful freedom to pursue goals while ensuring that variance in measurable player behaviors reflects purposeful constructs. If there is not enough freedom to play, the experience can lose its ability to be engage [87], by reducing the potential added value of GBAs compared to a less expensive assessment achievable with traditional methods [17].

Further research into GBA participants' reactions, i.e., the attitudes, affects, and cognitions about the assessment process, is essential [75]. Indeed, a meta-analysis by Duckworth et al. [9] suggests that test-taking motivation accounts for a large portion of the variance in the results of tests and academic scores that have often been attributed to intelligence. In addition to the subjective investigation through questionnaires, it is necessary to include correlation studies between the user's psychological states and physiological signals. Studies have shown that physiological signals can indicate player engagement [88, 89] and flow experiences [90]. Product and in-game data from a GBA can benefit from more detailed and reliable information through alternative and additional evaluation tools to overcome the limitations of standard approaches [36]. For example, physiological measures use sensors that calculate test anxiety taking into account measures of electrodermal responses, respiration, somatic activity, and the cardiovascular system. Using physiological measures to assess anxiety during evaluation situations appears to have a considerable advantage over self-report measures [44]. Physiological measures are immune to the inherent problems of self-report measures, such as falsification and social desirability [91]. Finally, we address an important point: there are currently no agreed standards for the psychometric properties of game-based ratings for both product and in-game data [37]. This aspect is crucial since GBAs must produce scores with reliable psychometric properties and, secondarily, develop a positive affective experience [63]. In the analysis of complex constructs (e.g., collaborative problem-solving in game-based social simulation) [92], instead of the traditional summation of scores, it will be advantageous to have a psychometric model for the entire response pattern, for example, an (modified) IRT model or a Bayesian network [51, 54].

However, to thoroughly and reliably use the possibilities offered by psychometric approaches that distance themselves from classical methods, future studies will have to implement the specific purposes of GBAs by slavishly controlling significant variables, such as the manipulation of the level of immersion (i.e., photorealistic environments vs. abstract environments), difficulty and adaptability, usability, rules, personal background, dependencies between actions at points in time, different situations that arise as players interact with a game, also including alternative data collection strategies, such as physiological data.

References

1. Hommel, B.E., Ruppel, R., Zacher, H.: Assessment of cognitive flexibility in personnel selection: validity and acceptance of a gamified version of the wisconsin card sorting test. Int. J. Sel. Assess. **30**(1), 126–144 (2022)
2. Hausknecht, J.P., Day, D.V., Thomas, S.C.: Applicant reactions to selection procedures: an up-dated model and meta-analysis. Pers. Psychol. **57**(3), 639–683 (2004)
3. Weiner, E.J., Sanchez, D.R.: Cognitive ability in virtual reality: validity evidence for VR game-based assessments. Int. J. Sel. Assess. **28**(3), 215–235 (2020)

4. Meijer, J., Oostdam, R.: Test anxiety and intelligence testing: a closer examination of the stage-fright hypothesis and the influence of stressful instruction. Anxiety Stress Coping **20**(1), 77–91 (2007)
5. Oostdam, R., Meijer, J.: Influence of test anxiety on measurement of intelligence. Psychol. Rep. **92**(1), 3–20 (2003)
6. Tett, R.P., Simonet, D.V.: Faking in personality assessment: a "multisaturation" perspective on faking as performance. Hum. Perform. **24**(4), 302–321 (2011)
7. Shute, V.J., Rahimi, S.: Review of computer-based assessment for learning in elementary and secondary education. J. Comput. Assist. Learn. **33**(1), 1–19 (2017)
8. Borghans, L., Meijers, H., ter Weel, B.: The importance of intrinsic and extrinsic motivation for measuring IQ. Econ. Educ. Rev. **34**, 17–28 (2013)
9. Duckworth, A.L., Quinn, P.D., Lynam, D.R., Loeber, R., Stouthamer-Loeber, M.: Role of test motivation in intelligence testing. Proc. Natl. Acad. Sci. **108**(19), 7716–7720 (2011)
10. Laureiro-Martínez, D., Brusoni, S.: Cognitive flexibility and adaptive decision-making: evidence from a laboratory study of expert decision makers. Strateg. Manag. J. **39**(4), 1031–1058 (2018)
11. Landers, R.N., Tondello, G.F., Kappen, D.L., Collmus, A.B., Mekler, E.D., Nacke, L.E.: Defining gameful experience as a psychological state caused by gameplay: replacing the term 'Game-fulness' with three distinct constructs. Int. J. Hum. Comput. Stud. **127**, 81–94 (2019)
12. Landers, R.N., Sanchez, D.R.: Game-based, gamified, and gamefully designed assessments for employee selection: definitions, distinctions, design, and validation. Int. J. Sel. Assess. **30**(1), 1–13 (2022)
13. Hunicke, R., LeBlanc, M., Zubek, R.: MDA: A formal approach to game design and game re-search. In: Proceedings of the AAAI Workshop on Challenges in Game AI, p.1722. San Jose, CA (2004)
14. Deterding, S.: The lens of intrinsic skill atoms: a method for gameful design. Hum. Comput. Interact. **30**(3–4), 294–335 (2015)
15. Deterding, S., Dixon, D., Khaled, R., Nacke, L.: From game design elements to gamefulness: de-fining "gamification". In: Proceedings of the 15th International Academic MindTrek Conference: Envisioning Future Media Environments, pp. 9–15 (2011)
16. Landers, R.N., Collmus, A.B.: Gamifying a personality measure by converting it into a story: convergence, incremental prediction, faking, and reactions. Int. J. Sel. Assess. **30**(1), 145–156 (2022)
17. Landers, R.N., Armstrong, M.B., Collmus, A.B., Mujcic, S., Blaik, J.: Theory-driven game-based assessment of general cognitive ability: design theory, measurement, prediction of performance, and test fairness. J. Appl. Psychol. **107**(10), 1655 (2022)
18. Peters, H., Kyngdon, A., Stillwell, D.: Construction and validation of a game-based intelligence assessment in minecraft. Comput. Hum. Behav. **119**, 106701 (2021)
19. Quiroga, M., Román, F.J., De La Fuente, J., Privado, J., Colom, R.: The measurement of intelligence in the XXI century using video games. Spanish J. Psychol. **19**, E89 (2016)
20. Foroughi, C.K., Serraino, C., Parasuraman, R., Boehm-Davis, D.A.: Can we create a measure of fluid intelligence using puzzle creator within portal 2? Intelligence **56**, 58–64 (2016)
21. Chan, C.K., Yang, Y.: Developing scientific inquiry in technology-enhanced learning environments. In: Second International Handbook of Information Technology in Primary and Secondary Education, pp. 161–80 (2018)
22. Dede, C., Grotzer, T.A., Kamarainen, A., Metcalf, S.: EcoXPT: designing for deeper learning through experimentation in an immersive virtual ecosystem. J. Educ. Technol. Soc. **20**(4), 166–178 (2017)
23. Zainuddin, Z., Chu, S.K.W., Shujahat, M., Perera, C.J.: The impact of gamification on learning and instruction: a systematic review of empirical evidence. Educ. Res. Rev. **30**, 100326 (2020)

24. Lindstedt, J., Gray, W.: Extreme expertise: exploring expert behavior in Tetris. In: Proceedings of the Annual Meeting of the Cognitive Science Society, vol. 35, no. 35, pp. 912–917 (2013)
25. Mislevy, R.J., Oranje, A., Bauer, M.I., von Davier, A.A., Hao, J.: Psychometric considerations in game-based assessment. GlassLabGames (2014)
26. DiCerbo, K., Behrens, J.: From technology-enhanced assessment to assessment-enhanced technology. Annual meeting of the National Council on Measurement in Education, Vancouver, British Columbia, Canada (2012)
27. Kim, Y.J., Shute, V.J.: The interplay of game elements with psychometric qualities, learning, and enjoyment in game-based assessment. Comput. Educ. **87**, 340–356 (2015)
28. Auer, E.M., Mersy, G., Marin, S., Blaik, J., Landers, R.N.: Using machine learning to model trace behavioral data from a game-based assessment. Int. J. Sel. Assess. **30**(1), 82–102 (2022)
29. Olsen, J., Aleven, V., Rummel, N.: Statistically modeling individual students' learning over successive collaborative practice opportunities. J. Educ. Meas. **54**(1), 123–138 (2017)
30. Mislevy, R.J., Behrens, J.T., Dicerbo, K.E., Levy, R.: Design and discovery in educational assessment: evidence-centered design, psychometrics, and educational data mining. J. Educ. Data Min. **4**(1), 11–48 (2012)
31. Gris, G., Bengtson, C.: Assessment measures in game-based learning research: a systematic review. Int. J. Serious Games **8**(1), 3–26 (2021)
32. Krath, J., Schürmann, L., Von Korflesch, H.F.: Revealing the theoretical basis of gamification: a systematic review and analysis of theory in research on gamification, serious games and game-based learning. Comput. Hum. Behav. **125**, 106963 (2021)
33. Sulla, F., Aquino, A., Rollo, D.: University students' online learning during COVID-19: the role of grit in academic performance. Front. Psychol. **13**, 825047 (2022)
34. Ruiperez-Valiente, J.A., Gaydos, M., Rosenheck, L., Kim, Y.J., Klopfer, E.: Patterns of engagement in an educational massively multiplayer online game: a multidimensional view. IEEE Trans. Learn. Technol. **13**(4), 648–661 (2020)
35. Fetzer, M., McNamara, J., Geimer, J.L.: Gamification, serious games and personnel selection. In: The Wiley Blackwell Handbook of the Psychology of Recruitment, Selection and Employee Retention, pp. 293–309 (2017)
36. Bellotti, F., Kapralos, B., Lee, K., Moreno-Ger, P., Berta, R.: Assessment in and of serious games: an overview. Adv. Hum. Comput. Interact. **2013**, 1–11 (2013)
37. Barends, A.J., de Vries, R.E., van Vugt, M.: Construct and predictive validity of an assessment game to measure honesty–humility. Assessment **29**(4), 630–650 (2022)
38. McCord, J.-L., Harman, J.L., Purl, J.: Game-like personality testing: an emerging mode of personality assessment. Personality Individ. Differ. **143**, 95–102 (2019)
39. Vanden Abeele, V., Wouters, J., Ghesquière, P., Goeleven, A., Geurts, L.: Game-based assessment of psycho-acoustic thresholds: not all games are equal!. In: Proceedings of the 2015 Annual Symposium on Computer-Human Interaction in Play, pp. 331–41 (2015)
40. Harman, J.L., Brown, K.D.: Illustrating a narrative: a test of game elements in game-like personality assessment. Int. J. Sel. Assess. **30**(1), 157–166 (2022)
41. Lowman, G.H.: Moving beyond identification: using gamification to attract and retain talent. Ind. Organ. Psychol. **9**(3), 677–682 (2016)
42. Mislevy, R.J., Corrigan, S., Oranje, A., DiCerbo, K., Bauer, M.I., von Davier, A., et al.: Psychometrics and game-based assessment. In: Technology and Testing: Improving Educational and Psychological Measurement, pp. 23–48 (2016)
43. Gödöllei Lappalainen, A.F.: Game-based assessments of cognitive ability: validity and effects on adverse impact through perceived stereotype threat, test-taking motivation and anxiety. Graduate Studies (2017)
44. Mavridis, A., Tsiatsos, T.: Game-based assessment: investigating the impact on test anxiety and exam performance. J. Comput. Assist. Learn. **33**(2), 137–150 (2017)

45. Kato, P.M., de Klerk, S.: Serious games for assessment: Welcome to the jungle. J. Appl. Testing Technol. **18**(S1), 1–6 (2017)
46. Lumsden, J., Skinner, A., Woods, A.T., Lawrence, N.S., Munafò, M.: The effects of gamelike features and test location on cognitive test performance and participant enjoyment. PeerJ. **4**, e2184 (2016)
47. Csikszentmihalyi, M.: Toward a psychology of optimal experience. flow and the foundations of positive psychology. Springer, pp. 209–26 (2014). https://doi.org/10.1007/978-94-017-9088-8_14
48. Csikszentmihalyi, M.: Flow. The Psychology of Optimal Experience. New York (HarperPerennial) (1990)
49. Sanders, T., Cairns, P.: Time perception, immersion and music in videogames. In: Proceedings of HCI 2010. BCS Learning & Development, vol. 24, pp. 160–167 (2010)
50. Stanciu, C.G.I.A., Stănescu, A.T.D.F.: Development of an integrated game based assessment approach-the next generation of psychometric testing. Eur. J. Sustain. Dev. **8**(5), 270 (2019)
51. Fu, J., Zapata, D., Mavronikolas, E.: Statistical methods for assessments in simulations and serious games. ETS Res. Rep. Ser. **2**, 1–17 (2014)
52. Rupp, A.A., Levy, R., Dicerbo, K.E., Sweet, S.J., Crawford, A.V., Calico, T., et al.: Putting ECD into practice: the interplay of theory and data in evidence models within a digital learning environment. J. Educ. Data Min. **4**(1), 49–110 (2012)
53. de Klerk, S., Veldkamp, B.P., Eggen, T.J.: Psychometric analysis of the performance data of simulation-based assessment: a systematic review and a Bayesian network example. Comput. Educ. **85**, 23–34 (2015)
54. von Davier, A.A.: Computational psychometrics in support of collaborative educational assessments. J. Educ. Meas. **54**(1), 3–11 (2017)
55. Shute, V.J., Leighton, J.P., Jang, E.E., Chu, M.-W.: Advances in the science of assessment. Educ. Assess. **21**(1), 34–59 (2016)
56. Levy, Y.: Continuous-time stochastic games of fixed duration. Dyn. Games Appl. **3**(2), 279–312 (2013)
57. Iseli, M.R., Koenig, A.D., Lee, J.J., Wainess, R.: Automated assessment of complex task performance in games and simulations. Proceedings of the Interservice/Industry Training, Simulation and Education Conference, Orlando, FL (2010)
58. Brown, M., Anderson, S.L.: Designing for disability: evaluating the state of accessibility design in video games. Games Cult. **16**(6), 702–718 (2021)
59. Aguado-Delgado, J., Gutierrez-Martinez, J.-M., Hilera, J.R., de-Marcos, L., Otón, S.: Accessibility in video games: a systematic review. Universal Access Inf. Soc. **19**(1), 169–93 (2020)
60. DiCerbo, K.E., Shute, V., Kim, Y.J.: The future of assessment in technology-rich environments: psychometric considerations. In: Learning, Design, and Technology: An International Compendium of Theory, Research, Practice, and Policy. Springer, Cham (2023)
61. Burt, C., Crowe, L., Thomas, K.: Validation of a gamified measure of safety behavior: the SBT. Safety and Reliability–Safe Societies in a Changing World, pp. 263–70. CRC Press (2018)
62. Delisle, J., Braun, C.M.: A context for normalizing impulsiveness at work for adults with attention deficit/hyperactivity disorder (combined type). Arch. Clin. Neuropsychol. **26**(7), 602–613 (2011)
63. Landers, R.N., Marin, S.: Theory and technology in organizational psychology: a review of technology integration paradigms and their effects on the validity of theory. Annu. Rev. Organ. Psych. Organ. Behav. **8**, 235–258 (2021)
64. Washburn, D.A.: The games psychologists play (and the data they provide). Behav. Res. Methods Instrum. Comput. **35**(2), 185–193 (2003)

65. DeVellis, R.F., Thorpe, C.T.: Scale Development: Theory and Applications. Sage publications (2021)
66. Cortina, J.M.: What is coefficient alpha? An examination of theory and applications. J. Appl. Psychol. **78**(1), 98 (1993)
67. Yang, Y., Green, S.B.: Coefficient alpha: a reliability coefficient for the 21st century? J. Psychoeduc. Assess. **29**(4), 377–392 (2011)
68. Shu, Z., Bergner, Y., Zhu, M., Hao, J., von Davier, A.A.: An item response theory analysis of problem-solving processes in scenario-based tasks. Psychol. Test Assess. Model. **59**(1), 109 (2017)
69. Jaffal, Y., Wloka, D.: Employing game analytics techniques in the psychometric measurement of game-based assessments with dynamic content. J. e-Learn. Knowl. Soc. **11**(3), 101–115 (2015)
70. Gundry, D., Deterding, S.: Validity threats in quantitative data collection with games: a narrative survey. Simul. Gaming **50**(3), 302–328 (2019)
71. Rideout VJ, Foehr UG, Roberts DF. Generation M 2: Media in the Lives of 8-to 18-Year-Olds. Henry J Kaiser Family Foundation (2010)
72. Sanchez, D.R., Langer, M.: Video game pursuit (VGPu) scale development: designing and validating a scale with implications for game-based learning and assessment. Simul. Gaming **51**(1), 55–86 (2020)
73. Brockmyer, J.H., Fox, C.M., Curtiss, K.A., McBroom, E., Burkhart, K.M., Pidruzny, J.N.: The development of the Game engagement questionnaire: a measure of engagement in video game-playing. J. Exp. Soc. Psychol. **45**(4), 624–634 (2009)
74. Ryan, R.M., Rigby, C.S., Przybylski, A.: The motivational pull of video games: a self-determination theory approach. Motiv. Emot. **30**(4), 344–360 (2006)
75. Ryan, A.M., Ployhart, R.E.: Applicants' perceptions of selection procedures and decisions: a critical review and agenda for the future. J. Manag. **26**(3), 565–606 (2000)
76. Yohannis, A.R., Prabowo, Y.D., Waworuntu, A.: Defining gamification: from lexical meaning and process viewpoint towards a gameful reality. In: International Conference on Information Technology Systems and Innovation (ICITSI), pp. 284–9. IEEE (2014)
77. MacLeod, C., Koster, E.H., Fox, E.: Whither cognitive bias modification research? Commentary on the special section articles. J. Abnorm. Psychol. **118**(1), 89 (2019)
78. Jang, J.-S.: ANFIS: adaptive-network-based fuzzy inference system. IEEE Trans. Syst. Man Cybern. **23**(3), 665–685 (1993)
79. Jang, J.-S.R., Sun, C.-T., Mizutani, E.: Neuro-fuzzy and soft computing-a computational approach to learning and machine intelligence. IEEE Trans. Autom. Control **42**(10), 1482–1484 (1997)
80. Tekofsky, S., Van Den Herik, J., Spronck, P., Plaat, A.: Psyops: personality assessment through gaming behavior. In: Proceedings of the International Conference on the Foundations of Digital Games. Citeseer (2013)
81. Cohen, R.J., Swerdlik, M.E., Phillips, S.M.: Psychological testing and assessment: an introduction to tests and measurement. Mayfield Publishing Co. (1996)
82. Sailer, M., Hense, J.U., Mayr, S.K., Mandl, H.: How gamification motivates: an experimental study of the effects of specific game design elements on psychological need satisfaction. Comput. Hum. Behav. **69**, 371–380 (2017)
83. Sailer, M., Homner, L.: The gamification of learning: a meta-analysis. Educ. Psychol. Rev. **32**(1), 77–112 (2020)
84. Koivisto, J., Hamari, J.: The rise of motivational information systems: a review of gamification research. Int. J. Inf. Manage. **45**, 191–210 (2019)
85. Dichev, C., Dicheva, D.: Gamifying education: what is known, what is believed and what re-mains uncertain: a critical review. Int. J. Educ. Technol. High. Educ. **14**(1), 1–36 (2017)

86. Putka, D.J., Beatty, A.S., Reeder, M.C.: Modern prediction methods: new perspectives on a common problem. Organ. Res. Methods **21**(3), 689–732 (2018)
87. Mollick, E.R., Rothbard, N. Mandatory fun: consent, gamification and the impact of games at work. The Wharton School research paper series (2014)
88. Jelinek, H.F., August, K.G., Imam, M.H., Khandoker, A.H., Koenig, A., Riener, R.: Heart rate asym-metry and emotional response to robot-assist task challenges in post-stroke patients. In: Computing in Cardiology, pp. 521–4. IEEE (2011)
89. Kivikangas, J.M., Chanel, G., Cowley, B., Ekman, I., Salminen, M., Järvelä, S., et al.: A review of the use of psychophysiological methods in game research. J. Gaming Virtual Worlds **3**(3), 181–99 (2011)
90. Plotnikov, A., Stakheika, N., De Gloria, A., Schatten, C., Bellotti, F., Berta, R., et al.: Exploiting re-al-time EEG analysis for assessing flow in games. In: IEEE 12th International Conference on Advanced Learning Technologies: IEEE, pp. 688–9 (2012)
91. Zeidner, M.: Test Anxiety: The State of the Art. Plenum Press, New York (1998)
92. Gjicali, K., Finn, B.M., Hebert, D.: Effects of belief generation on social exploration, culturally-appropriate actions, and cross-cultural concept learning in a game-based social simulation. Comput. Educ. Educ. **156**, 103959 (2020)

Author Index

A
Angelelli, Paola   142

B
Balsamo, Michela   192
Bonfiglio, Natale Salvatore   78
Brattico, Elvira   30

C
Calvio, Antonella   18
Campo, Fulvia Francesca   30
Carlomagno, Francesco   30
Carlucci, Leonardo   192
Cerciello, Francesco   159, 183
Ciotola, Sonia   159, 183
Cirasa, Carla   117
Conti, Daniela   117

D
Di Fuccio, Raffaele   168
di Furia, Marco   101
Difino, Melania Rita   18

E
Esposito, Ciro   168
Esposito, Clara   159, 183

F
Fantinelli, Stefania   168
Finestrone, Francesca   63
Frolli, Alessandro   159, 183

G
Guarini, Piergiorgio   63

I
Iaia, Marika   142
Iuso, Salvatore   18

K
Kikuchi, Satoru   3

L
Lacedonia, Donato   18
Larsari, Vahid Norouzi   91
Lella, Clarissa   168
Limone, Pierpaolo   47

M
Marinelli, Chiara Valeria   142
Mascia, Maria Lidia   78

N
Nakayama, Minoru   3

P
Peconio, Guendalina   101
Penna, Maria Pietronilla   78
Petito, Annamaria   18

R
Ragni, Benedetta   101
Rega, Angelo   159, 183
Renati, Roberta   78
Ricci, M. C.   159, 183
Rollo, Dolores   78
Rossi, Martina   63

S
Savino, Francesco Pio   63
Serio, Gianluigi   192

Severo, Melania 18
Sulla, Francesco 168

T
Toto, Giusi Antonia 47

U
Uto, Masaki 3

V
Vizzi, Francesca 142

Y
Yamamoto, Hiroh 3

Z
Zaffino, Annalisa 18
Zoccolotti, Pierluigi 142

GPSR Compliance

The European Union's (EU) General Product Safety Regulation (GPSR) is a set of rules that requires consumer products to be safe and our obligations to ensure this.

If you have any concerns about our products, you can contact us on ProductSafety@springernature.com

In case Publisher is established outside the EU, the EU authorized representative is:

Springer Nature Customer Service Center GmbH
Europaplatz 3
69115 Heidelberg, Germany

Batch number: 08244160

Printed by Printforce, the Netherlands